FAMILY
HISTORY
for beginners

FAMILY HISTORY
for beginners

KAREN FOY

The
History
Press

In memory of my mum and dad – without whom
my own unique blend of family history would not
have been possible.

Front cover photograph courtesy of Frances Harries.

First published 2011

The History Press
The Mill, Brimscombe Port
Stroud, Gloucestershire, GL5 2QG
www.thehistorypress.co.uk

British Library Cataloguing in Publication Data.
A catalogue record for this book is available from the British Library.

ISBN 978 0 7524 5838 0

Typesetting and origination by The History Press
Printed in Great Britain

ACKNOWLEDGEMENTS

Many thanks to all at TheGenealogist, Findmypast and The National Archives who helped provide some of the fabulous document images for illustration – I was extremely grateful for your speedy replies. Thank you to Penny Law, editor of *Family History Monthly*, for recommending my 'writing abilities' and sincere thanks to Katharine Reeve and The History Press for commissioning this book – the opportunity is really appreciated.

Lastly, I would like to thank those supportive family and friends that always show an interest in my work – you know who you are – but most of all, my husband Jeff whose constant words of encouragement never fail to spur me on.

CONTENTS

Introduction   11

Chapter 1: *First Steps*   15
Getting started • Interviewing relatives • Unearthing family
memorabilia and documentation • Preparing a plan of attack and
charting your information • Tracing living relatives • Preparing to
visit an archive

Chapter 2: *Tools for the Task*   24
Equipment • Filing and storage systems • The benefits of family history
software programs

Chapter 3: *From the Cradle*   32
Birth, marriage and death certificates • Locating and using indexes •
Marriage and divorce • Parish records and bishops' transcripts • Baptism
and burial records • Tackling illegitimacy • Religion • Catholic and
Nonconformist records

Chapter 4: *The Census*   52
The Census explained • How to get the most from the information
provided • Overcoming problems and discrepancies in data • Poll books
and electoral registers

Chapter 5: *Filling the Gaps*   62
School registers, log books and public school records • Apprentice
records • A life of crime • Records and repositories • Imprisonment •

Transportation • Death by hanging • Trials and the justice system •
The workhouse • Poor Law unions • Newspaper and media coverage
• Living museums

Chapter 6: *All in a Day's Work*   75
Popular occupations of the eighteenth and nineteenth centuries •
Domestic service • The medical profession • Law enforcers
• Policemen and the legal profession • The clergy • The entertainment
industry • Railway workers • Canal workers • Postmen • Labourers
and farmers • Freemasons

Chapter 7: *Location, Location, Location*   93
Maps and street plans • Tithe maps: what they are and where to find
them • Poverty maps • Historical/trade directories • The history of
your home

Chapter 8: *Emigration*   105
Reasons for emigration • The Highland Clearances • Religious
recruitment • Irish instability • Australian immigration • Ships'
manifests and passenger lists • Assisted and unassisted passengers •
Burials at sea • Ellis Island • Passports • Child migration

Chapter 9: *A Cultural Mix*   120
The importance of a name • Scottish, Irish and Welsh research •
Reasons for immigration to Britain • Citizenship • Huguenot
ancestors • Quaker ancestors • Indian ancestors • Jewish ancestors

Chapter 10: *In the Forces*   134
Army, navy and air force careers • major conflicts • Available records
and where to find them • Medal indexes, service records, campaigns
of war • Prisoners of war • The Commonwealth War Graves
Commission • Military museums

Chapter 11: *Serving the Nation*   163
National service • The Home Front and rationing • The Home
Guard • The Land Girls • Evacuees • Conscientious Objectors

Chapter 12: *Fame and Fortune*   *170*
Famous ancestors • Aristocratic ancestors • Heraldry

Chapter 13: *To the Grave*   *174*
Funeral customs • Mourning etiquette • Burial plots • Gravestone
symbolism • The National Burial Index and burial registers • Coroners'
inquests • Obituaries • Wills and probate

Chapter 14: *Preserve and Protect*   *185*
Personal documentation and how it can aid your research • Deciphering
old handwriting • Storage, preservation and care of family memorabilia
• Understanding photographs • Understanding trade cards • Medal
preservation and display

Chapter 15: *Collate and Collaborate*   *197*
Creating a lasting legacy for future generations • Information
checklist • Writing up your information • Top tips and what to avoid
• Print on demand • Presentation alternatives • Paper or electronic
format, newsletters, blogs, websites, time capsules, scrapbooks and printed
books • Ancestry's 'bookbinding' service • Social networking, message
boards and mailing lists • Joining a family history society • Family history
fairs • DNA testing • Family reunions

Chapter 16: *Anchoring Your Ancestors: Historical Timelines* 209
Monarchs • British prime ministers and their terms of office • Homes:
furniture, style and architecture • Key dates in world history • Inventions

Appendix 1: Useful Websites   *215*

Appendix 2: Useful Addresses   *217*

Bibliography   *220*

Index   *222*

INTRODUCTION

Family faces are magic mirrors. Looking at people who belong to us, we see the past, present and future.

Gail Lumet Buckley

If you have ever been put off tracing your family tree because you thought it was a tedious exercise in gathering names and dates then, happily, you have been misled. Don't get me wrong; yes, you do need to gather facts but this journey also requires you to wear many hats from detective to diplomat, perfectionist to pioneer.

The popular BBC TV series asks 'Who Do You Think You Are?' and, in essence, your mission is to find the answer. From whom did you inherit the colour of your eyes, or that Hollywood-style square jaw? To which ancestor do you owe your sporting prowess and artistic abilities? Who were these ancestors and how did *their* lives shape *yours*?

Along the way you will find they each have their own stories to tell: expeditions and adventures, triumphs and tragedies. This network of threads – the warp and weft on the loom of life – will weave a tale that you cannot help but be intrigued by. You share the same blood so you share the same story and what you need to begin with are facts.

In very basic terms, genealogy is the study of your descending family tree through the generations from a specific ancestor or ancestors. For most people, a paper trail exists – it is just a matter of finding it – and how far back you can take it is unique to your family and the clues they left behind.

It is a misconception that you have to be retired to enjoy researching your family tree. There is no doubt that endless hours with no time constraints would be lovely, but whatever our age our busy twenty-first-century lives mean that we all have commitments, from work obligations to looking after the grandchildren.

Dabbling in genealogy is a pastime anyone can take pleasure in and, although it is guaranteed to get you hooked once you start, it is important to break your research into manageable, bite-sized pieces. Perhaps get other members of your family involved and create a lasting legacy for future generations to enjoy.

My own experiences as a writer and history researcher have led me to realise that no single publication can cover everything that the budding family historian might want to know. What you do need is a guide that will answer your early questions, explain what records are available and what they look like, decrypt the numerous abbreviations and give you a helping hand over those stumbling blocks which we all face when adding 'branches' to our trees. This book aims to do just that – it does not claim to cover every aspect of this massive subject but is based on the questions which the 'ordinary' man or woman is likely to ask when they embark on this fascinating hobby. And it really is a fascinating hobby because, in effect, it is your own life that you are researching and, without the highs and lows, trials and tribulations, love and heartache that your ancestors experienced you would not be here. Even if this book helps you to find out one fact about your forebears that you did not already know, then I will have done my job; but I can guarantee that once you start down this road of untangling your roots, the compulsion to find out more about your story will become extremely hard to suppress.

Walking into a record office for the first time can be a daunting task, and for some maybe even a little disappointing if you leave empty-handed after hours trying to find your way around the vast array of documents. But don't be put off; there's a wealth of information available if only you know where to look, and with a little preparation – and understanding of what it is that you might be looking at – you can glean a great deal from your visits.

The main thing is to be realistic: you won't complete your family tree overnight. There are very few short cuts, especially if you want to do things properly, and although you can undertake this project on a budget, be prepared for a number of expenses along the way. But fees to obtain copies of documents and travel costs to visit archives and museums are a small price to pay for the intrigue of being a 'history detective', which often proves to be an absorbing and rewarding experience.

Genealogy can be as time-consuming as you want it to be, but even when you say that you will just spend a quick half an hour on research on a given day, it is surprising how easily that half hour can turn into much more. As a result, many of the resources suggested in this book are internet based – some free and some requiring subscriptions or pay-per-view – allowing you to get the most out of your limited research time. It must also be stressed that there is nothing like seeing original documents to confirm your provisional conclusions and I can guarantee that at some point you will be tempted to see for yourself the location where your ancestors lived or worked or perhaps even the churchyard in which they are buried.

Whatever resources you decide to use, the most important aspect is to have fun and enjoy the challenge of piecing together your giant family jigsaw puzzle. But beware: what starts as just a pleasant pastime can often turn into a lifetime's labour of love.

What are my options?

At the outset you need to decide your main aim. As you travel backwards from your two parents, to your four grandparents and eight great-grandparents, the number of direct ancestors doubles with each generation (*see* chart). Add in siblings, their marriages and offspring, and before you know it you have so many names to deal with that you cannot recall whether Uncle Sid is married to Aunt Betty and your tree becomes a tangle. The

Calculating Great Grandparents

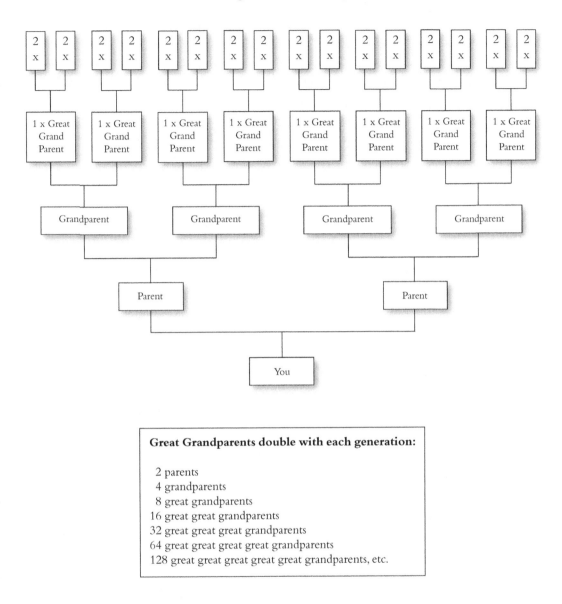

> **Great Grandparents double with each generation:**
>
> 2 parents
> 4 grandparents
> 8 great grandparents
> 16 great great grandparents
> 32 great great great grandparents
> 64 great great great great grandparents
> 128 great great great great great grandparents, etc.

choice is yours and as you gain experience and understanding, the fog will lift and you will be able to see relationships more clearly. But in the meantime, why not choose a research route that best suits your needs?

The Male Line: Take this path from father to grandfather to great-grandfather, adding in their wives and families, and you will have an obvious surname to tackle and a 'beacon' to follow. If you have an unusual surname then this is an added bonus.

The Female Line: This route can be more of a challenge as you head back from your mother to your grandmother to your great-grandmother, swinging from family to family with each changing name. Your aim is to pinpoint each maiden name to help you in your quest.

The Extended Family Tree: This direction allows you to include the collateral branches of a family which refers to *all* descendants and their spouses, often linked by your earliest known ancestor.

None of these avenues are set in stone and as you progress you can move around the various branches of your tree as you try to overcome research hurdles or are drawn to a particular area of interest.

Chapter 1

FIRST STEPS

You have decided to dip your toe in the water. You are getting acclimatised to the world of genealogy and looking at what is already known about your family in greater depth. You may be surprised at just how much information is lying around in drawers, or tucked away in the minds of your older relatives. It is now your job to collect it all together, sift fact from fiction and make new discoveries with the aim of sharing your findings with all who help you in your mission. This could be a long journey; be prepared for a fascinating ride and perhaps some surprises along the way.

What type of family documents could I expect to unearth?

Hidden away in old shoe boxes long-forgotten treasures lie. Alongside fragile folded birth, marriage and death certificates could be newspaper cuttings, correspondence, diaries and war medals, all with their own stories to tell. Photographs, postcards, apprentice indentures and scrapbooks reveal details of life in a different era, whilst wills or family bibles record significant dates in faded ink penned in your ancestor's own handwriting. There are so many clues stored in the backs of drawers or in suitcases in the loft and if you are serious about preserving your family history then it is essential that you root them out and encourage other family members to do the same – you may well uncover a family archive that you didn't know existed.

Family letters can give clues to business transactions, journeys taken and even languages spoken.

Why is it important to interview relatives?

Older relatives have the advantage of being able to recount details of ancestors further back in your family tree – they could have grown up, lived or worked alongside these forebears and are able to characterise them from their own experiences and recollections. They can describe their appearance and personalities first hand, explain where they lived and the trade or occupation in which they were employed. It is likely that they'll also have a myriad of facts that you could not hope to get from any official documentation. Bear in mind that some of the stories may be family hearsay, expanded and elaborated on over the years, but it is essential that you note everything down as there may just be a grain of truth in there that can help you with your research at a later date. Whilst some older relatives may be eager to share their experiences, others may not – the key is to try and make them curious about your project and what you may achieve rather than suspicious.

Which is the best way to interview a relative?

Each method has its benefits. An 'interview' conducted face to face is ideal for letting your ancestor regale you with tales of the past. Allow plenty of time for your visit as you may well wander from one subject to another when distant memories trigger recollections about certain family members. Try to keep some kind of order by asking specific questions and, as always, write it all down.

Some researchers have found recording the interview to be helpful, enabling them to concentrate on the interviewee rather than on the writing. Ask the relative's permission first, test your recording device beforehand to ensure that it is working properly and place it in an unobtrusive place so that it does not become a distraction. This system also has the added benefit of providing you with a sound library of your relative's voice – an appealing resource for future generations.

For me, by far the best way of extracting as much information as possible is to send your relative a questionnaire. This allows them to complete it at their leisure when they can sit down and really think about their answers. Include a stamped addressed envelope for them to return it to you or arrange to pick it up at a later date when you can follow it up – face to face – with further questions about what they have written, enabling you to get the best of both worlds.

For most people the opportunity to recount tales of the past is a pleasurable experience, but always remember to consider your interviewee's feelings as some memories may be difficult or emotional. If you don't probe too hard at first, they may be more willing to open up at a later date when they have got used to reliving those memories.

After every visit always write or telephone to express your thanks for their help. Even if your questioning resulted in no new information being found, it enables you to ask for their help again in the future should the need arise.

What questions should I ask to get the most productive answers?

Always structure your questions so that more than just a 'yes' or 'no' answer has to be given. Establish family members, siblings' names, dates of birth, marriage and death and even addresses or areas in which they lived. Also enquire about those issues that are not so easily discovered, such as middle or nicknames, unusual events associated with their lives and their hobbies or interests. The following examples should help to get you started.

- Who was the oldest family member you can remember from your childhood? Can you describe them?
- What was your religion growing up and what church, if any, did you attend?
- Describe the house you lived in as a child. What was the address? Did you have electricity, a telephone or bathroom facilities?
- Can you remember your grandparents? What was their style of dress and can you describe their personalities?
- Did you attend any family weddings? Where was the marriage held, who were the 'happy couple' and can you remember anything about the other guests?
- Are there any major events that you remember happening in your childhood? How did they affect you?
- Have you ever appeared in the newspaper and if so, what for?
- Is there a family story which stands out for you and why?
- Was their a particular occupation or trade which ran in your family? Who was employed in this line of work?
- What was your first job, what did it involve and how long were you employed there?

DON'T FORGET!

Never assume anything;
your forebears may surprise you.

My children are eager to be involved; would you give them specific tasks?

Perhaps start by getting them to compile a list of questions which *they* think should be answered – you may be surprised at how intuitive they are.

Or why not set them the challenge of finding any related memorabilia that your wider family may have inherited? Children are not shy about asking to see something and adults are more likely to make the effort to find these mementoes and explain their history to an interested member of the younger generation. Treat it like a treasure hunt and you may just strike gold.

There seems to be so many lines of enquiry to follow up, what is the best way to start?

Armed with the results of your family survey, where possible try and get out and about to corroborate any basic information you have found. Visit local churchyards to confirm birth and burial dates listed on family gravestones – the details can often throw up some interesting and intriguing information – and remember to scout around to see if there are other headstones with similar family names which may turn out to be linked as you widen your search. Some churches also have an open-door policy, so pop inside and see if your family name is on any of the inscriptions inside. This method paid off for me when I discovered bell-ringing connections within the family as our surname was included on a commemorative plaque. If you're fortunate enough to uncover any new leads, find the contact details of the vicar or churchwarden then write or ring for further information once you get home.

Church plaques. Details of individuals and events are often recorded on commemorative plaques within the church. This example shows a list of church bell ringers including my ancestor. Remember to look for information inside the church as well as outside in the churchyard – you may be surprised at what you find.

So now you should be bulging with reams of information and you have not even touched an official document yet. It is time to get organised.

What is the best way to log these initial dates and details?

By combining the information from relatives and any documents or ephemera you have found you can record the details in what is technically known as a 'pedigree' – an outline showing the descent of your family from a particular ancestor. This basic chart will be something you can refer to as you add other generations and siblings.

First, plot out a drop line chart (*see* chart) on a large piece of paper starting with the ancestor furthest back. Get into the habit of recording husbands to the left and wives to the right and show the children descending from this union in order of their birth. Multiple marriages should also be recorded in order, left to right. At first, it can be quite difficult fitting everyone in but after a couple of attempts you should end up with a clear and concise chart which only records names and dates of birth, marriage and death. Remember to allow one chart for each branch of the family and keep each generation on the same horizontal level. You now have a 'map' to follow and already there should be gaps of information pointing you to those areas you need to research.

Links to the Past

Drop Line Chart

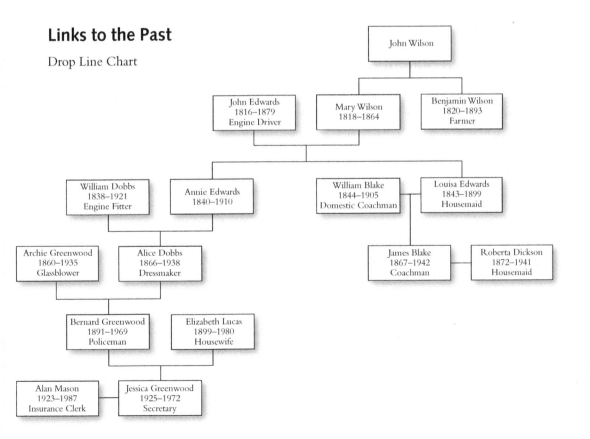

I'm unable to fit all the information I know onto my chart; have you any tips?

A drop line chart is a way of displaying the general facts and is not supposed to show every last detail about your ancestors' lives. Try using abbreviations to convey your information. Below is a list of some of the most common abbreviations used on family trees. Don't be tempted to make up your own; there are times when you will have to leave your research and there is nothing more frustrating than coming back to your work and not understanding the meaning of the acronyms you have used.

b.	born
bapt./chr.	baptised or christened
m.	married (an equals symbol = can also be used to indicate marriage)
div.	divorced
nat.	child of an unmarried couple
d.	died
bur./crem.	buried or cremated
d.inf.	died in infancy
k.i.a.	killed in action
c.	circa – used when approximating a date

What is an Ahnentafel chart?

This is a genealogical numbering system that allows you to list your ancestors in a particular order. It enables you to record the information compactly without the need for a diagram and includes the name of each individual along with the dates and places of birth, marriage and death where known. The numbering system can be complicated but, once grasped, has the potential to allow you to record a large amount of data and to easily see your ancestors in a 'generation' layout.

First Generation

1. You

Second Generation

2. Your father
3. Your mother

Third Generation

4. Your father's father
5. Your father's mother
6. Your mother's father
7. Your mother's mother

Fourth Generation

8. Your father's father's father
9. Your father's father's mother
10. Your father's mother's father
11. Your father's mother's mother
12. Your mother's father's father
13. Your mother's father's mother
14. Your mother's mother's father
15. Your mother's mother's mother

Understanding family relationships

Family relationships can be determined either by blood – where everyone is related through common descent of an ancestor to include parents, siblings, grandparents, cousins – or by marriage. Half-brothers and -sisters share one biological parent so would be related by blood, whilst step brothers and sisters would be related by marriage.

I'm often confused when determining the relationships of cousins, what does each term mean?

It often takes a bit of thought fathoming how one person is related to another, but I've found the easiest way to remember it is thus:

First cousins are the people in your family who share two of the same grandparents as you; **second cousins** have the same great-grandparents as you, but not the same grandparents; **third cousins** share two great-great-grandparents.

But when cousins descend from a shared set of ancestors by a different number of generations, then this is known as 'removed' so:

Cousins once removed are separated by one generation e.g. your father's first cousin would be your first cousin once removed; **cousins twice removed** are separated by two generations e.g. your grandfather's first cousin would be your cousin twice removed.

Tracing living relatives

With the aid of family knowledge and very little investigation many of us can already 'travel' back 100 years and establish some key figures in our family history, but not everyone is in that position. Separation – at birth or as the result of wars, conflict, emigration or family feuds – can tear families apart, but if you feel the time is right to discover more about your living relatives then there are several easy steps that can get you on the right road.

Visit your local archive library to search their telephone directories and electoral registers for your relative's last known address. Consider placing a newspaper advertisement. Word your request accordingly to avoid upsetting anyone – depending upon the reasons for your separation.

Internet sites such as friendsreunited.co.uk may be able to connect you with old school friends who know the whereabouts of long-lost cousins, whilst their sister site genesreunited.co.uk could also be of help.

The people finder at 192.com/people allows you to search electoral rolls from 2002 to 2010 to track down those relatives that you may have lost touch with in recent years. The family tracing service provided by the Salvation Army has an eighty-five per cent success rate – why not give them a try?

What Next?

Don't dismiss the importance of your own library. Not only ideal for local history research, they usually have a set of publications which can link you to destinations further than those within your own county in the shape of the telephone directory. Wherever you are on your travels, it is well worth popping in to the library and making a list of the people with the particular surname that you've been researching. These indispensable tomes can provide you with the contact details of possible relations and, whether you write them a letter detailing your family history quest or pluck up the courage to telephone them direct, you may come across someone who can shed light on your ancestors and their descendants. This method is particularly useful if your ancestors culminated in a specific town or village or, you have an unusual surname, but is not as effective if your family name is *Jones* and your area of research is North Wales.

I'm now ready to take my research to the next stage but I feel a little sceptical about visiting my local archive. How do I overcome this?

Admittedly, your first visit can be a little daunting. Shelf upon shelf lined with books, rows of microfilm readers and cabinets full to the brim with film reels labelled with what seems like the most complicated numbering system in the world can baffle any beginner – but don't be put off. The archivists and assistants are happy to share their knowledge on everything from where to view a tithe map to how to untangle your microfilm from the reader. They are used to answering the queries of everyone from the expert to the apprentice and welcome 'new starters' by familiarising them with the layout of the archive and explaining which records will be of most benefit at this early stage.

Are there any arrangements I should make before I visit?

Most archives require you to provide some form of identification before you're allowed access and granted a 'reader's ticket', so remember to take something along like a driver's licence, passport or domestic bill. Add a notebook, pencils (not pens), a sharpener, digital camera and coinage for photocopying charges.

If you don't make some kind of plan about what information you hope to find your trip could be wasted for want of proper preparation. Write down your requirements and make some brief notes about what you already know so that you can refer to these during your search. Do not set yourself too many challenges on your first visit – use some of the time to have a wander around, get acclimatised to your surroundings and familiarise yourself with the types of records, books and resources they hold that could be of interest to you in the future.

Can I take photographs of documents in a local archive?

I've found that the rules vary from one place to another. Some allow you to take photographs for personal use as long as you turn off your flash and sign a copyright and data protection form. Others may require a small fee but it is always best to enquire when you ring to make your appointment.

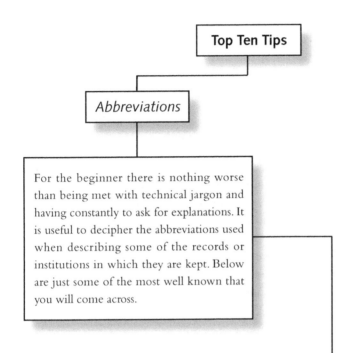

Top Ten Tips

Abbreviations

For the beginner there is nothing worse than being met with technical jargon and having constantly to ask for explanations. It is useful to decipher the abbreviations used when describing some of the records or institutions in which they are kept. Below are just some of the most well known that you will come across.

CRO	County Record Office
FFHS	Federation of Family History Societies
GRO	General Record Office
IGI	International Genealogical Index
IHGS	Institute of Heraldic and Genealogical Studies
LDS	Church of the Latter Day Saints (Mormons)
PRONI	Public Record Office of Northern Ireland
NAS	National Archive of Scotland
SoG	Society of Genealogists
TNA	The National Archives formerly the PRO or Public Record Office

Chapter 2

TOOLS FOR THE TASK

Research is formalized curiosity. It is poking and prying with a purpose.

Zora Neale Hurston

The key to researching your ancestors is to follow a simple recipe. First, you need a huge dollop of patience; mix this with lashings of perseverance and a splash of determination before finally sprinkling on a handful of luck. As long as you bear this in mind, your tree should gradually begin to grow as you track down those elusive pieces of information that can sometimes be found in the most unlikely places.

All the equipment in the world cannot find those much-sought-after details for you but they can help you to keep your findings organised, point you in the right direction and collate what information you have found, often enabling you to see your problems from a different angle.

I don't have a computer. Is it worth me continuing?

You don't necessarily need one. People regularly researched their family history before computers were available for home use, and if you are able to travel easily from one archive to the next using their facilities, microfilms and transcriptions, then you too can get some fantastic results.

That said, access to a computer does make life a little bit easier. It speeds up the process, gives you the ability to search and order copies of documents online as well as cutting down the hours and expense of travelling. Additional benefits include the ability to type up your story on the word processor, use email to keep in touch with new relatives and contacts as well as scanning and printing photographs in order to preserve your originals. Of course, there's nothing quite like confirming your facts at the archives and seeing the original document for yourself; but perhaps when you weigh up travel costs against the prices of today's basic desktop and laptop computers, you may find it worthwhile making this investment.

What equipment do I need?

Whatever approach you decide to use you *must* keep your data organised: notepads, pens and pencils are essential for jotting down your thoughts and findings. When you start, ring binders and folders with plastic pockets will provide the ideal storage facility for your photocopies and print-outs, but as you progress and your stash of documents grows you may want to consider other means of storage for items like certificates, letters and family ephemera which need preserving for future generations (*see* Chapter 14: Preserve and Protect).

How do family history software programs make organisation easier?

There is an abundance of family history/genealogy programs on the market and to the new starter the choice can be a little confusing. If you know of someone who already uses this kind of software, ask their advice about what they have found to be the pros and cons of their particular program and get them to show you its potential first hand.

Consider visiting a family history fair where there is always a variety of software available for purchase with knowledgeable and enthusiastic people on hand to explain the intricacies – and do not forget to scan the family history magazines where there are often reviews of the latest systems used by like-minded devotees.

All programs allow you to arrange your data into some kind of order and, once input, to jump back and forth between the generations, adding in new information as you find it. Depending on your choice, you can view lines of descent, siblings and their families, add details of military careers, notes on their cause of death or describe occupations. All the information you have retrieved can be input against each individual instead of having dozens of pieces of paper to rifle through. At the click of a button you can print out your tree or add in photographs of each family member as you acquire them. The possibilities are endless, and there are usually regular updates or improved versions available as new features are added.

I would definitely recommend investing in a software package – once bought, you'll wonder how you ever managed without it.

How do I use this new software? Do I need to install it on my computer?

Put the CD into your CD Rom drawer and follow the on-screen instructions for installation. In the majority of cases, the program will then be on your hard drive so that each time you want to use it you can click on an icon on your desktop which will take you straight to your uploaded information. The benefit of this is that you do not need to keep loading the CD every time you use it. The downside is that it will take up some of your computer memory – but very little considering the working capacity and potential it has. Do not be put off by this.

Each CD will have an online help guide on how to get started, but the golden rule – which applies to all your research – is to input the information about yourself and gradually begin to work backwards adding parents, siblings and grandparents for each generation. Once your tree begins to take shape you can concentrate on each individual to build a bigger picture of their lives. It will soon become apparent what information is missing which will then point you in the direction of your next area of research.

Which software would be best for me?

Finding the software that fits your criteria is purely down to personal preference. The majority of programs allow you to add, view and edit family data then print it out in a variety of formats – what makes each one different is the additional features they provide. Take advantage of the free trials offered and try before you buy. Whilst testing, jot down your requirements to help you find the right one.

Consider your ultimate goals: do you want to share your findings with other family historians online? If so, look out for those programs which offer the ability to upload your information with ease or even the possibility of how to create your own web page. Would you like to create a book with the data you've gathered? Some programs focus on how to print your information in book format with a variety of layouts and features to enhance your work. Are you limited for storage space and simply want a program to store data in an electronic format? Look out for software that is easy to use with an uncomplicated on-screen layout.

Perhaps you want to create wall-sized family tree charts where you can add photos. Consider your printing requirements and look at the other types of display features offered – can you create a slide show on your computer desktop or does it allow you to add video and audio clips? Or simply, are you a new computer user? Does the program have a paper manual or are all the 'help' instructions on screen?

These are just some of the questions you'll need to consider to get the best for your money. Every year, new updated versions of each company's software are produced and there is now more focus on 'helping' with your research by including 'research logs', 'to-do lists', the ability to compare your data, help pinpoint what information you need to find next and suggestions about the resources where you might find it. Take your time and don't be shy about asking others for their opinions.

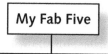

My Fab Five

Legacy is a powerful yet easy-navigable program that offers multiple views of your family tree and a 'source citation' feature which enables you to document your sources of information to aid future research. There is the option to upgrade to their deluxe version, map your ancestors in different locations around the globe and calculate relationships not only by blood but also by marriage. My personal favourite. www.legacyfamilytree.com

Family Tree Maker has enhanced integration with ancestry.com and the ability to view timelines and interactive maps so that you can highlight events and places in your ancestors' lives. Its high performance interface allows you to quickly navigate between the various features and individuals in your tree. www.familytreemaker.com

RootsMagic is perfect for anyone who likes the idea of beautifully displaying their family data for future generations. Featuring decorative charts, shareable CDs and the option to publish your own book, this easy to use program has something for everyone who likes to enhance the visual aspect of their tree. www.rootsmagic.com

Family Historian has exceptional multimedia facilities – ideal for those who like to integrate their photographs into their data – as well as enabling you to create ancestor, descendant, hourglass, everyone and their unique 'All Relatives' diagrams. www.family-historian.co.uk

The Master Genealogist is ideal for those who like to add every last detail about the family members in their tree. Once mastered, the program allows you to evaluate and document all the data you have found and is flexible for both the novice and professional researcher. www.whollygenes.com

What can I expect to see on screen when I open my family history software?

The usual layout will show three generations on the screen at any one time, e.g. yourself and your spouse, your parents and their parents. Birth, marriage and death dates will be visible depending upon which individual is highlighted. There is then the option to click further into the details gathered on each person, allowing you to add everything you know about them from their appearance on the censuses and the length of their military career to details of their occupations and the organisations to which they belonged. Each program has different ways of displaying this but by holding your cursor over each piece of information you can easily begin to find your way around and understand the potential it offers.

From experience, what advice can you give about using genealogy programs?

Although each program has its own features, many of the tasks they aim to achieve are the same – the following tips can be applied to most products.

Only ever input names, dates and facts that you know to be true – this will save confusion later on. If there is a section – perhaps a 'to-do' list – which allows you to write details which you have yet to confirm, add these here or devise a system where you add your 'uncertainties' in a notes section on the program. This will help you to keep track of what investigations you have yet to carry out.

Always, always, always save your work after each session and consider backing up your Gedcom file to another disc or flash drive, or even emailing the file to a family member for safe keeping. There's nothing worse than losing all your hard work through a computer crash or other technical glitch.

Every once in a while print out all your findings using a narrative report facility on your program – it's always worth having a paper copy back-up of this. Similarly, print out a descendant chart which helps you to see your family tree at a glance.

If your program allows, import photographs of your ancestors next to their information. As your tree grows, this makes it visually much easier to navigate around the screen.

A mapping facility can be a real bonus. Learn how to use it and you can chart the movements of your family.

What is a Gedcom file?

Gedcom stands for Genealogical Data Communication and is the format in which your family history file is saved. Just as a text document is suffixed by the abbreviation *.doc* or an image by *.jpg* after its file name, your saved family tree information will be followed by *.ged*.

These Gedcom files are universally compatible with all family history software and online networking sites where you may wish to upload your tree. If you find that a particular software program is not for you, you can easily export your information using the Gedcom facility to another program without having to manually input all of your information again.

What are my filing alternatives?

Ring binders with plastic wallets which can be moved around within the folder are great but can become a bit unwieldy as they fill up with dozens of print-outs and notes, so be selective about what you file and try not to duplicate your information. Try colour co-ordinating your filing system for each branch of your tree, enabling you to find quickly the individual you need. Similarly, whilst carrying out research, add your findings to colour co-ordinated or labelled notebooks, dividing into four: father's father, father's mother, mother's father, mother's mother. You will then, in effect, have four trees to work on with different surnames to research. Remember, your list of surnames will grow with each new marriage so this early division of your tree will help you to remember which names are linked with which branch.

Should I keep paper copies?

A software program does cut down on the need for paper records but it's entirely up to you. Try to avoid lots of scraps of paper though. It is essential to jot down notes and questions that you need to answer, but once you do, transfer this new information to your main file or program and dispose of the note, otherwise you'll be swamped with a wave of queries and you won't be able to remember whether you've solved them or not.

Computer users can still make use of the blank forms intended for manual filing systems when visiting record offices and archives. Their pre-printed layout makes recording and transferring facts easy and ensures that you have noted all the details ready for input onto your computer program at a later date.

Whatever system you use – manual or computerised – the rule is still the same: be methodical in your record keeping and meticulous when taking notes and make your writing legible. Returning home to find you can't even read your own writing can be extremely frustrating.

What does 'identifying the source' mean?

Every time you find a piece of information, whether it is a birth date, a monumental inscription or an obituary, you should always try to make a note of the 'source' or resource from where the information came. For example, a birth date may be discovered from a birth certificate so you would write a brief reference to this fact; a monumental inscription could have been found on the family headstone in St Mathew's Church, Chester, whilst an obituary may have been discovered in the *Lancashire Gazette* of 3 May 1902. If you ever need to verify these facts, a quick look at your source notes will help you locate the original details again easily. Most genealogy computer programs have the facility to add this extra information at the click of a button.

Why should I document my sources?

Documenting your sources is all part of your 'historical housekeeping' and although you may think 'why bother?' it can save you hours of needless research in the long run. If you've searched through a decade of marriage records to try and establish the marriage date of your ancestors but been unsuccessful, you must still make a note of the years and registers examined. If not, a few months later when you decide to reinvestigate the marriage you could waste your time going over old ground. It is just as important to record what you have not found as what you have.

How do I categorise various sources?

Primary sources are family historians' bread and butter and refer to original documents and books which allow us to build our trees with certainty. Despite this, it would be ridiculous to ignore the addition of **secondary** sources: the facts and figures which are given to us second hand. These take the shape of indexes and transcriptions of original sources and, although many of them will be excellent, they can be open to human error with spelling mistakes and inaccuracies which can 'infect' your tree in a similar way to a computer virus. The wrong information has the potential to lead you off in the wrong direction and even result in you researching someone who does not belong to your family. So, where possible, take the information you have discovered in a secondary source and follow it up with a viewing of the original or cross reference the details with another source to confirm your facts.

Personal websites and blogs can really help boost the 'body count' in your own tree as you discover a branch which has already been researched, but always do your own investigating of the information you have found to ensure you agree with all that has been written. Contact the website owner, ask how the information was discovered and share what you know – combining your energies may uncover some facts that will be of interest to you both.

Have you tried?

Buy yourself two or three fairly large notebooks and allot one for each century. In the top right-hand corner of each page write the year date, i.e. in a book labelled '1800s' start at 1800, 1801, 1802 and work your way through to 1899. Each time you come across a significant date in your family tree, i.e. a birth, marriage, death, date of employment, military enlistment etc., write it down in the appropriate year. The key is to write down only those dates which have been confirmed and guaranteed as accurate.

You may think that this can be achieved in your computer program, which to some degree it can for each individual, but this 'paper format' method is indispensable for helping to compare the lives of your various ancestors against each other at different periods in history. For example, you will be able to see that your Uncle Roger was born in the same year that your great-great-grandmother died, and that your Aunt Lucy got married. All of these people could be from different branches of your tree and it would be very difficult to achieve this combined knowledge – at a glance – in your computer software.

DON'T FORGET!

There may be periods when your own busy life makes it difficult to find time to fit in as much research as you'd like, but it's essential that your work to date is organised enabling you to pick up where you left off when you return. Don't be selective about the facts that you include. You may not like the idea that your great-great-grandfather had a criminal record or that great-aunt Eleanor had an illegitimate child as the result of an affair, but it is part of your history and an equally important aspect which helped shape your family story.

Chapter 3

FROM THE CRADLE

The farther back you look, the farther back you see.

Winston Churchill

One of the most important parts of recreating an account of your ancestor's life is to gather a series of dates and place names which represent key markers in their timeline. These markers include birth, baptism, marriage, death and burial dates which appear on documents such as civil registration certificates, parish records and bishops' transcripts. Building up these pieces of evidence helps to form the 'coat hanger' onto which you can hang all the other information you'll acquire along the way.

Now that I've gathered together family details and drawn up a brief chart, what do I do next?

It is essential to confirm the facts that your relatives have given you to ensure that you are not off on a wild goose chase researching the wrong person. Beginning with a 'certainty' – perhaps a person's birth date that you absolutely know is correct – you can begin to work backwards. You will need to acquire their birth certificate to confirm who the individual's parents were and then find the marriage of these parents to establish what the mother's maiden name was and who both parties' fathers were. This technique is used through every generation and is how you begin to add 'branches' to your tree. Since with each generation the number of grandparents doubles, with every marriage a new name will enter your tree in the form of the wife's maiden name, making each union a fascinating discovery and potential gold mine of links to other families.

Where possible, try to start your research with the most unusual surname – it's easier to follow the ancestral lines of the 'Helmsleys' than it is to follow the 'Smiths'. At some point, you may well have to tackle your 'Smith' branch but by that time you'll have a greater knowledge of how and where to search for information and will have built up a tree which makes linking your Smith ancestors into it that little bit easier.

What is civil registration and what does BMD stand for?

In 1837 – the year that Queen Victoria came to the throne – civil registration was introduced to England and Wales. On 1 July, the country was divided into registration districts, each controlled by a superintendent registrar and, in turn, a registrar general, making it law that all births, marriages and deaths were documented. In Scotland, this procedure officially began on 1 January 1855, whilst in Ireland it was not introduced until 1864. The letters BMD refer to the **b**irth, **m**arriage and **d**eath certificates which can be requested to gain the information about a specific person recorded under civil registration.

What information does each certificate include?

Your first look at a copy of the birth, marriage or death certificate of an ancestor and the acquisition of new knowledge about your family's past can be an exciting experience.

Birth certificates give the child's forenames, the date and location of the birth, the name and occupation of the father and the name and maiden name of the mother along with her usual address. Also included are the details of the informant for registration.

Marriage certificates give the names and ages of the couple with their addresses and occupations along with the names and occupations of their fathers. Each certificate includes the date and place of marriage with the names and signatures (or marks) of two witnesses – these could be friends or other members of the bride or groom's family.

Death certificates record the identity of the deceased, their age, date and place of death, their occupation and address as well as the actual cause of death. The name and address of the informant for registration is also included.

How do I find a BMD certificate and where do I order it from?

These certificates can be located using indexes in which each year is split into quarters and every entry is labelled with the district in which the event took place, a volume and page number. Search the indexes at The National Archives or online at ancestry.co.uk, findmypast.com, freebmd.org.uk or BMDindex.co.uk. Alternatively, you can visit your local record office or family history society who may have a paper version for you to check through. Scotland's indexes can be viewed at The National Archives of Scotland or online at scotlandspeople.gov.uk.

With this information you can then apply for a copy of the original certificate by completing the form with reference numbers from the index on the General Register Office (GRO) website at gro.gov.uk/gro/content, by post or at the register office at which the event was registered.

Based in Southport, the GRO is the central source of certified copies of register entries in England and Wales. Issued in a certificate format, births, marriages and deaths registered since 1837 can be applied for here, as well as adoption certificates and certain records for some British Nationals who were born, married or died overseas.

Certificate Considerations

Events are filed by the date registered – not the date that they occurred.

From 1874 a fine was imposed if a parent registered a newborn outside the permitted period of six weeks from birth, so some families actually lied about the date of birth of their child to avoid paying the penalty.

On a marriage certificate the newly weds were never asked to give proof of their actual names; some were married with their nickname or shortened name rather than the one issued on their birth certificates.

Just because your ancestor signed his own signature rather than made his mark with a cross did not necessarily mean he could read. Many people knew just how to write their own name but not how to read.

On a death certificate, if the cause of death is not followed by the word 'certified' then this would usually mean that a doctor was not called in to officially confirm the deceased's passing. Often the poorer classes could not afford a doctor's fees.

From 1875, the relationship between the deceased and the informant of the death had to be stated on the death certificate. This gives genealogists the opportunity to find new family links.

Keep an open mind when referring to the age of the deceased; sometimes an informant would not be entirely sure of their age.

Will I need to order BMD certificates for each of my ancestors?

Not necessarily – but do think carefully about what information you wish to find. You may be able to establish some facts from the census (*see* Chapter 4) so try to get the most from your research. For example, rather than sending for each individual's documents it may be more beneficial to acquire an older sibling's birth certificate to see if the home address changed over the years, especially if they were born nearer the earlier part of civil registration when the same information provided on (say) the 1841 census would be very sketchy.

Marriage certificates are essential for determining the names of each of the couple's fathers and provide the starting point for another generation, but if you know the location at which the union took place then parish marriage records can often be viewed on microfilm at your local archive and photocopied for a fraction of the cost of a certificate.

Death certificates will not help in the same way. Although vital for establishing a cause of death, they won't necessarily add extra generations to your tree unless the informant was a family member that you were not yet aware of. From 1866 onwards, the age at death was added to the indexes enabling you to calculate the approximate birth date for the deceased. You may then decide not to send for this individual's birth certificate depending upon whether you can find details of their parents by other means.

MARRIAGES REGISTERED IN JANUARY, FEBRUARY, MARCH 1839

NAME		SUB-REGISTRARS DISTRICT	VOL	PAGE
DANIELS	James	Kensington	3	181
—	Lot	Manchester	20	478
—	Mary	Manchester	20	464
—	Mary	Norwich	13	374
—	Samuel	Cheltenham	11	205
—	Sarah	Bakewell	19	269
—	Sarah	Nottingham	15	701
—	Susannah	Bristol	11	527
—	Thomas	Axbridge	10	485
—	William	Liverpool	20	157
—	Winifred	Wigan	21	431
DANN	James	Kensington	3	195
—	James	Norwich	13	438
—	Sophia	Brighton	7	355
DANNETT	Sarah	Gainsbro	14	407
DANSIE	William	Edmonton	3	63
DANSON	Ann	Garstang	21	235
—	Jane	Lancaster	21	267
—	Margaret	Wigan	21	456
DANTON	Julia Emma	Bedminster	11	50
DARBEY	Caroline	Oxford	16	125
—	Maria	Dudley	18	302
DARBY	Ann	Shoreditch	2	280
—	Daniel	Birmingham	16	292
—	Daniel	Towcester	15	467
—	James	Dudley	18	299
—	James	Newington	4	254
—	John Thomson	Wandsworth	4	374
—	Maria	Walsall	17	216
—	Sarah	St. Pancras	1	211
—	William	Tiverton &c.	10	423
—	William Edward	Williton	10	743
DARBYSHIRE	John	Whitechapel	2	385
—	John	Wigan	21	444
—	Mary	Leigh	21	288
—	Philip	Altrincham	19	3
DARCH	Elizabeth	Barnstaple	10	25
DARE	Eliza	Risbridge	12	525
DAREY	Richard	Bethnal Green	2	9
DARK	Harriet	Keynsham	11	101
—	William	Stoke Damerel	9	471
DARKE	Elizabeth	Exeter	10	135
—	Sarah Elizabeth	St. Geo. Han. Sq.	1	23
DARKEN	Emily	Blofield	13	47
DARLEY	George	Sculcoates	22	349
—	Jane	Sculcoates	22	341
—	Joseph	Lincoln	14	577
—	Mary	Hull	22	229
—	Mary	Doncaster	22	69
—	William Henry	Dover	5	141
DARLING	Ann	Newcastle on Tyne	25	254
—	Hannah	Durham &c.	24	45
—	Matthew	Sheffield	22	412
—	Rebecca Flora	St. James West.	1	85
DARLINGTON	Elizabeth	Stockport	19	194
—	Martha	Wem &c.	18	242
—	Richard	Ecclesfield	22	101
—	Samuel	Birmingham	16	259
—	Sarah	Atherstone	16	239
DARLISON	Thomas Clifford	Foleshill	16	344
DARNELL	Maria	Leicester	15	99
—	Thomas	Islington	3	130
—	William	Stepney	2	338
DARNILL	Sarah	Glanford Brigg	14	485
DARNOCK	William	Cambridge	14	3
DARNTON	Thomas	Stockton &c.	24	150
DARRELL	Harriet	York	23	527
DARRICK	Mary	St. Columb	9	98
DARRINGTON	Harriet	Salisbury	8	515
DARRUGH	Daniel	Sheffield	22	402
DART	Sarah	Totnes	9	524
DARTS	William Edward	Greenwich	5	240
DARVEL	John	Hendon	3	99
DARVILL	Mary Ann	Eton	6	405
DARWEN	Edward	Manchester	20	424
DARWENT	William	Wolstanton	17	241
DARWIN	Charles Robert	Newcastle under Lyme	17	93
—	Jacob	Thirsk	24	449
—	Sarah	Sheffield	22	406
—	William	Skipton	23	474
DASCOMBE	Thomas	Clifton	11	279
DASH	Edward	Dursley	11	299
—	Samuel	Brighton	7	356
DATE	John	Kingsbridge	9	401
DATSON	Sarah	Milton	5	363A
DAUBENY	William	Stow on the Wold	11	421
DAUBNEY	James Hamlet	Kensington	3	179
DAUGHTERS	Maria	West London	2	205
DAUGHTREE	James	Portsea Isle	7	195
DAUGHTRY	Thomas	Chesterfield	19	331
DAULTON	Ann	Foleshill	16	353
—	John	Northampton	15	357
DAUNTER	Edward	Worcester	18	509
DAVENEY	Larkey	Liverpool	20	281
DAVENPORT	Betty	Barton &c.	20	79
—	Davies	Congleton	19	66
—	Edward	Aston	16	225
—	Elizabeth	St. Olaves	4	344
—	Elizabeth	Bury	21	174
—	Grace	Manchester	20	445
—	Hannah	Barton &c.	20	75
—	Harriet	Bury	21	173
—	Henry	Rochdale	21	388
—	James	Stockport	19	189
—	John Marriott	Bicester	16	41
—	Mary	Leek	17	55
—	Mary	Wigan	21	441
—	Richard	Bolton	21	92
—	Sarah	Wigan	21	460
—	Sarah	Birmingham	16	255
—	Thomas	Newington	4	289
DAVES	Agnes	Bedford	6	31
DAVEY	Catherine	Redruth	9	288
—	Charles	Chard	10	558A
—	Eliza	Plomesgate	12	471
—	Elizabeth Anne	Bristol	11	525
—	Ephraim Skingle	Epping	12	133
—	Frances	Thetford	13	461
—	John	Bath	11	31
—	John Leaberry	Huntingdon	14	229
—	Maria	St. Germans	9	134
—	Mary	Redruth	9	273
—	Mary	Tiverton &c.	10	412
—	Mary	Newmarket	14	189
—	William	Lambeth	4	227
—	William	Bodmin	9	39
DAVID	Edward	Bridgend	26	382
—	Eli	Cardiff	26	408
—	Elizabeth	Llanelly	26	609
—	Evan	Narberth	26	687
—	Jannet	Dolgelley	27	205
—	Margaret	Shoreditch	2	254
—	Morgan	Neath	26	469
—	Thomas	Neath	26	482A
—	William	Llanelly	26	594
DAVIDSON	Ann	Chertsey	4	39
—	Elizabeth	Penrith	25	89
—	Elizabeth Christiana	Stockton &c.	24	148
—	Emma	Otley	23	357
DAVIDSON	Emma	Manchester	20	401
—	Esther	Newcastle on Tyne	25	283
—	Jane	Brampton	25	21
—	Jane	Bellingham	25	181
—	John	Halifax	22	179
—	John William	Bermondsey	4	5
—	Margaret	Longtown	25	65
—	Mary	Brampton	25	21
DAVIE	Amelia	Witham	12	375
—	John	Liverpool	20	148

BMD Index. Here, the marriages from the first quarter of 1839 are shown, listing the name of each individual, the registration district in which the marriage took place and the volume and page numbers where the entry was recorded. The details of Charles Robert Darwin's marriage can be seen here; it took place in the Newcastle under Lyme area. By using the information found on these indexes you can track down your own copy of one of your ancestor's marriages enabling you to discover who they married, the actual date and location, their occupations and the names and occupations of their fathers. Courtesy of thegenealogist.co.uk and General Registers Office.

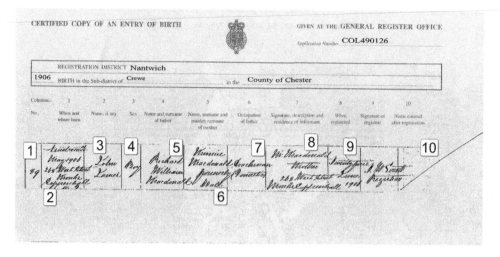

(*Right*) Copy of official marriage certificate. (1) This refers to the registration district location and will be listed as such in the indexes. This will be followed by the building or address where the marriage took place, a repeat of the registration district and the county. Often the parish name is mentioned. There are variations according to religious denomination. (2) This number refers to the entry number of the event. (3) This shows the date of marriage. (4) This column names the bride and groom. These are not necessarily the names they were given at birth, but can be those by which they were most commonly known. (5) The ages indicated here should be treated with caution. The term 'of full age' was supposed to mean that a party was over 21 but this was not necessarily true (*see* Chapter 3). (6) 'Condition' denotes marital status. A bride listed as a widow may be recorded under her former married name and not her maiden name. (7) Occupation at time of marriage was recorded except during the early twentieth century when women's occupations went unrecorded. (8) The couple's address at time of marriage. (9) The natural father's name was always recorded here; never a stepfather or other family member. Illegitimate children could finally name their father or adopt a name to avoid the stigma of illegitimacy. (10) The father's occupation. (11) The place of marriage. (12) More details about the marriage: after banns, by certificate, by common or special licence etc. (13) Signatures or marks of the couple. (14) This line indicates that no changes have been made.

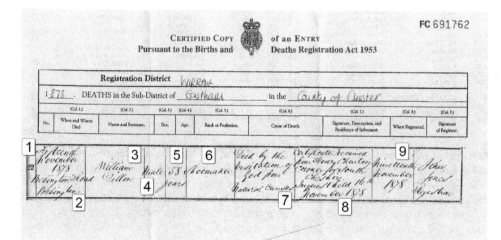

(*Left*) Copy of official birth certificate. (1) Entry number: a number between 1 and 500 was given to every birth event. (2) Date and place of birth. A time may indicate a multiple birth. (3) The child's forenames. If none is recorded this could indicate a stillbirth, an illegitimate child destined for adoption or simply that a name had not yet been decided upon. (4) The sex of the child. (5) Before 1850, the inclusion of an illegitimate child's father was at the registrar's discretion. After 1850, the father's name and occupation were left blank. After 1875, unmarried parents could add the father's details by mutual agreement but both parties would sign the register; therefore two signatures in the informant column indicates that the parents were unmarried. (6) An unmarried mother will have one entry in this column since she will still be using her maiden name. If she has been married more than once any previous married names will be included. This changed in 1969, after which previous married names did not have to be shown. (7) A line indicates that the father had no occupation or that the informant did not know it. (8) This is the signature of the parent or other informant; if this person were unable to write they would mark a cross. Many people could write their own name but could not read well enough to check that the information recorded was correct. (9) This is the date of registration, not of birth. There can be a substantial gap between the two. (10) This column allows for the changing of a name after registration.

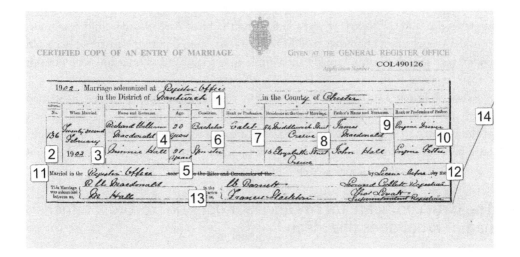

(*Left*) Copy of official death certificate. (1) The entry number could be anything between 1 and 500 in the early registers with five entries per page. Two members of the same family may appear with the same reference number if they died together in an accident or around the same time of a disease. (2) The date of death was recorded here; the place could of course be anywhere and not necessarily the address of the deceased. (3) This column records the name of the deceased. Again, this could be that by which they were most commonly known and may not match their birth certificate. A baby that died shortly after birth may be recorded only by surname. (4) The sex is given here; mistakes have been known to be made. (5) The age of the deceased should be treated with caution; the individual may have lied (perhaps in order to marry earlier) or the informant may have been misinformed. (6) This is the deceased's last known occupation; it may not be that at which they had worked for the majority of their life. (7) This column recorded the medical term for the cause of death. The earlier the certificate, the simpler the description is likely to be. The information could be given by a doctor, certified by an inquest, certified by a post mortem but no inquest or uncertified. By 1845 a doctor was present at the majority of deaths. (8) The informant could have been someone in attendance, the occupier of the house or the master of an institution. (9) Most deaths were registered within a couple of days. If the death was unexplained then it could go unregistered until after an inquest.

I'm unable to find a birth/marriage/death in the index; what am I doing wrong?

Sadly, prior to 1874, there was no penalty for failing to register an event so there will be cases which have 'slipped under the radar'. But there are other possibilities that you should consider. For example, could your ancestor have been born, married or died outside England and Wales?

Look for alternative spellings of the surname you are tracking down – many people could not read or write and, combined with various accents, the precise name could have been 'lost in translation' by the registrar.

If you are using ages from the census to calculate the year of birth, why not try widening the period in which you're searching – your ancestor could be younger or older than they actually claimed on the census.

If tracking down a marriage, check that the bride had not previously been wed and is, in fact, registered under her widowed surname and not her original maiden name. If you are trying to find the marriage of parents using the birth date of their child as a guide, consider that the first child may well have been born long before the marriage, so again widen your search period. Equally, the couple may have lived as man and wife but not actually married at all.

As we all know, deaths can take place at any time and this may well have happened for your ancestor. He or she could have been travelling or visiting family in another part of the country, so expand your search further afield to find the place where their deaths were registered. If an inquest was carried out upon the death of your ancestor, the event may well have been registered a while after the death occurred.

The birth certificate for my ancestor does not record a father's name. What does this mean?

There is a strong probability that your ancestor was illegitimate. If the father had died before the birth then the mother would perhaps have been listed as widowed and the father's name would appear alongside the word 'deceased'. Alternatively, the parents of the child may not have been married, although in some cases, the father was still named. Where possible, follow up this discovery with a check of the censuses to see if your ancestor was listed as living with any 'parents' or, if he or she married, investigate whether the father's name was included on the marriage certificate.

In cases of illegitimacy, parish records will list the mother's name only on the baptism records of her child and may even have the words 'bastard', 'spurious' or 'illegitimate' as definition. You may be fortunate enough to be given a clue such as 'reputed son of…'; the child may have two surnames (one for each of his parents) or the father's name will be included in the middle names of the child. Initially, it can be disheartening to think that a whole branch of your tree may not be accessible because of this lack of information, but all is not lost. Before you completely write off this side of the family, do some other investigations of your own.

DEATHS REGISTERED IN APRIL, MAY, JUNE, 1849

NAME		SUP REGISTRARS DISTRICT	VOL	PAGE
BROCKLEHURST	Mary	Belper	19	376
	River Ridgway	Stockport	19	246
	Samuel	Macclesfield	19	96
	William	Wortley	22	533
BROCKLESBY	Frances	Lincoln	14	332
	Mary	Boston	14	196
BROCKLEY	Elizabeth	Foleshill	16	305
	Mary	Wolstanton	17	234
	Richard	Stockport	19	215
BROCKLISS	Ann	Brackley	15	160
BROCKMAN	George	Germans St	9	66
	Julius Tatton	Bradford Yk	23	174
BROCKSHAW	George	Lukes St	2	212
BROCKWAY	Fanny Maria	Bedminster	11	58
BROCKWELL	Caroline Eliza	Kingston	4	154
	Joseph	Oxford	16	78
BRODERICK	Jeremiah	Marylebone	1	199
BRODHURST	Hannah Maria	Blaby	15	39
BRODIE	Andrew	S Shields	24	159
	Jane	Tynemouth	25	338
	Jane	Tynemouth	25	337
	Jessey Alexandrina	York	23	558
BRODRICK	Mary	Liverpool	20	194
	Michael	Sheffield	22	460
BRODWELL	Thomas	Pateley Bridge	23	408
BROGDEN	Ann	Bradford Yk	23	107
	George	Bradford Yk	23	106
	Joseph	Ripon	23	417
	Joseph	Manchester	20	538
	Mary	Preston	21	455
	Nancy	Bradford Yk	23	68
BROGGI	Clara	Pancras St	1	210
BROKENBROW	Emma	Bath	11	52
BROKENSHIR	Harriet Maria	Shoreditch	2	287
	Nicholas	Falmouth	9	52
BROLAN	James	Wellington Sp	18	170
BROMAGE	Ann	Hay	26	271
	Betsey	Pershore	18	332
	John	Presteigne &c	26	207
	John	Crickhowell	26	262
	Richard	Hay	26	273
	Thomas	Warwick	16	404
	Thomas	Abergavenny	26	15
BROMBELL	John	Atcham	18	8
BROMEHEAD	Charles Alexander Crawford	Chesterfield	19	415
BROMELEY	James	Ashton	20	39
BROMELL	Richard	Holsworthy	9	223
	William	Stratton	9	179
BROMFIELD	James	Lymington	8	143
	Jane	Tiverton &c	10	201
BROMHAM	James	Henley	16	64
	Martha	Henley	16	61
BROMIGE	Frank William	Pancras St	1	287
BROMILEY	Ellen	Bolton	21	138
	Jane	Bolton	21	90
	Martha	Manchester	20	581
	Mary	Bolton	21	135
	Samuel	Bolton	21	135
	Thomas	Bolton	21	135
BROMLEY	Alexander	Lambeth	4	213
	Ann	Auckland	24	4
	Annis Maria	Wolstanton	17	228
	Edward	Milton	5	315
	Elizabeth	St Lukes	2	200
	Elizabeth	Medway	5	296
	Elizabeth	W Derby	20	854
	Elizabeth	Liverpool	20	445
	Harriet	Malling	5	283
	Isaac	Wolstanton &c	17	234
	James	Wolstanton	17	236
	James	Stoke on T	17	150
	John	Hendon	3	163
	Martha	Boughton Gt	19	38
	Mary	Chorlton	20	169
	Mary	Stoke on Trent	17	131
	Mary Ann	Pancras St	1	232
	Peter	Leigh	21	397
	Richard	Geo St Southk	4	319
	Sarah	Henley	16	59
	William	Leigh	21	398
	William	Liverpool	20	419
BROMWELL	William	Bedford	6	31
BROMWICH	Catherine	Rugby	16	327

NAME		SUP REGISTRARS DISTRICT	VOL	PAGE
BROMWICH	Edwin	Poplar	2	231
	Thomas	Birmingham	16	198
BRONTE	Anne	Scarbro'	24	384
BROOK	Alfred	Huddersfield	22	288
	Ann	Otley	23	386
	Betty	Huddersfield	22	271
	David	Huddersfield	22	281
	Edwin	Otley	23	385
	Elizabeth	Sheffield	22	450
	Elizabeth	Sheffield	22	451
	Elizabeth	Langport	10	304
	Elizabeth	Wakefield	22	529
	Elizabeth	Huddersfield	22	253
	Elizabeth	Huddersfield	22	250
	Elizabeth	Ecclesfield	22	115
	George	Huddersfield	22	211
	Henry	Bradford Yk	23	165
	Henry Edwin	Geo St Southk	4	343
	Isaac	Bradford Yk	23	130
	James	Huddersfield	22	253
	Jane	Huddersfield	22	255
	John	Barnstaple	10	29
	John	Ecclesfield	22	112
	John	Ecclesfield	22	118
	John	Bradford Yk	23	173
	John	Bradford Yk	23	177
	John	Huddersfield	22	274
	Jonas	Leeds	23	360
	Joseph	Chard	10	269
	Joseph	Huddersfield	22	289
	Joseph	Huddersfield	22	251
	Joseph	Halifax	22	146
	Joshua	Huddersfield	22	259
	Mary	Torrington	10	213
	Mary	Wakefield	22	507
	Nancy	Huddersfield	22	249
	Naomi	Bradford Yk	23	151
	Richard	Brighton	7	218
	Robert	Bosmere	12	238
	Samuel	Hayfield &c	19	449
	Samuel	Sherborne	8	75
	Samuel	Halifax	22	167
	Samuel	Halifax	22	143
	Sarah	Wortley	22	538
	Sarah	Ecclesfield	22	116
	Thomas	Sherborne	8	76
	Thomas	Dewsbury	22	28
	William	Tadcaster	23	501
	Male	Medway	5	300
	Male	Hunslet	23	212
	Female	Huddersfield	22	290
	Female	Hunslet	23	212
BROOKBANKS	Richard	Aston	16	138
BROOKE	Ann	Leeds	23	371
	Ann	Gainsbro'	14	239
	Caroline	Depwade	13	26
	Ellen	Stockport	19	202
	Enoch	Bradford Yk	23	158
	George	Salford	20	805
	George	Gainsbro'	14	239
	Harriet	Birmingham	16	263
	Jane	Bradford Yk	23	123
	John	Tenbury	18	375
	John	Halifax	22	137
	Laura	Pancras St	1	243
	Margaret Anna Elizabeth	Elham	5	118
	Martha	Macclesfield	19	92
	Mary	Wortley	22	538
	Salome	Guiltcross	13	117
	Sarah	Stockport	19	214
	Sarah Maria	Chelsea	3	37
	Thomas Henry	Plymouth	9	259
	Thomas Wyatt	Doncaster	22	69
	William	Bradford Yk	23	125
BROOKER	Elizabeth	Tonbridge	5	407
BROOKER	George	Tonbridge	5	407
	George Edward	Dover	5	88
	James	E Grinstead	7	277
	James Colbert	Hunslet	23	235
	Jonathan	Wallingford	6	194
	Joseph Augustus	Brighton	7	217
	Lydia	Wokingham	6	224
	Michael	Kingston	4	166

BMD Index. The birth, marriage and death indexes work in the same way allowing you to locate the relevant civil registration certificate. This example records the death of Anne Brontë in 1849 in Scarborough. The indexes are also invaluable in identifying an event if it took place in an area away from your ancestor's normal habitat. Courtesy of thegenealogist.co.uk and General Registers Office.

Before the formation of the Poor Law Unions of 1834, each parish was responsible for its poor. Overseers, clergy and churchwardens would often work in unison establishing a place of legal settlement which decreed that a legitimate child could take his father's place of settlement even if it was different from his place of birth, whilst an illegitimate child could claim settlement in the place where he was born. This could then result in the overseers sending a pregnant girl back to her own place of settlement so that the parish did not have to take responsibility for the child.

Sometimes, formal investigations were carried out before the birth of the illegitimate child to establish who the father was. These details were then recorded in the overseer's account books so that he could pay the lying-in and later maintenance costs of the child.

The overseer's position also enabled him to apply for a warrant to bring any alleged fathers to the quarter sessions courts to stand before the Justice of the Peace. These sessions were held four times a year and minute books usually recorded the proceedings and the information regarding the father and his place of residence. If the case against him was proven, a document known as a 'bastardy bond' was signed which absolved the parish from any responsibility for the child and required payment of maintenance until the child reached the age of 7. These bonds also required the signature of two guarantors, one of which was usually the man's father – which has the potential to add a new name to your family tree. These types of records may hold clues as to the parentage of your ancestor and those documents that remain are likely to be held at your local archive.

Illegitimacy was a stigma and a 'cross to bear' for both the child and its mother. In many cases, you will not be able to establish the true identity of the father but there could be clues which will point you in his general direction. If family knowledge has passed down the name of a possible candidate then follow up this potential lead – he may have apprenticed the child in a 'family' trade or even mentioned his offspring in his will.

In some cases of illegitimacy a father suddenly appeared on a later marriage certificate; treat such instances with caution. Although these certificates were official documents and are looked upon as primary sources, at times our ancestors lied. Admitting to illegitimacy was humiliating so inventing a father spared the individual embarrassment.

We have all read novels or watched costume dramas where the housemaid has become pregnant by a liaison (consensual or otherwise) with the wealthy head of the household, his son or other 'upstanding' member of the community. The social divide did not look kindly upon this fraternising between the classes and often the woman was left an outcast whilst the offending male was bundled off abroad or given a commission at sea until the gossip around the incident had died down. Some men had no intention of admitting to or providing for the unwanted child, but for others – where there had been true feelings involved – you may find examples of gifts given during the child's early life: payments made for schooling, or the sudden fortune of a lucrative military career in adulthood.

Although having a child out of wedlock was frowned upon, it was also a regular occurrence. Some families would arrange informal adoptions between both parties, making this very difficult to trace, before an official system was established in the twentieth century. Others would try to hide the fact by sending their daughter away to live with relatives during her confinement whilst the mother would play the 'pregnant role'. Upon the daughter's return the baby would be passed off as a sibling. This infant may then have grown up calling her actual grandparents 'mother and father' whilst her real mother would have been classed as an older sister. This is always worth considering if there are discrepancies within your family tree and large gaps between the births of children.

What is a 'foundling'?

A foundling is a child who has been abandoned by its parents. From the establishment of London's Foundling Hospital in 1739, institutions would take in deserted youngsters to give them a place to live and were an early form of children's home. By the age of 14, boys were usually apprenticed or joined the forces while the girls entered domestic service. London's Foundling Hospital produced records of its admissions between 1741 and its closure in 1954, which are kept at the London Metropolitan Archives (LMA) (cityoflondon.gov.uk/LMA). Find out more about life as a foundling and the work of the hospital exhibited at the Foundling Museum, 40 Brunswick Square, London or online at foundlingmuseum.org.uk.

Perhaps there were similar institutions in the area where your ancestor was brought up – track down local history publications which should enable you to pinpoint their location and give you a background story of their work.

Can I find the birth year of my ancestors by their ages on their marriage certificates?

In many cases you can, but be aware of the phrase 'of full age' which was used to imply that the bride or groom was 21 years or over and old enough to marry without the consent of their parents. Use this age as a guide to a particular date range when calculating the birth and widen your search on either side of this to find the exact year. If a couple were desperate to get married, one of the pair could have been a minor. Vanity also played its part as women would often knock a few years off their ages whilst men would add a few on. You will come across numerous occasions in your family history research when our forebears liked to confuse us.

Despite searching the indexes I'm still having trouble finding the birth of one ancestor. Where else could I look?

Try the website BMDRegisters.co.uk where the non-parochial, foreign and maritime registers can be found. Listing over 8.25 million entries from 1636–1950, the collection includes births, marriages and deaths aboard ships, maternity records and Nonconformist records which cover Methodists, Baptists, Quakers, Wesleyans, Roman Catholics and many others – ideal if you have had difficulty tracking down an individual in the Anglican parish registers. The records are free to search but if you wish to perform advanced searches or download documents then a small fee is required.

Calendar Calculations

Throughout the centuries, various diaries or almanacs have been used to mark time and fix events and religious festivals within the yearly cycle. Originally, people would set these dates to tie in with easily observed natural occurrences like the changing seasons or varying weather, but the fact that these happenings were not reliable meant that an alternative had to be found.

In 45BC, Julius Caesar established the Julian calendar which was used in Britain and her colonies until 1751. His formula consisted of creating eleven months of 30 or 31 days and 28 in February (except on a Leap Year when this rose to 29). The calculations differed from the solar calendar by only 11.5 minutes per year, but over the centuries these minutes added up, and by the 1500s the Julian calendar was ten days behind its astronomical equivalent.

The Gregorian calendar was created by Pope Gregory XIII in 1582 to correct this problem, and although Britain did not take on this new schedule, many other countries did. One of the main differences between the two calendars is that the Julian has a leap year every four years whereas the Gregorian does not have a leap year if the number is not dividable by 400 or ends in 00. Therefore, 2000 was a Leap Year but 1900 was not.

In 1751, when Britain eventually decided to adopt the Gregorian system, eleven days had to be lost in that first year to set it in line. These were taken from the month of September when the British Calendar Act declared that Wednesday 2 September would be followed by Thursday 14 September. In the old Julian calendar, the first day of the year was 25 March – or Lady Day as it was known – so to complete the calendar changeover, 1751 ran from 25 March to 31 December, allowing the following year to begin on 1 January. If you are able to track your ancestry back to this period, be aware that events in this year were often dated as 1750/51 when the calendar conversion took place.

My female ancestor was widowed and remarried but I cannot find any mention of her second marriage in the index. Why?

Upon marriage, a woman takes the surname of her husband forfeiting her maiden name. If widowed, and later remarried, she would be listed under her widowed surname and not revert back to her maiden name, so take this into account when searching the indexes. A similar situation may occur on a birth certificate where a mother's maiden name is shown. If she had been married before any children were born to a second husband, the record would read, for example: 'Mary Clark, Late Jones, Formerly Smith' – meaning Mary Clark is her married name at present, she was previously married to a man named Jones and her maiden name was Smith.

What is a marriage licence and how does this differ from a 'traditional' banns marriage?

Today, there is a wealth of choices available when planning a marriage, from church services and registry office weddings to gatherings in hotels or unusual venues. But from 1215 the church required the announcement of a union and the opportunity for anyone who objected to voice their opinions. As a result this declaration was made in the form of 'banns' which were read for three consecutive weeks before the marriage took place.

From the fourteenth century onwards, those looking for an alternative were faced with obtaining a marriage licence which would allow them to marry immediately and waive the banns notice period. There was a fee for this service and an agreement in the form of a 'bond' to establish that there was no impediment to the marriage. Details of the bondsman – usually a relative or friend to oversee the event – were also recorded. A licence did not have to be obtained in the county from which the couple were originally from, so this was ideal for those who wanted to marry away from home.

My female ancestor is believed to have divorced in the early 1900s. How can I confirm this?

Before 1858, divorce could only be granted by a Private Act of Parliament and was not an option for the ordinary classes, so the ability to legally separate from one's spouse was not really considered a realistic alternative until the twentieth century. Why not visit findmypast.com and take a look at their divorce and matrimonial cases of 1858 to 1903? There is a pay-per-view facility, ideal if it is only one specific record for which you are searching. The abbreviation 'PMD' in the 'marital condition' column of a marriage certificate stands for 'previous marriage dissolved'.

What are parish records?

In the sixteenth century, Henry VIII unwittingly gave a major boost to future genealogical researchers by ordering that ministers should keep a log of all baptisms, marriages and burials in each respective Anglican parish. These registers tell us the date and parish in which an event took place, names, ages and parents' surnames.

Although this practice began in 1538, very few records survive before 1600 and some originals have been lost altogether. A duplicate set of these documents was also made which are known as bishops' transcripts and, together with the originals, they enable the possibility to trace our families from 1837 and the start of civil registration (and the introduction of BMDs), back to Tudor times.

Index to divorce and matrimonial causes from 1866. These indexes are a finding tool for other divorce records. Once you locate an ancestor in this record set, refer to the help and advice section at www.findmypast. co.uk/helpadvice/ knowledge-base/ wills-divorces/ index.jsp#divorce_ to further your research.

How would I find transcriptions of these parish records or view the originals?

Record offices usually hold copies of the registers or microfilmed versions of their area; the Society of Genealogists (sog.org.uk) holds the largest collection of registers in the country, whilst many family history societies have transcribed and indexed their

Sept. 1655	Marriages	Feb. 1656

1655.

11 Arthur Foxley to Katherin Tompson, widow
12 [1] Morgan Phillips to Grizzill Atkins
13 Mathew Horner to Ann Hayes, widow
17 John Furnis to Mary Crake
18 Thomas Hill, gent., to Mrs. Elinor Webb, spr.
Henry Saldat to Elizabeth Hayes
26 Hamlett Joyce to Susanna Gibson, spr.
29 Randolph Andrews to Alice Powell, widow

October.

2 Rowland Jones to Elizabeth Humphrey, spr.
3 James Snell to Mary Boone, widow
6 Nicholas Loue, gent.,[2] to Elizabeth Bugges, spr.[3]
Thomas Keppin to Lucyna Newton, spr.
8 Mathew Watkins to Frances Potter, spr.
Thomas Barber to Elizabeth Snell, spr.
9 [4] Peter Smith to Elizabeth Caades, widow
9 Richard Ball, gent., to Elizabeth Arther, spr.
Richard Baker, gent., to Elizabeth Maynerd, widow
Andrew Foot to Elinor Labarr, widow
10 James Knot to Ann Ruden, spr.
11 John Bewicke, to Joyce Shippee, spr.
15 William Copper, yeoman, to Jane Farrell, widow
16 Richard Farlow to Christian Redman, widow
18 John Doe to Anne Rogers, spr.
22 Henry Hatton, esq.,[5] to Elizabeth Polsted, widow

November.

2 Nathaniell Overton, gent., to Hannah Bignall, spr.
William Frost, yeoman, to Sarah Hare
5 William Coleman to Rebecca Robinson
Robert Heard to Dorothy Findall
6 John Hollawell to Margrett Goulding, widow
William Bromley to Hellen Grigson, spr.
Richard Mynd to Jane Applegate,[6] spr.
Evan Joanes, yeoman, to Margrett Bickerton, spr.
Henry Ticknall to Constance Moore, widow
Robert Chillman to Jane Williams, widow
19 James Partridge, yeoman, to Elizabeth Pattison, widow
Richard Eyans, gent., to Margarett Aisgill, spr.
21 John Watson to Mary Boyett, spr.
22 Thomas Cowell to Mary Ward, spr.
27 Richard Napton to Ann Robinson, widow
29 Robert Plumer to Mary Brice, spr.

December.

1 Samuell Peps, gent.,[7] to Elizabeth Marchant De S[nt.] Michell, spr.[8]

1655.

John Page to Elinor Howard, spr.
John Collins to Margrett Bennett, widow
4 Henry Jarvice to Mary Townesen, spr.
5 William Lowen to Elizabeth Reynolds
John Horseman to Sarah Langdale, widow
10 Richard Ward to Elizabeth Shorter, spr.
William Atkinson to Margery Watkins, spr.
11 Robert Parker to Elizabeth Franklin, widow
Tobias Martyn to Margrett Harrison, widow
Edward Goldney to Susanna Butler, spr.
Daniell Booker, gent., to Mary Fenn, spr.
14 William Browne to Ann Richardson
15 William Page, gent., to Abigaile Kethrich, spr.
18 Richard Presey to Elizabeth Ivores, widow
William Daueney, yeoman, to Jane Wrighter, widow
Henry Hawke, yeoman, to Ann Roper, spr.
John Norton to Elizabeth Mooleham
20 Francis Robinson, yeoman, to Mary Marsden, spr.
24 Robert Atreed to Margrett Williams, widow
27 Patrick Chambers to Auderey Wood, widow
William Eaton to Elizabeth Lucus, spr.
29 John Atford to Margrett Russell, spr.
Isaack Walker to Margrett Cooke

1656.

January.

1 Francis Joanes to Sibella Salter, spr.
3 William Burt to Anne Mesinger, spr.
Thomas Raybee, yeoman, to Dorcas Smith, spr.
4 George Kate to Margarett Wigins, spr.
7 Felix Carter to Elizabeth Mayson, spr.
10 Richard Bennett to Anne Whright, spr.
14 Nicholas Tatham, yeoman, to Elizabeth Bayley, spr.
17 Georg Griffith to Jane Mosse, spr.
28 John Heading to Anne Bladen, spr.
30 James Morgan, gent., to Elinor London, widow
John Nash, gent., to Mary Knipe, widow

February.

4 John Hunt to Elizabeth Baker, spr.
6 Richard Mathews, yeoman, to Margery Wells, spr.
14 Thomas Wright, gent., to Elizabeth Bridges, spr.
16 Thomas Hall to Mary Symons, spr.
18 Peter Linley to Anne Wilkinson, widow
William Winter to Elizabeth Coole, spr.
Edmund Gray to Jane Doncastell
19 Richard White to Sarah Cooke, spr.
Isaac Richardson to Katherine Fox, spr.

[1] Banns published 27 August, 3, 10 September 1654; marriage dated 12 September 1655.
[2] S. of Dr. Nicholas Love, headmaster of Winchester, 1601, by Dousabel, dau. of Barnabas Colnett, of the Isle of Wight; matric. Oxford (Wadham Coll.) 1626, M.A., 1636; barrister-at-law (Lincoln's Inn), 1636, bencher, 1648; recorder of Basingstoke, 1643; a six clerk in chancery, 1644; M.P. for Winchester, 1645-53, and 1659; one of the judges for the trial of Charles I., but did not sign the death-warrant; excepted from the act of oblivion, and fled to Switzerland at the Restoration; d. at Vevey, 5 November 1682, and bur. there in the church of St. Martin.
[3] This marriage is recorded also in the registers of Westminster Abbey.
[4] Altered from "8."
[5] S. of Roger Hatton, of London, by Anne, dau. and co-h. of — Palmer, of Leicester; of Micham, co. Surrey; knighted 14 December 1660; J.P. for Surrey.
[6] Altered from "Applegath."
[7] El. s. of John Pepys, of London and afterwards of Brampton, co. Huntingdon (s. of Thomas Pepys the elder, by Mary Day); b. 23 February, and bapt. at St. Bride's, Fleet Street, 3 March 1633; educated at St. Paul's School, London, and Cambridge (B.A., 1653, M.A., 1660); went to live with the family of his relative Sir Edward Montagu (see his M 7 November 1642, and note thereto), 1656; clerk of the acts of the navy, and clerk of the privy seal, 1660; F.R.S, 1665; surveyor-general of the victualling office, 1665; M.P. for Castle Rising, 1673, for Harwich, 1679, 1685; deprived of his offices and imprisoned in the Tower on the charge of promoting the Popish Plot, 1679-80; P.R.S., 1684-6; secretary of the admiralty, 1686; lost his appointment at the revolution; again imprisoned for a short time, 1692; d. s.p. 26 May, and bur., at St. Olave's, Hart Street, London, 4 June 1703; his will pr. 25 June 1703; his famous Diary, giving in shorthand an account of events from 1660 to 1669, remained in MS. at Cambridge until 1825, when it was deciphered by John Smith, and published under the auspices of Richard (Neville) 3rd Baron Braybrooke.
[8] Dau. of Alexander Marchant, Sieur de St. Michel, by Dorothea, 2nd dau. of Sir Francis Kingsmill, of Ballybeg, co. Cork, knt., widow of Thomas Fleetwood; d. 10 December 1669.

Parish Records. Examples of parish records can be found in handwritten ledgers or bound, typewritten books which have been compiled at a later date. This example from the London Parish Record transcripts shows an entry for Samuel Pepys whose marriage took place to Elizabeth Marchant De St Michell on 1 December 1655. How far back are you able to trace your family line? Courtesy of thegenealogist.co.uk.

local records, making locating an event that bit easier. To find out what is available try consulting the *Phillimore Atlas and Index of Parish Records* at your archive library or invest in your own copy from genealogysupplies.com to view examples of pre-1832 parish boundary maps, 1834 county maps and details of how to locate both original records and copies.

A National Burial Index is available on CD or online at findmypast.com but bear in mind that neither is yet complete – so do not be disheartened if you cannot find that elusive ancestor just yet.

How would I use parish records to search for ancestors born before 1837?

Take, for example, a fictitious Robert Reed who appears on the 1851 census, aged 35 and gives his place of birth as Crewe in Cheshire. By subtracting his age from the census year you would get an approximate birth date of 1816 – well before the start of civil registration. You would now locate the parish record baptisms for Crewe, Cheshire and search for Robert Reed there. If you were successful, you could expect to find a note of his baptism, the names of his parents, their abode and perhaps even his father's occupation. This information would help take you back another generation allowing you to try to locate his parents on an early census, establish their ages and then apply the same methods to find their baptisms. Alternatively, you could switch to the marriage records to track down their marriage.

In all situations, if you fail to find details of an event, search the records of neighbouring parishes. Local and county archives will hold collections of their parish records – some will have been indexed while others will not. Use a search engine to discover if the records you need to investigate have been put online or contact web shops such as parishchest.com or genealogysupplies.com to buy your own copy of an area's transcribed registers on CD Rom – extremely useful if you have a large number of ancestors who stayed in one particular area of the country.

DON'T FORGET!

Baptism entries are different from birth dates and it's wise not to confuse the two. Baptisms would usually take place a few days or weeks after the birth but in some cases, especially in Nonconformist groups, you may discover that large families went in for multiple baptisms with a whole age range of children being baptised on the same day. If you cannot find the entry for your ancestor, expand your date range and attempt to find the entries of other siblings to help narrow your search.

ST. OLAVE, HART STREET, LONDON.

May	12	Mrs Ann White, wid., buryed at St Dunston's, East: side chauncell
	23	Mathew s. Mathew & [sic] Millington: church yard
	24	Eliz. d. Abraham Gardner & Eliz. True, a base borne child: new church yard
June	6	Mary d. Thomas & Mary Pike: ch. yard
	10	John s. Nathaniell & Martha Rodburne
	27	Mr John Loggins, grocer, ffrom Mr Watkins in Cheyne Alley: new vault
	29	a stillborne child of Mr John Oviat, m^rc't, & Mrs Bridgett his wife: ch. yard
Aug.	5	Thomas s. Thomas & Eliz'beth Knight: ch. yard
	13	John s. John & Mary Greenwood: ch. yard
		Mary Cotten, ffrom St Leonard, Shorditch: old vault
	17	Roger s. Henry & Jane Watson: chvurch yard
	30	Joseph Obison, aprentice to Mr Wats: ch. yard
Sep.	7	Sarah d. Mr Ralph Ingram, mrc't, & Mrs Sarah his wife: old vault
		Susan Tivill, servant to M^r Wm. Thornbury, buryed in Mr Thornburye's vault
	10	John Walker, a labourer from Mr Frood's: church yard
		Thomas s. Tho. & Mary Potter, from ye Tower Liberty: church yard
	12	Samuell s. Samuell & Ann Hide: old vault
	15	Henry s. Wm. & Susanna Arnoll: old vault
	20	John s. Jno & Mary Wilkins: ch. yard
	23	Elizabeth wife of Humphry Bell: new vault
	29	Wm. Luck, ffrom Mr Kent's: vavlt
Oct.	2	Mr Saml Gardner, m^rc't, ffrom ye Tower Liberty: old vault
	5	Mary d. John & Mary Twigg: church yard
	10	Eliz. d. Nathan'l & Eliz. Hudson: church yard
	16	Thomas s. Wm. & Elizabeth Fitch, from Mr Hasle's: church yard
	22	Mary d. Frauncis & Mary Gythings: ch. yard
		a ffemale child of Robert & [sic] Eliot, vnbaptiz'd: church yard
	30	John Crosley, cooper: church yard
Nov.	13	Elizabeth wife of Samuell Pepys esq^r, one of his Ma^{tis} Comishon^{rs} of ye Navy, obit x Novem^r & buryed in ye chauncell xiij instant
	15	Mary Harmer, a servant mayde of M^r Wm. Beakes: south isle, church
	22	Martha d. Thomas & Katherine Holker: midle isle, church
	28	Ann wife of Wm. Clements: new ch. yard
Dec.	2	Lidia d. Mr Jno Stone & Mrs Mary his wife: church yard
		Thomas Brand, porter: church yard
	8	Frauncis Thoris, lodger at Mr Meakins: old vault
	10	Elizabeth d. Wm. & Joyce Phillips: ch. yard
	11	Susan wife of Will Newman: vault
	12	a male child, vnbaptized, of Rich. & Hannah Gibson: church yard
	13	Susan Watts, ffrom Algate pish: old vault
	30	Mrs Rebecca Midlemore, ffrom Doct^r Trenches, buryed at St Clement's: church
		Mary wife of Jno Pomphret: old vault
Jan.	2	Elizabeth Ratcliffe, wid., buryed in Alhall', Barkin: north isle, church
	5	Edm^d Trench, doct^r of phisick, buryed at Alhall' Stainings: south isle, church
	6	James s. Mr James Carckas & Mrs Issabella his wife: midle isle
	9	Rozaman Ouerhill, ffrom ye Costom house: church yard
	19	a ffemall child, vnbaptized, base borne, of Susan Cox, servant to Jno Smith, butcher: church yard
	25	Jno Davis, servant to Walter Willson, vinctn^r: church yard
	26	Susam Cox, servant to Tho. [sic] Smith, butcher: new church yard
	29	Ann Faulkner, serv^t to ye widd. Crockford: church yard
Feb.	16	Wm. Aylin, a servant to Esqr Blunt: ch. yard

Parish Record. This record from the London Parish Record transcripts allows us to discover Elizabeth Pepys' burial date of 15 November 1669 in the chancel of St Olave's church in Hart Street, London. By following a trail of records you can chart your ancestor's story, adding snippets of information that will help you build a timeline of events. Courtesy of thegenealogist.co.uk.

What is the International Genealogical Index?

In 1830, Joseph Smith founded the Church of the Latter-day Saints after witnessing a series of visions where he was led to a golden tablet inscribed with the Book of Mormon which told of the early history and religion of America. Although Smith was murdered fourteen years later, his religious work and belief that Christians were 'latter-day saints' was perpetuated by Brigham Young. One of their principal aims was to record the history and pedigrees of its members, a documentary archive which grew into one of the most comprehensive genealogical databases in the world.

As a result of a project started in the 1920s, the International Genealogical Index (IGI) is now searchable on the Latter-day Saints' site at familysearch.org. Although incomplete, a wealth of information is available here in the form of an index of births, marriages and deaths which has been compiled from church records dating back to medieval times and has the benefit of helping to tie your ancestor to a particular parish. It also includes details of baptisms and christenings from all over the British Isles and beyond (but no burials).

Dig deeper and you will find that the worldwide resources on this site enables you to search ancestral files, the 1881 census of Britain, the 1880 census of the United States and the 1881 census of Canada, as well as US Social Security Death Indexes and much more.

The church's latest venture is the upgraded record search pilot site to which new data is being added all the time. With English baptisms and marriages from 1700–1900, bishops' transcripts and registers of electors gradually being uploaded, it is a real luxury to have access to these resources at your fingertips.

The Church of the Latter-day Saints has research centres located around the country where their extensive records are searchable on CD or microfilm for those who wish to visit in person. You can order copies of any of the sources stored in their Family History Library in Utah despite not being a member of the church. Find out more at lds.org.uk.

What other parish register indexes are available to help me find the marriage of my ancestors?

Why not try the Boyd's Marriage Index for England between 1538 and 1837 which you can view online at originsnetwork.com; or the Pallot Marriage Index that dates from 1780–1837 and although mainly covers the London area, there is some coverage of other counties – you can search this at ancestry.co.uk and also at the Institute of Heraldic and Genealogical Studies at ihgs.ac.uk. If the marriage in question took place north of the border, take a look at the old parochial records between 1553 and 1854 at scotlandspeople.gov.uk.

What is the Strays' Index?

A 'stray' refers to an event such as a census entry, baptism or even a court appearance which has taken place outside the county or area where the person was born or usually lived. Most family history societies have compiled their own index so if your ancestor seems to have disappeared contact the relevant FH society and ask for advice on how to view this useful resource.

What are Nonconformist records?

These records apply to the huge variety of congregations who did not belong, or 'conform', to the Church of England. This includes Methodists, Baptists, Presbyterians, Independents and Quakers. The Church of England was established in the sixteenth century when Henry VIII broke away from the Roman Catholic Church, but over time, not everyone agreed with the ideals and beliefs of the Church of England so they established their own congregations. These 'rebels' were initially persecuted and called 'dissenters', but by 1851 over a quarter of the English population had shifted their allegiance to a Nonconformist faith. They were usually intelligent, freethinkers who fought for a better Britain and were not afraid to stand up for what they believed in.

Many Nonconformist records can be searched online at The National Archives – initial investigations are free of charge but advanced searches and downloads require a small fee. Records from the London Metropolitan Archives detailing the baptism, marriage and burial records of Britain's most famous Nonconformists – alongside those of thousands of ordinary men and women – were digitalised in 2010 and can be seen at www.ancestry.co.uk.

Below are just some of the religious movements and the dates from which they refused to conform to the Anglican Church. One branch of my family was Methodist – perhaps your ancestors belonged to one of these denominations.

- 1560 – Presbyterians
- 1582 – Congregationalists
- 1612 – Baptists
- 1640 – Unitarians
- 1650 – Quakers (Society of Friends)
- 1729 – Methodists
- 1837 – Mormons (Church of the Latter-day Saints)

Nonconformist Record. This example shows the birth certificate of Florence Nightingale in 1820. It gives her parents' names and place of birth as well as details of who was present at the birth and the name and address of the registrar. Before civil registration in 1837, parish records are an important source of tracing information on baptisms, marriage and burials. Nonconformist congregations included Baptists, Methodists, Presbyterians, Protestant Dissenters, Independents and some Roman Catholics, so if you can't find your ancestors listed in the Church of England registers then perhaps the Nonconformist records is where you should look. Courtesy of thegenealogist.co.uk and RG5 The National Archives UK.

How do I find my Catholic ancestors?

Between the mid-1500s and 1829, Catholicism in Britain was illegal. Adherents were forced to operate 'underground' in private houses and did not always consider it safe to keep records. The Catholic Relief Act of 1829 removed many of the restrictions on worship and procedures. Some Catholic records can often be found alongside the Nonconformist records but first contact the Catholic Record Society (catholic-history. org.uk/crs) whose volumes are all indexed individually, or familiarise yourself with the resources available at catholic-history.org.uk. The National Archives is always a great place to contact for assistance but your county record office should also be able to tell you what documents have survived in your region. If your ancestors were Scottish Catholics then you may be able to take advantage of the collection of parish baptisms from 1703–1955 which is online at scotlandspeople.gov.uk. Soon to be added are Catholic marriages, confirmations, deaths, burials and even lists of 'coverts' – opening up a whole new avenue of research that may previously have been difficult to follow.

Did You Know?

'Our BMD Registers collection provides hidden birth, marriage and death records from previously unpublished registries, and many include three generations of a family,' explains Beth Snow from thegenealogist.co.uk. 'They're invaluable for research prior to census and BMD records. The data includes images of early birth certificates and registers and are unique to The Genealogist. Included are Nonconformist records, early birth registries, maternity records, fleet marriages, burials, overseas BMDs, BMDs aboard ships and British churches abroad, covering the period 1654–1950.'

Top Ten Tips

Since the introduction of civil registration in 1837 there have been a number of changes to the information recorded and required by law. Below are just some of the modifications which were made.

1   From 1866 the death indexes record the age of the individual upon death.
2   From September 1911 the birth indexes show the mother's maiden name.
3   From 1921, a woman was allowed to marry her deceased husband's brother after the Deceased Brother's Widow Marriage Act was passed.
4   In 1926 the Adoption of Children Act established an Adopted Children's Register.
5   From 1927 the registration of stillbirths became compulsory.
6   From 1929 it became illegal for anyone under the age of 16 to marry. Previously boys had been allowed to marry at the age of 14 and girls at the age of 12 with their parents' consent up to the age of 21.
7   From 1931 it became legal for an aunt to marry a nephew or an uncle to marry a niece.
8   In 1949, births and deaths which took place in aircraft anywhere in the world but were registered in Britain or Northern Ireland were recorded in the Register of Births and Deaths in Aircraft.
9   From 1969 the death indexes now included the date of birth of the deceased.
10 In 1969 the minimum age for marriage without parental consent was reduced from 21 to 18.

Chapter 4

THE CENSUS

The census is, without doubt, one of the most useful genealogical resources, forming the backbone of our nineteenth and early twentieth century research.

Completed every ten years since 1841, it enables us to get a real insight into life in the past. Always start with the most recent release and work backwards. Now that these documents are fully digitalised (ancestry.co.uk is a veritable one-stop shop for the family historian) online access allows you to proceed with these investigations from the comfort of your own home.

On what dates did the census take place?

Each decade the census was taken to record everyone living in a household on a specific date. These records were subject to closure for 100 years due to the sensitive personal information that they contained. For the censuses currently open the exact dates were:

Sun 6 June 1841	Sun 3 April 1881
Sun 30 March 1851	Sun 5 April 1891
Sun 7 April 1861	Sun 31 March 1901
Sun 2 April 1871	Sun 2 April 1911

What is a census enumerator?

The enumerator was employed to collect and collate information about the inhabitants who resided at each household, institution or vessel on census night. These details were supplied on forms known as **schedules** which he would then write up in his enumerator's book in the order number of each schedule. It is at this point that he may have found it difficult to interpret a householder's handwriting and could have misspelled or mis-transcribed information which can lead to discrepancies between certain family details across the decades. It was not until the release of the 1911 census that we were able to witness our ancestors' own handwriting on the census forms.

1881 Census of Staffordshire. This example shows Laurence Wedgwood (great-grandson of Josiah Wedgwood) and his family at their home Orsett House in Barlaston. (1) The schedule number. A **schedule** was a form left by the enumerator with each household for the head to complete. (2) This double line denotes the start of a new household. (3) The information here can include a house name or simply the name of the area. It was common for the house number to be omitted. (4) The following two columns recorded whether a building was inhabited. (5) From 1851 onwards the inhabitants were listed with the head of the household first, followed by his spouse, children, visitors and servants. 'Do' stood for 'ditto'. (6) The 'condition' of an inhabitant referred to their marital status. (7) From 1851 exact ages were supposed to be given, but keep an open mind and allow a couple of years each way. (8) Occupations could be abbreviated, for example 'Ag Lab' instead of agricultural labourer. (9) The place of birth was recorded but again is not always accurate. (10) Any disabilities were listed here. (11) A census **piece** is a collection of bound books filled in by the enumerator. The number at the top right was stamped after binding and known as the **folio number**. The page number is irrelevant as it refers to the individual book before binding. Courtesy of thegenealogist.co.uk. RG11/2695 The National Archives UK.

As you progress with your research you are likely to hear the terms 'piece' and 'folio' when referring to the census. A **piece** refers to the collection of individual enumerators' books bound together for that district; a **folio** is a sheet within one of those books. In the upper right-hand corner of every sheet is a stamped number referred to as the 'Folio number'.

What information could I expect to find on each document?

The census is a real 'window' into another world, providing a detailed layout of everyone in the household on census night including lodgers, domestic servants and visitors, along with their ages, marital status, occupations and place of birth. You will also find a note of the location in which they lived if not their full street address.

Remember: don't place too much significance on the spelling of a name. Sadly, the early Victorian censuses were taken at a time when up to half of the population was

1911 census recording famous suffragette Emily Wilding Davison as an example of how a name can be misspelt – making the reader aware not to dismiss alternatives and to be flexible with their search terms.

- Surname is spelt 'Davidson' – note the additional d – the record was found by searching with findmypast.co.uk's 'variants' search functionality box ticked
- Davison's age is also recorded incorrectly as 35 (she would actually have been 38 in April 1911)
- Davison's birthplace is also recorded incorrectly as Long Wosley (her birth was actually registered in Greenwich)

(Courtesy of RG14/489 The National Archives UK.)

illiterate or semi-literate. Not all of our ancestors could spell accurately and their name could have been transcribed incorrectly by the enumerator – so don't be in a hurry to discount John Thomson as the relative John Thompson you've been hunting for just because the 'p' is missing from his surname.

Equally, your ancestor's place of birth may differ from one census to another. If only a county is recorded continue your search on subsequent decades to see if further clues as to the town or village have been added.

Identifying relationships is usually straightforward but perhaps consider that the person listed as a lodger, boarder or visitor may, in fact, be a stepchild or even the cohabiting partner of a widowed head of the household.

Many householders were reluctant to admit that a family member had medical disabilities as the census wording would tar them as an 'idiot'. When the description changed to 'feeble minded' in 1901, the number of recorded acknowledgements of mental illness increased.

1851 and 1861 census returns showing how they differ from later censuses. These returns record the family of Robert Morris, who appears on the 1911 census on the following page – a nice contrast to show the extra information that the latter census can provide. Courtesy of findmypast.co.uk. and RG9/2716 The National Archives UK.

1911 census featuring Robert Morris (family appears on previous page in 1851/61 census) written in the individual's own hand.
- A really lovely example that shows just how much extra information you can get from the 1911 census if your ancestor is that way inclined – packed with details about his life.
(Courtesy of RG14/22536 The National Archives UK.)

How do the censuses differ?

The 1841 census was the first official census to have all the names of the household, their ages and occupations, listed together. Be aware that the ages of those over 20 were rounded down to the nearest five years i.e. someone who was 52 would be recorded as 50. Those under 20 had their exact age recorded.

The actual place of birth was not recorded; instead a 'yes' or 'no' was added to the column 'Born in the same County'.

From 1851 and in each subsequent census more information was given, including greater detail on the parish, municipal ward, town, hamlet and ecclesiastical district. The head of the household was listed first, with his wife and children following in descending order of age, finishing with lodgers and domestic servants. Each person's marital status and occupation was added and a place or county in which they were born. There is also a column to record whether the person was 'blind or deaf and dumb'.

Access to each census is usually restricted to 100 years (although the 1911 census for England was released early) so we will not be able to view the 1921 census until around

2020. The records of the 1931 census were completely destroyed by fire in 1942, and there was no census completed in 1941 because of the Second World War.

Have there been other censuses?

The first census was carried out in 1801 with others following in 1811, 1812, 1821 and 1831, but very few of the original enumerators' records were kept; those that did survive were restricted to a district rather than a whole county – but it is well worth an enquiry at your local archives library to see which records they may hold.

The information is likely to be sketchy but invaluable for anyone connected with these areas, containing details such as the name of the head of the household, their occupation, the number of males and females in the house and even the number of windows in the property. This last piece of information was vital as people were still paying a Window Tax (depending upon their circumstances) up until 1851 when it was finally repealed and replaced by House Duty.

Does the census differ in England, Ireland, Scotland and Wales?

In Wales, from 1891 onwards, extra information was added to include whether the inhabitants of a property spoke Welsh; similarly, in Scotland from this date, it was recorded whether Gaelic was spoken. From 1901, the ability to use Irish Gaelic was recorded, whilst in the Isle of Man those who were able to speak the Manx language were expected to declare it.

The Irish 1901 and 1911 censuses give only the city or county of birth rather than the parish, whilst their earlier censuses contain no birthplace at all.

Additional questions in the 1911 census are beneficial to our research as they ask how long a woman's current marriage has lasted, the number of children which have been born alive within it and how many are still alive – essential for helping to track down marriage dates and further family members.

Where would I be able to search the census?

As well as The National Archives, which holds a complete set of censuses, your local record office is likely to have a digitalised copy or microfilm version of the original.

Many online indexes and transcriptions enable you to search for your ancestor on the census: ancestry.co.uk, thegenealogist.co.uk, findmypast.co.uk and familysearch.org are just some of those available to you. Sites vary, with some offering free access to certain records whereas others require a small subscription or pay-per-view charge. Use these indexes and transcriptions as a guide and always opt to view the original document on-screen once you have found the individual you are searching for. By doing this, not only do you cut down the chance of duplicating any errors or spelling mistakes, but you'll also see at a glance any additional information about each member of the household as well as who is living at the same address and in the neighbouring street.

All digitalised Scottish censuses from 1841 to 1901 (the 1911 Scottish census is due for release after March 2011) are available at the official government pay-per-view site scotlandspeople.gov.uk.

Unfortunately, most of Ireland's censuses before 1901 were destroyed in a fire in 1922. Nothing remains of the 1881 and 1891 returns although there are fragments of censuses from other years making research a little hit and miss. It is always worth enquiring at the record office closest to the area where your ancestor is believed to have lived to see what records they hold.

Does Ireland's lack of census records mean that branches of my tree are now closed to me? How could I overcome this problem?

Admittedly it does make research a little harder – but not impossible. There are many other options available to you which can give positive results. Take Dublin, for example. Acquire your ancestor's birth or death certificate and establish their address at the time of the event. Follow the trail by using historical street and trade directories to pinpoint the addresses of your family members. From this you will be able to establish the type of area your ancestor lived in and whether it was made up of houses at the higher end of the scale or tenement blocks. This, in turn, will give you an idea of the life your ancestor led – their one-room dwelling could point to them falling on hard times, experiencing poverty and struggling from day to day, whilst their abode in a more affluent part of the city may help you establish their financial stability and high status within the community.

It is true that over the decades Ireland has suffered some dark times – from the potato famine of the mid-1800s to the tuberculosis epidemic which wiped out one-sixth of the country's population in 1905 – and it is likely that your Irish ancestors experienced some of the trauma. Many chose the path of emigration to start a new life (*see* Chapter 8) whilst others were not so lucky and were stuck between 'a rock and a hard place' of either the city slums or the workhouse. Consider checking the workhouse records which are held at The National Archives of Ireland (nationalarchives.ie) – you may uncover a wealth of information including your ancestor's date of admission, age, and occupation and sometimes even details of their spouse. Discharge dates are also likely to have been recorded which could mean that the individual had been transferred to another institution, left altogether or passed away.

Which is the most recent Irish census available for searching?

The Irish 1911 census is now online with completely free access. It allows you to search the records of all thirty-two counties (i.e. those of Northern Ireland and the Irish Republic) by name, age, gender and place and, like the English and Welsh 1911 census, features digital images of the household manuscripts filled out by the head of the household. Future improvements are hoped for in the form of a facility which also enables you to pinpoint your investigations, searching by occupation, religion, marital status and literacy. Find out more at census.nationalarchives.ie.

I'm having difficulty deciphering the handwriting on one particular page of the census; are there any tips you can give?

On some census pages the handwriting can be notoriously difficult to read. Try to find recognisable letters on the page and compare them to the words you're having difficulty with. Remember that in the mid–1800s, a double 'S' would often be written as 'fs', with the occupation of 'dressmaker' recorded as 'drefsmaker'; the letter 'Q' would often look like a fancy 'Z' and a long slanted 'J' was in fact a capital 'S'.

Watch out for the term 'Do' which appears frequently on most pages and is short for 'Ditto', i.e. if a mother was recorded as a dressmaker and her daughter followed in the same line of work, instead of repeating the description the enumerator would simply write 'Do' underneath.

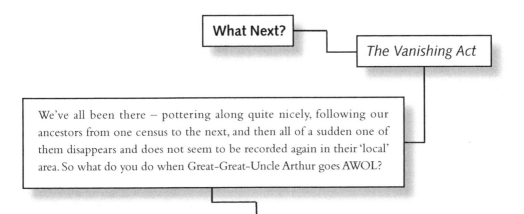

What Next?

The Vanishing Act

We've all been there – pottering along quite nicely, following our ancestors from one census to the next, and then all of a sudden one of them disappears and does not seem to be recorded again in their 'local' area. So what do you do when Great-Great-Uncle Arthur goes AWOL?

First you need to establish the last time he was known to have been alive. From this, work from the closest census to that date forward, also checking for any mentions in family letters, diaries, documents or whether he's recorded as a witness on any family marriage certificates. If applicable, find his spouse on the following census and check if she is listed as widowed. The most obvious reason for his disappearance could be that he simply passed away, so seek out obituary notices in newspapers or even if he left a will. But sometimes in genealogy, the family history fairy likes to throw a spanner in the works and make things a little more complicated so you may need to ask yourself a few questions to get at the truth.

Has he moved with his job to a different part of the country, and so is recorded on another county's census? Census registration districts do not always coincide exactly with county boundaries and a location close to a boundary may well fall into a different county's records. When trying to locate a missing ancestor on the census, widen your search to the adjoining county.

Is he a bigamist living with another family? This is not as far-fetched as it sounds – there were a surprising number of working-class couples who entered into bigamous unions during the Victorian era and your ancestor may well have been one of them. Has he emigrated overseas or gone off on his travels to see the world? (*See* Chapter 8.) Has he been convicted of a crime and been subject to imprisonment or transportation overseas? (*See* Chapter 5.) Has he joined the armed forces and been posted further afield? Is the period in which he has gone missing a time at which Britain's troops were taking part in conflicts around the globe? (*See* Chapter 10.) Has he fallen upon hard times and been forced to seek sanctuary in the workhouse? Has he become ill and been admitted to hospital – or even to an asylum?

Missing women could have been widowed and remarried with a new surname in the ten-year census gap. If it is a young child who has gone missing in the intervening decade, consider infant mortality rates at that particular time; did your ancestors live in an area that could have been affected by cholera or typhoid, or could a lack of money and a poor diet have resulted in a death from tuberculosis? Perhaps another relative may have relieved the burden of a large family by taking the child to live with them?

The census is a fantastic tool for plotting the lives of our ancestors at ten-yearly intervals, but as we all know a lot can change in a decade. Try to bear the above scenarios in mind when tracking down any 'mysterious disappearances' from your tree.

Are there other habitat-related records that are helpful to use alongside the census?

Poll books were registers of people entitled to vote in elections. Produced from 1696 to 1872, they contained the name and address of the person and their qualification to vote along with their chosen candidate. Voters had to be land or house owners (freeholders). These documents are ideal for tracking down where your ancestor lived between the census years as well as giving a clue as to their political inclinations.

In 1832, the Representation of the People Act introduced electoral registers to list everyone who was eligible to vote in parliamentary and local elections. Although they did not replace the poll books until 1872, when ballots became secret, they were produced annually (except in 1917 and between 1940 and 1944). Along with the same poll book information, electoral registers can include the names of tenants. The yearly publication of these registers makes them helpful in following the whereabouts of a family, whilst the inclusion of 'absent voters' may point you in the direction of ancestors who have joined the military leading to a search of service records. Remember that before 1928, when the Equal Franchise Act was introduced, not everyone could vote. This act of Parliament finally gave women over the age of 21 the same voting rights as men. Some digitalised data can be found online but enquire at your local archive to see what registers they hold.

Visit thegenealogist.co.uk, whose collection of poll books pre-dates the census records and goes back as far as the 1700s, making it a valuable resource for family historians who are eager to follow the trail back that little bit further.

BRADFORD

POLLING DISTRICT.

BOOTH, No. 2.

Names of Electors.	Residence.
HAWORTH TOWNSHIP.	
M...Akeroyd John Ogden	Grove,
M...Bancroft Abraham	Hole
M...Baraclough John	Haworth
W...Baraclough Francis	Haworth
M...Baraclough Joseph	Shaw
W...Beaver John	Sykes
M...Beaver John	Leeming
M...Beaver Paul	Leeming
W...Boocock William	Haworth
M...Booth James Hartley	Shaw
M...Booth Thomas	Shaw
W...Booth James	Haworth
W...Bronte Rev. Patrick	Haworth
M...Brooksbank William	Bradford
M...Butterfield Richard	Lumfoot
M...Butterfield John	Lumfoot
W...Crabtree John	Cold-knowl-end
M...Denby John	Bull-bill
W...Doughty Thomas	Thirsk, North-Riding
Doughty Isaac	Barcroft
W...Driver James	West Lane
M...Earnshaw John	Upper Town
M...Eccles William	Haworth
M...Farrar James	Walshaw
M...Feather George	Free School
M...Feather George	Upper Town
M...Feather James	Lower Town
M...Feather James	Pinhill End
M...Feather Edward	Best Lane Bottom
M...Feather Robert	Marsh
W...Feather Thomas	Marsh
M...Greenwood James	Woodlands House
M...Greenwood William, sen.	Oxenhope

Names of Electors.	Residence.
HAWORTH TOWNSHIP CONTINUED.	
M...Greenwood Willian, jun.	Oxenhope
M...Greenwood John	Isle
M...Greenwood John	Shoe Bottom
M...Greenwood Joseph Wright	Haworth Brow
Hardacre William	Colne, Lancashire
M...Hartley John	Haworth
M...Hartley Joseph	Hole
W...Hartley Joseph	Stairs
W...Hartley Bernard	Marsh
W...Hartley Timothy	Haworth
M...Heaton Michael	Royd House
M...Heaton Robert	Ponden
M...Hey John	Wadsworth House
M...Hird Jonas	Royd House
Hodgson Joseph	Bradshaw Lane
M...Holdsworth John	Best Lane Bottom
M...Holmes John	Moor Side
M...Holmes Timothy	Moor Side
M...Holmes Robert	Moor Side
Holmes Jonathan	Hawks Bridge
Holmes Jeremiah	Hall Green
Holmes Joseph	Stanbury
Horsfall Timothy	Haworth
W...Holmes Thomas	Chapel Lane, Keighley
M...Ingham Jonathan	Grove Street, Halifax
M...Lambert Tobias	Hall Green
M...Lister Thomas	Hollings Mill
M...Murgatroyd John	Best Lane Bottom
M...Murgatroyd Roger	Haworth Brow
W...Murgatroyd Thomas	Field Head
M...Moore John	Haworth
M...Ogden Jonas	Leeming Lane
M...Ogden Joseph	Leeming
M...Ogden Roberts	Lower Town
W...Ogden Joseph	Moorhouse
W...Ogden Nathan	Moorhouse
M...Overend Isaac	Sykes
M...Parker Thomas	Leeming
W...Pickles William	Haworth
M...Pickles Robert	Lower Town
M...Pickles John	Mill Hill
M...Pickles William	Stanbury
M...Pickles Robert	Upper Town
M...Pickles John	Wildgreave Head
M...Pickles Michael	Marsh

Poll Books. Ideal for pinning down your ancestors between the census years, poll books give the names of the electors, their place of residence and whether they were married or widowed. This 1835 example for West Riding in Yorkshire shows the district of Bradford and records widowed Patrick Brontë available for casting his political vote in Haworth. Notice that all the names in this list are males as females were not allowed to cast their vote until 1918 – eighty-three years later! Courtesy of thegenealogist.co.uk.

Chapter 5

FILLING THE GAPS

If you cannot get rid of the family skeleton, you may as well make it dance.

George Bernard Shaw

Your family tree should now be looking very healthy, flourishing with an array of names, dates, addresses and facts, and perhaps even details of forebears that you never even knew existed. But what next?

By this point there should be some individuals who stand out from the crowd and intrigue you, pushing you on to find out more and encouraging you to fill the gaps. Perhaps you have a birth and death date and a series of census entries but are wondering what that family member was up to in the intervening years. Were they academic, did they join the military, or excel in their chosen career? Or perhaps life was not so kind – they fell on hard times, suffered tragedy or even turned to a life of crime. The following chapters will show you just some of the other records that will allow you to investigate further.

How do I find out about my ancestor's childhood?

Initially, a census will allow you to establish where and with whom the child lived and if they were ever listed as a 'scholar' – a term used to describe those in receipt of an education. Armed with this information you'll need to investigate which schools they may have attended within the area and whether any school records, admission and attendance registers or school log books still exist. Any surviving documents are likely to be held at the county record office – a telephone enquiry should set you on the right track and, if successful, a visit in person is essential.

What is a school log book and how can they help me in my research?

Similar to a diary or journal kept by the teacher, the school log book can give a real insight into the educational activities of our ancestors. Some date back to 1862 when the government first required schools to keep a daily log of their activities in order for them

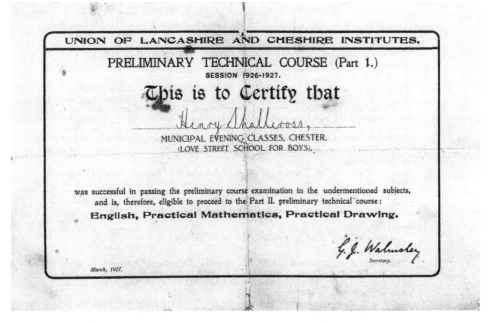

Educational certificates. Perhaps your ancestor passed a qualification at school, university or night school. Ask relatives if these kinds of family records have survived to uncover your ancestor's academic past.

to receive a state grant, but the contents rely on the diligence of the individual teacher. Most of what we know about Victorian teaching methods and the school day can be gleaned from these books along with details of new staff appointments, official visits and outbreaks of illnesses, providing an excellent resource and reference of the time. Unlike today, various festivals and harvests were considered reasons for school closure or lack of attendance. In rural areas potato planting was an important occasion for a family, with 'all hands' required to get the job done and provide food for the coming season. As such, this was considered an acceptable excuse to be absent from school and noted in the log books.

During the Second World War years many children from the towns and cities were evacuated to the countryside and it is within these pages that you may find clues of those children and families who were affected.

Although some teachers kept specific 'punishment books' to document the reasons which resulted in a child being caned, others chose to record these events in the log book and give the name of the offender, the infraction committed and the punishment doled out in the number of strokes from the cane – fairly barbaric by today's standards.

These books were not only essential if your ancestor was a pupil at the school but also if they were employed in a teaching capacity. Observe their penmanship, the way they described their pupils and the type of lessons taught. These can all give clues to your ancestor's personality – whether they were compassionate or harsh – their priorities, teaching methods and even their standing within the community.

SCHOLARS OF ST. PAUL'S SCHOOL. [1640-57

John Cade,
Pauline Exhibitioner, 1649–55 ; Queens' College, Cambridge, B.A. 1653 ; Fellow 1655.

Richard Cumberland,
Born 1631, in the parish of St. Bride, in London ; Pauline Exhibitioner, 1648–53 ; Magdalen College, Cambridge, B.A. 1653 ; M.A. 1656 ; Fellow of Magdalen ; Vicar of All Hallows, Stamford ; Bishop of Peterborough, 1691—1718 ; died 1718, aged 86. Author of *Disquisitio Philosophica de legibus Naturæ ; Essay towards the recovery of Jewish Weights and Measures* (dedicated to Samuel Pepys, his school-fellow and companion at College) ; and *Sanchoniathon's Phœnician History* (published posthumously).

John Wagstaffe,
Son of John W. of London ; Pauline Exhibitioner, 1649–58 ; Oriel College, Oxford, B.A. 1653 ; M.A. 1656. He succeeded to an estate at Hasland, "a little crooked man of despicable appearance " (A.O.) ; he died distracted in 1677, aged 44, and was buried in Guildhall Chapel. He was the Author of *Historical Reflections on the Bishop of Rome*, 1660, and *The Question of Witchcraft Debated*, 1669.

Samuel Nalton,
Poor Scholar 1649, when he petitioned for an Exhibition.

Benjamin Pulleyn,
Petitioned for an Exhibition in 1649, and again in 1652, when he received a grant of £10 ; Trinity College, Cambridge, IB.A. 1653 ; Fellow ; D.D. 1673 ; Regius Professor of Greek, 1674–86 ; possibly the Mr. Pullen whom Pepys met at the Apposition, February 4, 1663.

Richard Meggott,
Queens' College, Cambridge, B.A. 1653 ; M.A., S.T.P. 1669 ; Rector of St. Olave's, Southwark ; Chaplain in Ordinary to His Majesty ; Canon of Windsor ; Vicar of Twickenham, 1668–86 ; Dean of Winchester, 1679 ; died 1692. Preached at the School Feast, 1675–76, in St. Michael's, Cornhill.

— Christmas,
Mentioned in *Pepys' Diary* (November 1, 1660) as his schoolfellow ; he left the School before January 30, 1648–49.

William Corker,
Trinity College, Cambridge, B.A. 1654 ; Fellow of Trinity ; Proctor ; Senior Fellow ; Benefactor of St. Paul's School Library 1673 and 1682 ; he died in 1702, leaving considerable property to the College, which, in token of gratitude, placed a black marble stone over his remains in the ante-chapel, 1709.

Gabriel Towerson,
Pauline Exhibitioner, 1650–59 ; Queen's College, Oxford, B.A. 1654 ; M.A. 1657 ; Fellow of All Souls' 1660 ; Vicar of Welwyne, Herts, 1662 ; D.D. (from Archbishop Sancroft), 1677 ; Rector of St. Andrew Undershaft, London, 1692 ; died 1697. Author of many religious works (A.O.).

Robert Elborough,
Pauline Exhibitioner, 1650–53 ; Emmanuel College, Cambridge, B.A. 1655. Pepys dined with him after the Apposition, February 4, 1662, and "found him a fool as he ever was or worse." He was parson of St. Lawrence Poultney (a donative) at the time of the Fire, 1666 (*Pepys*). He was appointed to it in 1664.

Thomas Johnson,
Recommended for a Robinson Exhibition, 1650 ; Trinity College, Cambridge, B.A. 1654 ; M.A. 1661.

Samuel Pepys (Peapes),
Son of John P., tailor of London ; born 1632 ; recommended for a Robinson Ex-hibition, 1650 ; entered at Trinity College, Cambridge, as sizar, 1650, but removed to Magdalen College (sizar, October 1, 1650) before commencing residence, March 1650–51, where he was first elected to one of Spendluffe's Scholarships, and sub-sequently to one of Dr. Smith's ; B.A. 1653 ; M.A. 1660 ; married in 1655, and entered the service of Sir Edward Montague, whom he accompanied to Holland to fetch back Charles II., 1660 ; shortly after the Restoration he was appointed Clerk of the Acts of the Navy (June 1660) ; Clerk of the Privy Seal (July 1660) ; Younger

School and university registers are a great place to look if your ancestor was fortunate to have a good education. This example shows just how far back these records can be searched with the admission register of St Paul's School in London showing a brief biography of pupil Samuel Pepys who attended between 1646 and 1650. Courtesy of thegenealogist.co.uk.

I've been led to believe that my ancestor attended public school; are these records available for searching online?

The website familyrelatives.com has a fully searchable database of public school registers dating back to 1500, with over 138,000 listings of pupils and masters. Expect to find the surname of the pupil as well as the name, address and father's date of birth (and possibly death). You may even discover information about school sports teams, qualifications and achievements.

It was at the behest of King Edward VI that a number of grammar schools were founded to provide free education to the talented poor. Over the years this charitable system of aiding those of limited means changed to become a method of educating the country's young gentlemen who were expected to go on to find careers in the military, the church or the professions.

The public school system was independent from the state and eventually available to anyone who could afford it; although many decided to study at these institutions during the 1800s, by the 1900s pupils were increasingly called for military service. Details of their distinguished careers can often be found from this source. The site has a vast array of records, all of which are accessible for a yearly subscription fee of £30.

Perhaps your ancestor attended Cambridge University; ancestry.co.uk have now added the Cambridge alumni records from 1261–1900 to their extensive digital archives, allowing you to find the name, birth date and birthplace of the pupil, their parents, notable accomplishments, other schooling and later occupation – a fabulous resource for those with learned forebears.

What was an apprentice?

An apprenticeship was a position that allowed the learning of a trade, profession or craft over a fixed period of time (usually three, four or seven years) from a master or expert. The apprentice would then serve his time as a journeyman in a working role before eventually having the opportunity to become a master himself. Between 1563 and 1814, anyone who learnt a trade or craft had to serve an apprenticeship with an agreement in the form of 'articles' or an indenture drawn up and signed between the parents or guardian and the employer. If they survived, these indentures were usually passed down within the family, but repositories such as the London Metropolitan Archives, the Guildhall Library, the Society of Genealogists and some county archives do hold a selection of these records whilst apprentice indexes are viewable at The National Archives. Similarly, Apprenticeship books which have survived can provide the name of the apprentice, the name of the master, his trade and place of residence, the date of the indenture and the period of service.

Rebellious relatives and family secrets

Do not dismiss a seemingly wild or exaggerated family story without investigation; there is always the possibility that it may hold an element of truth. Note down all of the information you receive – no matter how fanciful it seems at the time – but treat it with an air of caution until you have established the facts. The idea of a 'black sheep' in the family or skeletons in the cupboard lurking within your family tree may sound exciting to you, but not all of your relatives will see the family wrongdoer in the same light. Their actions might have had devastating effects and caused deep embarrassment. You may find that decades or centuries ago, your family cast out a relative for a misdemeanour and agreed never to speak of a particular individual again.

You may have inadvertently stumbled across this family secret so probe gently for details to avoid the information-giver clamming up completely; never mock and always treat the subject with respect. What may seem like a comical episode to you could still be a serious matter to an older relative. With a little work and perseverance you have the ability to become the family hero who is finally able to set a story straight, but equally you have the potential to open old wounds which have remained hidden for decades. Tackle this area of your history like all other aspects of your genealogical research but remember to tread carefully to avoid unnecessary upset.

A LIFE OF CRIME

Not all of our ancestors held glowing employment records throughout their adult lives and changes in circumstances or events beyond their control may have sent them down a completely different route.

I believe that my ancestor was a convicted criminal who was transported to Australia. Where would you recommend that I start my search?

For a real step-by-step guide visit The National Archives online, where you will find an informative yet concise rundown of everything you need to know about transportation to Australia between 1788 and 1868: how to search for a named convict; how to find where a trial took place; and convict settlement in Australia. For those who would like to get to grips with the subject even more, there is an extensive reading list which will allow you to advance your understanding away from the computer screen.

Consider trying the Convicts to Australia site at http://members.iinet.net.au/~perthdps/convicts/census.html where a full research guide and searchable lists of convict ships, Western Australia convicts, pensioner guards and female convicts sent to New South Wales can be found. Do not forget to search through newspapers of the period to check for possible accounts of the court proceedings and details of the forthcoming transportation – remember that there may have been a significant time period between conviction and transportation.

In early 2009, ancestry.co.uk added to its comprehensive Australian Convicts Collection with the launch of their online Convict Registers of Conditional and Absolute Pardons, 1791–1846 and the New South Wales Certificates of Freedom, 1827–67. This, in effect, completes the journey from arrest to release of almost one-third of all convicts who were transported to Australia. With over 2 million Britons thought to have a convicted ancestor the likelihood of finding a connection here is fairly high.

Between 1788 and 1842, 80,000 convicts were transported to the New South Wales colony alone. The NSW Certificates of Freedom were given to those who had completed a 7-, 10- or 14-year sentence. 'Lifers' could receive a pardon but not a certificate.

There is a fascinating array of records in the whole collection including England and Wales criminal registers, convict transportation registers and even convict applications to marry. Delve deeper and you can find reports which document everything from the trial and the journey to the colony, to their lives as prisoners thousands of miles from home.

I believe that my ancestor was in the First Fleet to be transported to Australia. Where would I find information relating to them?

The convict immigrants of the First Fleet have been well documented and it is very possible that your family hearsay may well have a grain of truth as thousands of people today descend from these 'criminal' pioneers. Initially, start by searching the immigration and emigration records at ancestry.com or the aforementioned Convicts to Australia database.

It is worth bearing in mind that many of these people had committed very small crimes in comparison to some of those committed today which are given very lenient sentences. Back in the late 1770s you faced transportation for stealing a few yards of cloth or even a handkerchief.

What was the difference between a conditional and an absolute pardon?

A conditional pardon granted the convict their freedom but not the ability to return home; an absolute pardon gave them total freedom and full citizen rights both in and out of the colony.

Where in Australia were the penal colonies?

This list records just some of the main colonies across Australia:

1788	Botany Bay	1824–39	Moreton Bay, Brisbane
1788	Port Jackson	1788–1813	Norfolk Island. Situated 1,000
1804–24	Newcastle		km out to sea from mainland
1804–53	Hobart (Tasmania, then		Sydney, a second colony
	known as Van Dieman's Land)		opened here from 1825–55;
1822–33	Port Macuarie (replaced by		both were known for their
	Port Arthur, which opened in		harsh treatment of prisoners.
	1833).	1838–68	Rottnest Island

**Five Facts about
Australian Transportation**

1. In 1788, the first convicts arrived in Australia at Botany Bay before a permanent colony was founded at Port Jackson.
2. In many cases transportation was an alternative to execution, resulting in over 165,000 transportees to Australia over eighty years; 20 per cent were women.
3. Most male transportees were in their early twenties who included repeat offenders, political prisoners and trade union activists.
4. In 1868 transportation was abolished.
5. In 2007, it was estimated that 22 per cent of living Australians had a convict ancestor.

One of my ancestors is said to have been hanged. How do I research this?

First establish a date of death for this ancestor and, if possible, obtain a copy of their death certificate and see if it holds any clues as to the cause and location of death. Cross-reference the date with events around this time in local newspapers which could shed some light on the crime and the date of the hanging.

There may be someone in your family who could give you a few facts to aid your research but tread carefully; not everyone is willing to talk openly about what they perceive to be a 'black mark' on the family name – show sensitivity and understanding. Follow up your findings by checking if prison records are still available and look further back through the newspapers to see what was initially reported about the crime – there are often statements from eyewitnesses or even character references which could describe the type of person your ancestor really was.

Need more help? Then why not try Stephen Wade's in-depth guide *Tracing Your Criminal Ancestors* – you may well be surprised at what you are able to uncover.

How did the justice system operate?

Justices of the Peace, or 'JPs', were required to keep the peace in their area or county of jurisdiction. Usually prominent members of a community, early JPs would meet four times a year at what were known as quarter sessions, held around the ancient festivals of Epiphany, Easter, Midsummer and Michaelmas (although minor incidents were dealt with in between these periods at what were called petty sessions). Along with their colleagues, JPs would preside over a jury to consider a wide range of civil and criminal matters. They did not deal with crimes which would result in the death penalty as these would be heard at an assize court.

From hearing cases relating to the Poor Law and investigating disputes of bastardy to overseeing the maintenance of local public buildings and facilities, the JPs' remit was far-reaching, with all parish officials, overseers and constabulary reporting and, in effect, responsible to him for their actions. Bear in mind that these hearings were not just ancient practice but continued until 1970, when the Crown Court Act transferred their powers to the Crown Court system beginning the following year.

The records connected to court work can prove interesting for those who have legal professionals and criminals in their tree. The clerk of the peace would record proceedings in minute books and sessions files which can hold information such as the names of the jury and of the witnesses. Contact your county record office to see what documents they hold and whether they have been indexed. The National Archives may help you to pinpoint holdings and similarly, if your ancestor's work was in either Scotland or Ireland, contact the National Archives of each country for more details.

How were trials held in London?

The criminal justice system of London and Middlesex was presided over by the Lord Mayor who sat at the Old Bailey to hear the trials. Each Lord Mayor would serve one year of office between November and November. Newgate Prison was located next to the Old Bailey and was where prisoners were held awaiting both trial and later punishment – between 1783 and 1868 it was also a site of public execution. Visit the comprehensive site of oldbaileyonline.org to search their records between 1674 and 1913, where you may be able to discover the offence, verdict and punishment received by your criminal forebear.

DON'T FORGET!

Prisoners were also recorded on the census, with prisons usually documented separately on the first page of each enumeration district.

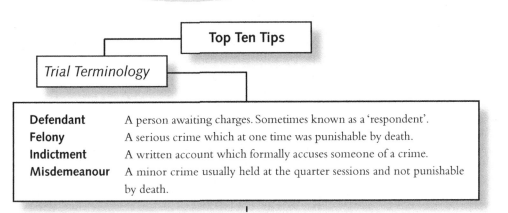

Top Ten Tips

Trial Terminology

Defendant	A person awaiting charges. Sometimes known as a 'respondent'.
Felony	A serious crime which at one time was punishable by death.
Indictment	A written account which formally accuses someone of a crime.
Misdemeanour	A minor crime usually held at the quarter sessions and not punishable by death.

Plaintiff	An individual or body bringing an action against another.
Prosecutor	The barrister who argues the case against the accused.
Testimony	Evidence given by a witness, also known as a 'statement'.
Verdict	The decision of 'guilty' or 'not guilty' made by the jury.
Sureties	People who guarantee that those accused who had been bound over would fulfil a condition. They would be required to pay a fee if this promise was not fulfilled.
Pardon	These came in the form of a free pardon, where the convict would receive no punishment, or a conditional pardon, where a convict would receive a lesser punishment.

THE WORKHOUSE

To understand how the introduction of the workhouse system came about it is important to appreciate the plight of Britain's poorer classes.

What was the housing situation like for the working-class family in Victorian Britain?

During the Industrial Revolution and the boom in manufacturing, towns and cities became overpopulated as families flocked from the countryside in search of permanent employment and the promise of regular money and food. Inevitably, this led to overcrowding in housing areas with many families sharing homes around communal courtyards. Lack of sanitation, adequate water supplies and sewerage systems brought about the spread of disease, and when a man's wage barely covered his rent and the support of a large family, he would not be able to afford medical supplies and treatment. Death, particularly infant mortality, was a constant threat. Although many fought hard they could not escape the slums in which they had become trapped or break away from the poverty that was now part of their everyday lives.

Try to discover more about the neighbourhood in which your ancestors lived by following them through the censuses. Compare how these locations changed using maps and consider contacting a local history group or library to determine how affluent or underprivileged these areas were.

What was a pauper?

This was a person unable to support themselves without the aid of charitable donations or funding designated for the poor.

What was the Poor Law?

In 1834, groups of parishes joined together to create the Poor Law union which, three years later, helped form the basis of the various registration districts when civil registration was introduced. For those unable to care for and support themselves – either through lack of income, unemployment, illness, infirmity or disability – the union built workhouses in which people who had fallen on hard times were required to live if they wanted a roof over their heads and food to eat. This would be the only form of poor relief, with each workhouse designed to be uninviting in an effort to make people find the means to cope outside. Despite this, along with the segregation of males and females and the introduction of 'prison-style' uniforms, for many, the conditions inside the workhouse were not as bad as the poverty they suffered outside.

How did poor relief differ in Scotland?

Before 1845, kirk sessions and heritors (local landowners) were responsible for the poor rather than the civil parish. The landowners would make voluntary contributions to the poor fund rather than being assessed for tax on their land or property, whilst the kirk would raise funds by making charges for performing baptisms, marriages and burials or by accumulating income from the collection plate.

After 1845, the Scottish equivalent of the workhouse was created – known as the poorhouse – with over seventy eventually built across the country. You can find out more at The National Archives of Scotland: nas.gov.uk/guides/poor.asp.

How did poor relief differ in Ireland?

Ireland established its own Poor Law Act in 1838. This enabled the country to be split into 130 Poor Law unions with a workhouse at the centre of each which could house the poorest and most needy. The potato famine had a massive effect on the country and those who were unable to escape via emigration to England or further afield had the threat of the workhouse bearing down upon them. By 1851, 4 per cent of the population had no option but to enter the world of the workhouse. Find out more at the National Archives for Ireland: nationalarchives.ie/research/poorlaw.html.

When did the Poor Law finally come to an end?

It was not until 1948 that the Poor Law was replaced with the creation of the Welfare State and the introduction of the National Assistance Act.

After discovering my ancestor listed as a workhouse inmate on the census, how could I find out more about this kind of institutional living?

The ultimate online resource is the website workhouses.com. You are guaranteed to learn something new about this sometimes grim yet crucial aspect of our social history every time you log on. From locating an institution in England, Ireland, Scotland or Wales to the Workhouse Acts and laws passed through its 200-year history, this extensive database should answer all your questions or at least point you in the right direction.

For a vivid description of institutional life then Simon Fowler's *Workhouse: The People, The Places, The Life Behind Doors* is an essential read. Using diaries, documents and correspondence to highlight how the poor sought assistance, it takes you behind the scenes and into the lives of the inmates, describes the conditions, routines, deprivation and even scandals, as well as giving an upbeat look at those who tried to improve the system. If your family history touches upon this world, then this book is for you.

What workhouse records are available?

Few workhouse records are available online. Some London workhouse records are searchable at ancestry.co.uk, but you will probably have to contact the local archive closest to where your original workhouse was based to find out what documents have survived.

Follow the links at workhouses.org.uk/index.html, which provides an essential guide to tracking down the information and what details you can expect to find.

Why did the sick or mentally ill often end up in the workhouse?

In the Middle Ages, the sick and infirm had been cared for in hospitals by monks and nuns, but this all changed with the Dissolution of the Monasteries during the reign of King Henry VIII. By the seventeenth and eighteenth centuries, if those with problems and disabilities could not be cared for by their family, they would often end up in the local poorhouse. Those categorised as dangerous were sent to private asylums.

It was not until 1845 that an act was introduced which declared that county asylums should be created for the insane poor. Many were admitted due to severe mental problems but there are numerous cases of young women who were sent to these institutions simply for getting pregnant out of wedlock. Contact your county archive for help in locating past asylums in your area to discover if any records of patients still exist. The National Archives of Scotland holds registers of all 'lunatics' admitted to Scottish asylums from 1805–1978, admission books from 1858–1962 (closed for seventy-five years) and lunacy minute books from 1857–1914, giving a glimpse into this poignant area of our past.

WIDENING YOUR SEARCH

How can newspapers help me with my investigations?

Local and national newspapers are a huge resource for the family and local historian. The freedom of the press kept the public informed of the events and incidents of the day, and with very little restriction on their content provided a fairly accurate record of what happened, who was involved and the location. Early copies may not have used photographs to illustrate these happenings but they did offer artistic images, sketches and engravings which can help bring a scene to life.

Throughout the nineteenth and early twentieth centuries, popular publications like the *Illustrated London News*, the *Graphic* and the *Sphere* were the *Daily Mails* and *Guardians* of the day – reporting on worldwide events as they unfolded. Do not assume that world affairs are not relevant to your family investigations; these newspapers gave accounts of living and social conditions, the latest transport systems – such as newly cut canals and the coming of the railways –which would have had a direct effect on your ancestors and the way they lived their lives. Newfangled gadgets and innovative labour-saving devices would be advertised alongside miracle cures for head colds, arthritis and upset stomachs – these products would have been available on the shelves of shops that your ancestors visited and, although exciting at the time, probably do not even exist today and are a real link to a past era.

Search through any local newspaper and it won't be long before you find a section on 'announcements' – usually where births, marriages and deaths are published. These occasions would be 'broadcast in the broadsheets' more so than they are today, and you can often find quite detailed descriptions of the bride's dress and guest list on her wedding day and comprehensive accounts of the deceased's career in their obituary. Alongside these are public notices of past or upcoming village events – your forebear may well be mentioned as the umpire of a cricket match, an entrant in a flower-arranging competition or a newly elected councillor. These snippets are priceless and will expand your family knowledge in a way that no other document can.

Ask yourself what you already know about your ancestors – did they see Queen Victoria when she made an official visit to their town or workplace, were they witness to an accident, did they see a new ship launched or take part in a suffragette rally? All of these events are likely to have been the news of the day and reported in the weekly paper. If you find anything related to your ancestor, read the coverage and consider whether any other news items will have been generated by the episode and try to track them down.

These incidents do not have to be life-changing or globally important but they do make up your 'story'. I followed a hunch when I found out that my ancestor was one of the first to get married in a newly built church in 1904. Not only was there information on this in the church itself but also an account of the event and details of the happy couple in the local newspaper – a real example of my family making their mark on history.

Remember the golden rule – genealogy is not just about names and dates, but also about people and places. Build that bigger picture.

Where can I get access to newspapers and are there searchable databases online?

Your local archive is likely to have the regional newspapers on microfilm and you can probably view the originals, which are usually bound in large tomes, smell slightly musty, are yellowing and brittle but instantly transport you back to another era.

The world's first fully illustrated weekly newspaper – the *Illustrated London News* – is available online, enabling you to view 160 years of material over 7,000 issues and understand more about the events that your ancestors read about, witnessed or may even have been involved in: http://gale.cengage.co.uk/product-highlights/history/illustrated-london-news.aspx.

I love online research but would really like to get a feel for what life was like during a particular period. Can you suggest any alternatives?

The internet is a fabulous tool, one that we would find difficult to live without, but there are times when you need to take what you have learnt online and go out into the world to find out more.

Whatever the period of interest to you, take a trip back in time by visiting one of Britain's living history museums and you will be amazed at how the experience will help answer some of those tricky questions that have been puzzling you about your ancestor's past, whilst also raising new queries which you will be freshly inspired to investigate. From trams and transport museums to glassblowing workshops and silk mills, Britain is scattered with 'living' archives where whole villages and towns have been recreated with a period feel. Blists Hill Victorian Town (ironbridge.co.uk), Beamish in County Durham (beamish.org.uk) and the Black Country Museum in the West Midlands (bclm.co.uk) could all hold the key, as well as providing a fascinating day out. St Fagans near Cardiff offers a Welsh experience, whilst the Highland Folk Museum (highlandfolk.com) may prove useful for those with Scottish heritage.

Ancient crafts, occupations, rural and urban lifestyles portrayed in exhibits, displays and hands-on workshops enable you to develop your understanding of a trade or skills practised by your forebears resulting in a whole touch, sound and smell sensation that you could not hope to experience sitting at your laptop.

Use your knowledge of the internet to track down those 'experiences' which will prove most useful to you – whether it is visiting a farm to understand the techniques of drystone walling or peddling a loom in a woollen mill. Step into your ancestor's shoes for the day and treat yourself to a trip out – all in the name of research.

Chapter 6

ALL IN A DAY'S WORK

Before the twentieth century, a large percentage of men were employed in agricultural work whilst the majority of women held positions as domestic servants. Despite the popularity of these posts there are very few records which pinpoint the work of an individual, so here your powers of deduction are required to discover more about such roles from history books detailing the period. You can gain a good insight into your ancestor's working day and the conditions they would have faced.

Whatever their occupation, the census is a useful tool to find patterns of employment from one decade to another. Note down your findings – do they direct you towards a particular trade or profession? It would take a whole publication in itself to describe the wealth of roles available but below are just some of the jobs – commonplace in the eighteenth and nineteenth centuries – that your forebears may have had.

DOMESTIC SERVICE

What was domestic service and what did it entail?

Most of us would be hard pressed not to find at least one member of our ancestral family who had been employed in domestic service. Throughout the eighteenth, nineteenth and early twentieth centuries, young women – some as young as 13 – would be expected to contribute towards the family income by finding employment. Daily help was required to ease the household work of general tradespeople, but the 'big house' or stately homes of the local gentry provided live-in work for suitable candidates from the area and further afield. It was thought that recruiting staff from outside the area would reduce the amount of gossip about family affairs between employees and local residents.

Advertisements for various posts, from ladies' maids and cooks, to nursemaids and scullery maids, were placed in the newspapers of the day. Some recruits were employed after visiting local mop fairs – gatherings where people who wished to find employment as farm workers, labourers, craftsmen or domestics would assemble in the hope that they would be chosen by employers or their representatives who were looking for new staff.

In exchange for board, lodgings and uniform, household staff were expected to work long hours and be 'on call' at all times. Some were fortunate enough to have a half-day off once a week to visit their families, but there was very little time for socialising. Domestic servants operated under a strict hierarchal system headed by the housekeeper who not only kept the accounts but ordered and distributed supplies; her male counterpart was the butler, who supervised all the male staff of the household.

Promotion to a higher position might bring with it the benefits of travel – perhaps as a lady's maid – the chance of better wages, or even the prospect of a marriage up the social ladder. But the majority of young women in service simply hoped for a good household, away from the poorer conditions endured at home, and remained in the same position until they were married.

In the 1841 census alone, over 750,000 women and girls are recorded as employed in some form of domestic service. In some cases – but not all – a larger workforce meant a greater spread of work. Single servants (sometimes described as 'factotums', a Latin word for a general assistant) had a whole host of activities to carry out, from childminding to daily chores.

By the end of the nineteenth century, the dynamic between master and servant was changing as workers began to want more from life. Some demanded more free time or access to books and learning, thought by some to be getting 'above their station'. The defining moment came with the outbreak of the First World War. Large houses and mansions were commandeered as hospitals or for military use. Most men – both employers and employees – were required for active service with some never returning home. Estates were broken up and sold. Women were given a freedom that they had not known before as they stepped into the jobs left by the men to take on worthy roles with better pay, in munitions factories and trades to support the war effort. Domestic service would never be the same again.

Are there any resources that allow me to search for an ancestor by occupation?

The Genealogist (thegenealogist.co.uk) allows you to use the 'keyword master' search facility to enter an occupation and obtain results from the English and Welsh censuses of 1841–1901.

Where would I find more details about my ancestor's employment?

Question living relatives for any vague recollections or stories which have been passed down within the family concerning an ancestor's period in service. Use these snippets of information to help you in your investigations. Establish their location of employment using the census and try to determine whether the property still exists. If you discover that they worked in a stately home of some importance, verify whether the property is open to the public and perhaps arrange a visit. Alternatively, write and enquire if the employment records of your ancestor have survived and whether you are able to acquire a copy or even view the document for yourself. Do not be put off if these records have not stood the test of time; many National Trust and heritage properties have recreated the servants' quarters and working areas, and by arranging a visit you can begin to picture the kind of life that your ancestor may have led, from the uniforms they wore to the tiny bedrooms in which they slept.

An inherited Trade Journal could shed light on your ancestor's occupation.

Although the documents of private houses usually remain at the property, there are other establishments which have donated their records to the county archives. It is always worth making an enquiry as you just don't know what estate papers, letters, account books and ephemera related to your ancestor's period in service are waiting to be discovered.

My great-grandmother was a nanny in a domestic household and is believed to have had training for the post. How could I find out more about her role?

By the nineteenth century the use of the term 'nanny' gradually began to replace that of 'nurse', with an upper-class household deemed incomplete without one. Growing family sizes increased the need for domestic labour and this female member of staff became an indispensable part of daily life.

In 1892, Norland College was established specifically for the purpose of ensuring that parents could employ highly trained nannies and nursery maids and, in turn, enhance their own social standing. Originally situated in a large stately property in rural Hungerford, the college is still in existence today but has now relocated to Bath. Norland Nannies could be recognised by their distinctive uniform of light-brown dress, hat and shoes with accompanying gloves and coat. The Norland motif of a large 'N' was embroidered on the left-hand side of their outfit, instantly distinguishing them from their counterparts and commanding respect. Visit norland.co.uk to find out more about Norland Nannies.

Depending on where your nanny was employed, prominent families with aristocratic backgrounds are easier to trace and their lives are usually well documented. Try searching for estate papers at The National Archives, then check for any personal correspondence for a mention of your nanny or perhaps even the duties she carried out. There may be references to the fact that the family frequently travelled abroad – requiring the nanny to accompany the children. Visit ancestorsonboard.com to see if she is listed amongst the passengers of an outbound voyage between 1890 and 1960.

Perhaps she was employed by one family for the majority of her working life – a real testimony to her ability to look after their children. Try checking the wills of her employers who may have left her a small bequest if she was considered to be indispensable. She may even have been granted a small pension or allowed to live in a property on their estate in retirement. Electoral rolls are searchable at your local record office and could help to track down her movements in later years.

My ancestor is believed to have worked for the royal family. How can I find out more?

Depending upon the period in which they were employed, the records of those individuals who have worked for the Royal Household are deposited with The National Archives. Staff were divided between the Lord Chamberlain's Department, which worked 'above stairs', whilst the Lord Steward's Department worked 'below stairs' and outdoors as kitchen maids, coachmen or grooms. By 1854, the Lord Steward's Department had been abolished to be replaced with the Master of the Royal Household whose records reside in the Royal Archives at Windsor Castle.

THE MEDICAL PROFESSION

Prevention and Cure

Despite continual developments in medical science, our ancestors would not have had access to the treatment methods we take for granted today. Many could not afford the services of the local doctor, whilst those who could may have found his treatments barbaric or even fatal. Old wives' tales of successful treatments for a number of ailments were passed down through the family as they experimented with herbs and natural remedies. Poultices were a soft, moist concoction, heated and spread onto a cloth then put onto the skin to treat an aching, inflamed or painful part of the body. Leeches – used for bloodletting for thousands of years – saw a live leech feed on a wound to remove an infection.

Garlic, with its antibacterial properties, was used to reduce inflammation; black cumin was called upon to treat coughs, allergies, influenza and stomach ache and, in an oil or powder format, to heal skin eruptions. Peppermint helped in the treatment of digestive problems including nausea and was especially beneficial to women in early pregnancy, whilst St John's wort was successfully used in the treatment of mild nervous disorders, the healing of wounds and kidney infections, but was hazardous if used in incorrect doses. Our ancestors really did take their life in to their own hands.

From doctors and nurses to dentists and midwives, the medical profession has become highly specialised; but before 1858, anyone could call themselves a medical practitioner. Patients suffered at the hands of 'quacks' whose experimental methods of treatment were often worse than the disease they were trying to cure. Remedies could kill or cure and the contraptions used to perform operations and procedures resembled ancient instruments of torture.

In 1858 the General Medical Council was established to improve the health and safety of communities by ensuring that proper standards were met in the practice of medicine.

Are there online databases for the medical profession?

The website familyrelatives.com has over 1 million records of medical indexes which can be searched using criteria such as surname, forename and date between 1853 and 1943. This is a particularly interesting resource as it also contains five years of records before the introduction of the General Medical Council in 1858.

Visit the website of the Royal College of General Practitioners (rcgp.org.uk). It has some extremely useful tips on how to trace your medical ancestors. Track down a copy of the Medical Register produced from 1859 to date which gives details of every doctor allowed to practise – expect to find not only names and addresses but often the medical school they attended and the qualifications gained. Now published online, search the registers from 1859–1959 at ancestry.co.uk. The books have been digitalised at four-year intervals and include details of foreign doctors who qualified in Britain.

DON'T FORGET!

Consider working backwards from the end of your ancestor's life. If you're certain they were employed in the medical profession, scour the newspapers for an obituary which may provide extensive details about his or her career.

CRIME PREVENTION

How did the Victorian police force develop and how would I find information about a constable's working life during this period?

For centuries Britain had endured crime, riots or misbehaviour with very few resources available to curb unlawful behaviour. By 1829 the situation was gradually improving, with London mustering 450 constables and 4,000 watchmen to patrol the city; but this was nowhere near enough for a population of 1.5 million. The Government realised they were in serious need of an even bigger workforce.

In 1829 Conservative Home Secretary Robert Peel introduced the Metropolitan Police Act, establishing the capital's police force. Seventeen divisions, each consisting of 144 constables and 4 inspectors, were managed from Scotland Yard and answerable to the Home Secretary. They became known as 'Peelers' or 'Bobbies' after their founder. From protecting public buildings to looking out for vagrants, gypsies or anyone vaguely suspicious, to the lighting of lamps, calling out the time – 'Ten o'clock and all is well' – and watching for fires, a peeler's job was certainly varied.

From the 1850s to 1900, a number of different titles were used within the force, from the basic 'police officers and watchmen' to the more unusually named 'superintendents of scavengers and inspectors of nuisances', all of which commanded varying degrees of pay. At the beginning of this period a constable could earn a mere 18s. a week, whilst a sergeant earned 22s. A superintendent was at the top of the scale, taking home £140 per year plus £50 for any expenses and the upkeep of his horse. Not surprisingly, records show a very high turnover of constables due to poor wages and working conditions, with many staying in the service for little more than a few weeks.

With the erection of new stations came the need for an inspector to reside there with his family and manage the facility. Single constables were often treated harshly with restrictions put on their private lives – even whilst off duty they could not leave the premises without permission from a senior officer in case they were needed in an emergency. Annual leave or rest days were no exception and to get married or to leave the borough they needed written permission from a chief constable. Even the wives of married officers did not escape the force's strict rules and had to search the female prisoners with the incentive of 1s. for each person searched. The sum of 2s.6d. was deducted from a married officer's wages for living in a main station and 1s. 2d. for a single man. Single constables paid 6d. to live in a cottage station and 1s. per day was taken from any constable off sick.

In the early 1900s each new recruit had to be less than 27 years old, at least 5ft 11in tall and with a minimum chest measurement of 36in. Wages had increased to £1.6s. a week for a constable and £2 a week for a sergeant.

The history of policing is a fascinating subject in its own right and for anyone with connections to this occupation there is a whole host of books out there which describe its development in much more detail than can be provided here. Sadly, there is no central source of records, but dedicated museums, such as the Greater Manchester Police Museum, provide a real insight into early policing. Particularly useful are the displays of police equipment and uniforms from the region helping you to date any photos you may have of your ancestor at work. Changes in the world of forgery and forensic science are also explained and a venture into the transport gallery, which contains a variety of vehicles dating from the 1950s, can help to bring the career of your ancestor to life.

Although police records can be quite patchy due to disposal during the reorganisation or amalgamation of police forces, it is well worth persevering. As always, The National Archives is indispensable to the family historian and holds examples of police warrant records, a brief history of the Metropolitan Police, reports on recruitment and even domestic violence records. Generally, personnel records are closed for seventy-five or eighty-five years after the enrolment of a recruit and there is no standard as to the details that were recorded, which varied greatly from force to force.

A database of women who joined the Metropolitan Police between 1916 and 1986 can be found at metwpa.org.uk in the Metropolitan Historical Collection which includes photographs and some service records. For detailed information about what is held in the Metropolitan Police archive, visit met.police.uk/history/archives.htm.

Use a directory such as the *Family and Local History Handbook* – an excellent guide packed with articles, research help, personal histories and a whole directory of addresses including many social history and occupation-based museums. Order yours at your local bookshop or online at genealogical.co.uk.

Museums which have archives open to the public by appointment include:

The Museum of Policing
County Police Office
Arpley Street
Warrington WA1 1LQ
museumofpolicingincheshire.org.uk

Thames Police Museum
Wapping Police Station
Wapping High Street
Wapping
London E1W 2NE
thamespolicemuseum.org.uk

West Midlands Police Museum
Sparkhill Police Station
639 Stratford Road
Sparkhill
Birmingham B11 4EA
westmidlandspolicemuseum.co.uk

What is the difference between a solicitor and a barrister and how can I find out more about an ancestor in the legal profession?

In England and Wales, solicitors and barristers both train in law but they serve different functions in its practice.

A solicitor can be appointed by a client to advise them of their legal rights and obligations and is usually an expert in a particular area, such as probate or litigation. An appointment with them is often the only method of gaining access to a barrister.

A barrister is a legal advisor or specialist court room advocate who independently represents their clients in court. He or she can be called upon to prosecute in one case and defend in another and is able to give an objective account of a situation, often making a great difference to the outcome of a case by impressing a jury in a criminal or civil court with his knowledge, understanding and successful cross-examination of the witnesses.

During the eighteenth and nineteenth centuries, 'taking the Bar' described passing the exams necessary to become a barrister. Law was considered a suitable profession for an upper-class man, thought to be a more socially acceptable and prestigious career than that of a solicitor, but as the years went by this gap between the two professions gradually narrowed.

Solicitors, barristers, attorneys and other legal professionals are recorded in the Law Lists which have been published annually since 1775, ceasing publication in 1976. Visit the Law Society Library online at library.lawsociety.org.uk and follow their guide. The society, which has regulated solicitors since 1843, also holds many other useful records; enquiries can be made at the Law Society.

From 1846, county courts were presided over by a judge. If your ancestor rose to this eminent position visit The National Archives at nationalarchives.gov.uk where you can find out more about the men who were appointed in this role. Why not check the Dictionary of National Biography or *Who Was Who* for notable and distinguished figures in this line of work.

Foster's List of 'Men at the Bar' is another publication searchable at the Society of Genealogists which contains details of all barristers in 1885 (sog.org.uk) or consider examining regional newspapers to see if your ancestor is mentioned in any local cases; if they were involved in high-profile proceedings they may have hit the national headlines. Check out the British Library Newspaper Library at bl.uk.

THE CLERGY

The parish church was at the heart of every Victorian community; perhaps your ancestor's vocation was within the church. The clergyman's income would have been drawn from the weekly collections, fees for performing marriages or funerals, tithes or rent from church-owned land known as a 'glebe', and his personality, dedication and contributions to the community would undoubtedly have had a massive impact on his parishioners and their opinion of his work.

Did you Know?

There were a number of occupational paths within the church that your ancestor may have chosen to follow.

Incumbent	The head clergyman who held office in the parish church, i.e. a vicar, rector, parson, etc. The parishes under his care would be known as benefices.
Deacon	This individual would assist the incumbent and although was in holy orders was not yet fully ordained as a priest.
Curate	A temporary appointment in a parish or an assistant to the incumbent.
Rural dean	Appointed by the bishop, this clergyman would be expected to run a small group of parishes in both rural and urban areas.
Priest	This position was below the rank of bishop but above that of a deacon. Remember, not all priests were Catholics and some were appointed within the Anglican Church.
Canon	Often retaining a role as a parish priest, the canon would also have been appointed as a member of a cathedral chapter.

The Clergy List was published from the early part of the nineteenth century and detailed all those working in the clergy at the time, from prison and military chaplains to those operating all over the British Empire. County libraries will often hold a copy of this valuable book.

Alphabetic listings of clergymen were produced from 1858 in the form of Crockford's Directories, which give brief biographies and the location of individuals over a certain period. A number of these have now been digitalised online at ancestry.co.uk, and at time of writing one can search the years 1868, 1874, 1885, 1898, 1908 and 1932. Most clergy attended university in Cambridge, Oxford or Dublin so if you can track down a college alumni record then you have the chance of discovering a wealth of details about the college attended by the individual, their graduation and degree taken as well as the churches in which they were later incumbent – excellent for tracking those who moved about the country or abroad.

Documenting the careers of all Church of England clergymen between 1540 and 1835, theclergydatabase.org.uk is an ever-growing website indispensable to family and local historians who want to find out more about the individuals connected to their parish church.

DON'T FORGET!

Check the front and back of the parish registers in the areas that your clergyman ancestor served – you may be surprised to find notes, inscriptions or dates relating to their incumbency providing an example of their handwriting and a glimpse into their personality.

Perhaps your ancestor was a churchwarden, responsible for the property and moveable goods of the parish church by keeping inventories and generally ensuring that the building and its contents were well maintained. Churchwardens were usually volunteers who received expenses but no wages and were appointed each Easter from reliable members of the community that were prepared to take on the responsibilities of the role. If the churchwarden's account book has survived you might uncover a vast amount of information – not only about your ancestor, but also about the parish in which he worked. You can begin to establish how long he worked in the role, the labour which was employed to maintain the church and the type of renovations carried out, the names of the women (often widows) who took in church washing and other jobs to supplement their meagre incomes, payments made to local traders and the names of those who required poor relief from the parish. These are fascinating documents and help to explain parish life of the period, whatever role your ancestor took within the church.

THE ENTERTAINMENT INDUSTRY

What would life have been like for anyone who worked in the theatre in the nineteenth century?

Show business undoubtedly had, and has, its highs and lows. A successful run could provide a healthy income but if little or no work was forthcoming some actors or actresses were barely able to live above the poverty line. The price of fame could often be a high one but for many, their lack of trade skills meant their wits and talent was all they had. Despite the fact that the wealthy loved the entertainment provided by a night at the theatre, the performers could still be looked down upon. This snobbery forced the stage performers and theatre crowd to be highly protective of each other within their little community, and where possible would always care for the welfare of their fellow actors if anyone was down on their luck.

Affairs of the heart often led to marriages within the community and people fell in love with not only their profession but also their fellow leading lady or man. When children came along, it was not unheard of for couples to change their acts to enable them to perform as a family – initiating the youngsters into the stage lifestyle at an early age.

Performers advertised their availability for work in publications such as *The Era* magazine and similar almanacs. Others supplemented their erratic income by branching out and extending their talents to fit a variety of genres by performing comedy, adapting their acts to the requirements of the music hall and even trying their hand at writing plays. From the outside, theatre life may have looked glamorous but the reality for the majority involved hard work and little stability.

Visit the website arthurlloyd.co.uk, one of the best resources for everything related to music hall and theatre history. Here you will find biographies of stage performers, images of old billboard posters, details of various acts and life behind the scenes. With over 2,000 online pages and a forum where you can post specific questions about the subject, you're guaranteed to find information and advice which will help further your own research.

Where is the best place to find out more about my ancestor's life on the stage?

Depending upon the success of their career, you may find information in *The Stage*. This magazine has an online archive which is searchable at archive.thestage.co.uk and includes articles on performers and their theatre appearances as well as obituaries of former stars.

If you know the theatre at which your ancestor performed then start your research here. Regional theatres often keep their own archives of past shows and the actors who performed in them. From this you can use your findings to help pinpoint advertising and reviews in the local newspapers. You may be rewarded with details of their show business career and information on where they would have been performing next – giving you even more clues to follow.

DON'T FORGET!

If your ancestor worked in entertainment during the mid-twentieth century, they may have belonged to Equity, the actors' union established in 1930 by a group of London performers. Go to equity.org.uk for more information.

TRADE AND TRANSPORT

All aboard: life on the railways

Throughout the nineteenth and early twentieth centuries the railways were the mainstay of Britain's travel infrastructure and provided work for hundreds of thousands of people. From the navvies who built the railways to the engine drivers who operated the trains and the staff who ran the stations, your ancestor may well have played their part in keeping the nation's passengers and freight on the move.

Finding these ancestors can be a little tricky and although there are many compilations of railway staff records it can be helpful to know some details beforehand. Try to establish what their actual role was, the railway company they may have worked for, their period of employment and where they were based. The National Archives is a great place to start, but also contact your county archive for more information on their holdings. The London Transport Museum (ltmuseum.co.uk) may be able to help with queries regarding city workers, whilst the National Railway Museum (nrm.org.uk) offers online help and guidance as well as details of their own archive collection if you wish to find out more about the history of this important transport system.

For those with an interest in the railways *and* the canals, visit the Railway and Canal History Society website at rchs.org.uk to find out how their exhaustive work can help you.

Making the cut: life on the canals

Britain's burgeoning canal network provided a diverse range of jobs in the construction, maintenance and navigation of these arterial waterways. Roles included those of navvy, boatman, waterman, wharfinger, bargeman, toll collector, docker, flatman, master bargeman, canal agent and canal clerk. If the census provides clues to your ancestor's role

Track Technology Timeline

Was your ancestor employed on the railways at any of these key moments?

1829 Robert Stephenson builds the early steam locomotive named the 'Rocket' and tests it at the Rainhill Trials.

1830 The Liverpool and Manchester Railway opens, offering the first passenger service between the two cities. The world's first 'intercity'.

1863 The Metropolitan Railway opens the world's first underground railway in London.

1876 The Kings Cross to Edinburgh journey time is cut to nine hours by the Special Scotch Express, later to become the famous Flying Scotsman.

1879 The London to Leeds train offers the first restaurant car service.

1890 The Forth Railway Bridge is opened across the Firth of Forth in Scotland and the first electric underground railway is opened in south London.

1904 The Plymouth to London mail train is the first engine to exceed 100mph.

1911 The first national rail strike takes place – was your ancestor involved?

1914 & 1939 The Government takes control of the railways during both wars. Extensive damage is inflicted on the railways and tracks during the bombings of the Second World War.

1948 The railways are nationalised seeing them split into the six regions of London Midland, North Eastern, Southern, Western, Eastern and Scottish.

1955 Over £12 million is invested to electrify the tracks and replace steam trains with diesel locomotives.

1961 Dr Richard Beeching is made chairman of the British Transport Commission and two years later he begins to close lines and stations across Britain – changing the face of the railways forever.

1968 Steam traction is finally removed from the tracks.

1994 Eurotunnel open the Channel Tunnel providing England with a rail link to France.

and location, you will be able to investigate further and discover more about his day-to-day activities, working conditions and pay.

Trade directories break each area down into its towns, villages and districts, listing the names of the inhabitants, merchants and traders as well as the services they provided – allowing you to determine the types of businesses that operated in and around the docks and who were the canal companies, carriers, customs officials, toll keepers and pilots.

From 1795 onwards, each vessel was required to be registered by the clerk of the peace who recorded who built the vessel, where it was registered, the name of the owner and the identity of the master. Canal boat registers usually cover the latter part of the nineteenth century but it is the luck of the draw as to what has survived in the collections of each individual archive. Log books give the name of the captain or owners and record the kind of cargo that was being carried, whilst gauging tables record the boat builder, the year the boat was built, its length, owner and where the vessel traded.

Documents detailing the canal transport system inherited from canal companies when they were nationalised or taken over by competitors (including railway companies) are held at The National Archives.

You may not have any photos of your ancestor at work but you can build up photographic evidence of similar workers, their costumes, and living and working conditions by visiting a related museum.

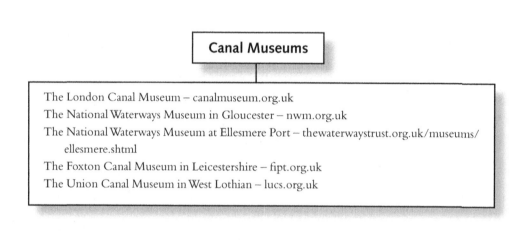

Canal Museums

The London Canal Museum – canalmuseum.org.uk

The National Waterways Museum in Gloucester – nwm.org.uk

The National Waterways Museum at Ellesmere Port – thewaterwaystrust.org.uk/museums/ellesmere.shtml

The Foxton Canal Museum in Leicestershire – fipt.org.uk

The Union Canal Museum in West Lothian – lucs.org.uk

Going postal: life as a postal worker

Long before the invention of the telephone, let alone the internet, our ancestors' only means of communication with family, friends and business acquaintances in other towns, villages or distant locations was by letter. Preservation of these documents can provide a captivating insight into a different world, but when was the importance of the postal system recognised, and could your ancestor have played their part in delivering the letters of the nation?

The General Post Office (or GPO) was created during the reign of Charles II as the sole carrier of post in England, Scotland and Ireland with established, organised and effective methods of delivery. London became the first city to trial a local system designed by William Dockwra which allowed items weighing up to 1lb to be delivered for 1d. (one penny). By stamping postmarks on each piece, it enabled post to be delivered on the same day that it was received in their offices.

In 1839 Rowland Hill introduced the greatest reform to the postal service by creating the Uniform Penny Post whereby, from May 1840, a prepaid postage stamp known as the Penny Black went on sale. His improvements to the system generated work for thousands of men and women, creating the essential service we know today.

How can I find out more about the career of my postal worker ancestor?

Between 1831 and 1956 a centralised register of every post office employee was produced and, although not all of the original appointment papers have survived, there are entries which detail the name of the individual, his date of employment and place of work which can all be researched at the British Postal Museum and Archive.

The Royal Mail Archive
Freeling House
Phoenix Place
LONDON
WC1X 0DL
Tel: 020 7239 2570
Email: info@postalheritage.org.uk
Website: www.postalheritage.org.uk

This is also the place to track down pension records, but bear in mind that before 1860 not all postal workers were entitled to a pension. If your ancestor worked in the capital, details of their grade and salary may have survived in the Establishment Books, which date from 1742.

The archives' extensive collection of photographs, artwork and posters is essential for helping you to add pictorial references about an employee's working day, from the uniforms they wore to the delivery routes taken. Paper ephemera, such as Post Office trade publications for staff, disciplinary and dismissal records, account books and salary lists, can add to your understanding of postal employment.

Agricultural ancestry: farmers and labourers

Before the Industrial Revolution swept the country, Britain had always been a nation of fishermen on the coast and farmers on the land. Farmers were self-sufficient but reliant on the seasons to ensure a good harvest and food for the winter, resulting in their lives being dominated by periods of feast or famine. The introduction of the Enclosure Acts, mechanisation processes and a growth in industrial trades brought changes to their way of life, and although many men were skilled in planting, sowing, harvesting and animal husbandry, the lure of better pay in the growing towns and cities had a huge effect on rural Britain. Sadly, there are very few records relating to farmers and agricultural labourers but you may gain clues to their status and size of their farm by comparing

STAFFORD.

Name of Owner.	Address of Owner.	Extent of Lands. (A. R. P.)	Gross Estimated Rental. (£ s.)
Warr, John -	Owen Street, Tipton -	—	125 6
Warr, John, jun. -	High Street, Tipton	—	56 -
Warren, Fred. -	Bilston	—	269 1
Warren, James -	Fenton	—	845 12
Warren, Mary -	Wolverhampton	—	195 12
Warren, Thomas -	Dunstall	84 1 17	201 -
Warrender, Samuel -	Wheaton Aston	3 2 29	22 -
Warrilow, J. -	Hanley	—	112 3
Warrington, Henry -	Stoke-upon-Trent	—	33 -
Warrington, Joseph -	Macclesfield	17 1 -	35 -
Warrington, P., Exs. of	Leekfrith	26 3 26	138 -
Warrington, William -	Uttoxeter	1 - 10	5 -
Washington, Owen -	Congleton	19 - 20	43 10
Washington, Timothy	Ashley	25 2 5	30 -
Wassall, Geo., Exrs. of	Brierley Hill	2 2 13	48 -
Waterall, Josh. -	Alton	1 - 3	60 2
Waterfield, John -	Wall Heath, Dudley	—	84 -
Waterfield, John, jun.	Tipton	—	27 12
Waterfield, Josh. -	Sedgley	—	72 10
Waterfield, Rachel -	Sedgley	—	122 2
Waterhouse, Bennett -	Sedgley	—	118 10
Waterhouse, Thomas -	Sedgley	—	1,043 10
Waterhouse, William -	Sedgley	—	33 -
Waterpark, Lord -	Doveridge Hall	42 - 2	116 -
Water Works Company	Birmingham	16 2 3	3,116 -
Water Works Company	Stoke-upon-Trent	81 3 -	999 13
Water Works Company	Wolverhampton	2 1 22	750 -
Mathew, J. M. -	West Bromwich	27 1 6	42 -
Watkin, Edward -	Dunstall	1 2 28	22 -
Watkin, Elizabeth -	Blymhill	1 1 8	15 8
Watking, John -	Burslem	—	325 10
Watkins, Edward -	Burton-on-Trent	6 1 25	26 -
Watkins, J. G. -	Droitwich	37 - 38	52 5
Watkins, Mrs. -	Walsall	3 - -	8 5
Watkins, Wm., Exrs. of	Brierley Hill	1 - -	34 5
Watkins, Wm., & Co.	Wombourn	14 3 22	335 -
Watson, Ann -	Leigh	2 2 20	24 12
Watson, George -	Rugeley	4 3 3	26 6
Watson, James -	West Bromwich	—	75 18
Watson, John -	Birmingham	—	26 -
Watson, John -	West Bromwich	5 - 20	229 15
Watson, John -	Yoxall	21 1 7	37 2
Watson, Stephen -	Rocester	15 3 35	64 -
Watson, William -	Cheadle	3 - 11	16 -
Watt, Arthur Chorley	(Horton)	973 3 17	1,468 3
Watt, James, & Co. -	Smethwick	19 1 2	2,083 8
Watt, James G. -	Radnor	2 2 28	218 4
Watt, Rev. Robert -	Cheadle	15 3 17	92 15
Watton, Alfred -	Burslem	—	68 10
Watton, John -	Burslem	59 - -	73 -
Watton, John -	Wolverhampton	—	9 -
Watts, Mr. H. F. -	Wavertree, Liverpool	5 2 32	24 7
Watwood, Thomas -	Gaol Square, Stafford	1 2 17	190 -
Waugh, Samuel -	Cheadle	2 - 13	25 10
Wayne, Rev. W. H. -	Much Wenlock	14 2 27	30 -
Weale, James -	Wheaton Aston	4 1 8	16 -
Weale, R., jun. -	Wheaton Aston	2 2 4	14 10
Weale, Reuben -	Wheaton Aston	6 - 5	23 -
Wearing, George -	West Bromwich	—	158 8
Weatherby, Mrs. Sarah	Norton-in-the-Moors	16 - -	56 10
Weatherer, Josh. -	Bednall	5 2 21	16 16
Weatherley, Thomas -	Eudon	75 - -	132 -
Weaver, Fred. -	Wolverhampton	—	533 18
Weaver, Susannah -	Wolverhampton	147 - 29	238 7
Weaver, William H. -	Penn	2 - 7	67 13
Webb, Ann -	Rickerscote, Stafford	2 - -	25 -
Webb, Captain C. -	Tamworth	163 1 5	446 19
Webb, Charles -	Elford	111 2 5	271 2
Webb, Charles -	Wetsey, Penkridge	4 1 39	20 -
Webb, Charles Henry	Birkenhead	510 3 25	998 2
Webb, E., sen., Exs. of	Wordsley	1 1 7	253 -
Webb, Edward -	Wordsley	4 - 6	190 15
Webb, Edwd. & Wm. -	Wordsley	5 - 6	1,001 10
Webb, Edwin -	Derby	9 1 6	29 10
Webb, Elizabeth -	Stoke-upon-Trent	—	100 7
Webb, Ellen, Exors. of	Etruria	4 3 1	13 1
Webb, Frederick -	Lichfield	26 1 37	41 6
Webb, Humphrey -	Church Eaton	399 3 -	746 6
Webb, J. H. -	Stafford	211 1 26	418 4
Webb, Jeremiah -	Quarry Bank	2 1 10	104 10
Webb, John -	Quarry Bank	2 - 9	144 -

Name of Owner.	Address of Owner.	Extent of Lands. (A. R. P.)	Gross Estimated Rental. (£ s.)
Webb, John Henson -	The Hough, Stafford -	31 1 13	233 2
Webb, Joseph -	Middle Claydon, Bucks	—	102 13
Webb, Joseph -	Wordsley (Kings Winford)	3 - 13	160 14
Webb, Joseph -	Wordsley	93 3 28	471 10
Webb, Joseph, Exs. of	Coalbournbrook	3 1 -	270 -
Webb, Rev. Joseph -	Guildford	1 1 15	4 4
Webb, Matthew -	Brownhills	1 - -	69 16
Webb, Robert -	9, St. George's Rd., S.W.	19 3 9	43 12
Webb, Sarah -	Lichfield	11 - 27	36 17
Webb, Theodore V. -	Great Gransden	79 2 7	153 6
Webb, Thomas -	Cheadle	8 - 5	35 -
Webb, Thomas -	Smallwood Manor, Uttoxeter.	176 3 34	364 -
Webb, Thomas -	Tutbury	47 - 14	272 4
Webb, Thomas -	Wordsley	3 1 6	78 -
Webb, Thomas, Trustees of.	Hatherton	7 - 5	22 10
Webb, Thomas, & Sons	Dennis Stourbridge	5 2 11	493 10
Webb, Rev. W. -	Tixall, Stafford	134 - 12	309 18
Webb, William -	Penn	1 1 39	10 15
Webberley, George -	Cheadle	1 1 6	11 -
Webberley, William -	Longton	—	325 7
Webster, Edwin -	Bloxwich	—	25 5
Wedge, Henry -	Australia	7 1 1	26 12
Wedge, John -	Walsall	4 - -	173 -
Wedge, Ed. -	Wolverhampton	30 1 13	223 6
Wedgwood, Enoch -	Wolstanton	—	471 3
Wedgwood, Fras. -	Barlaston Villa, Stone -	183 3 23	1,962 12
Wedgwood, J., Trs. of	Burslem	—	693 10
Wedgwood, Josiah -	Burlaston	—	120 13
Weetman, Joseph -	Tixall	43 3 8	63 12
Welby, Adlard -	Doveridge	39 3 11	192 19
Welch, Mr. -	Snow Hill, Birmingham	—	10 2
Weldin, Sarah -	Barton-under-Needwood	36 2 22	130 -
Wellington, William -	Walsall	1 - -	69 10
Wells and Hanson -	Walsall	1 2 -	75 -
Wells, Sarah -	Wednesbury	—	214 -
Wells, Thomas -	Wednesbury	—	786 -
Wells, Thomas -	Wolverhampton	55 3 27	317 16
Welsford, Mrs. -	Stoke-upon-Trent	—	113 15
Wenlock, Lord -	Escrick Park	2,752 1 12	4,070 10
Wenlock, Thomas -	Little Haywood, Stafford	5 2 5	21 -
Wenman, —, Exors. of	Codsall	4 - 36	9 10
Wennington, Mrs., Rs. of	Pelsall	7 2 16	83 13
Werge, Rev. John J. -	Somersal Herbert	22 2 25	79 6
West, Henry -	Leek	3 2 -	10 -
West, W. -	Lincoln College, Oxford	14 - 32	14 -
Westbrooke, Thomas -	Bloxwich	1 - -	43 15
Westhead, T. C. B. -	Barlaston	—	613 6
Westley, James -	Walsall	2 - -	172 10
Westley, John -	Walsall	1 - -	59 -
Weston, Benjamin -	Cheadle	5 3 37	15 -
Weston, Ellen -	Cheadle	5 - 8	12 -
Weston, James -	Cheadle	8 - -	8 -
Weston, James -	Tottenhall	2 - 3	26 -
Weston, James -	Kingsley	1 2 -	2 -
Weston, John -	Cheadle	18 2 2	41 10
Weston, T. John -	Standish	3 2 20	15 -
Weston, Thomas -	Uttoxeter	9 1 18	15 -
Weston, T., Trees. of -	(Bradley)	30 - 29	60 -
Weston, W. -	Ellastone	3 3 26	31 15
Westwall, Henry -	Leek	20 2 29	43 -
Westwood, Edward -	Oldswinford	2 1 22	36 15
Westwood, Jabez -	Bloxwich	1 - -	3 10
Westwood, Jeremiah -	Brierley Hill	1 3 20	159 5
Westwood, John -	Coldmore	1 - -	58 10
Westwood, John -	Walsall	1 - -	63 5
Westwood, Mrs. -	Bloxwich	1 - -	41 -
Westwood, R., Exrs. of	Walsall	1 2 -	46 5
Westwood, Susannah -	Brierley Hill	40 - -	100 -
Westwood, T., Exrs. of	Brierley Hill	36 2 89	90 -
Westwood, William -	Lichfield	1 - 35	16 6
Wetherall, John E. -	Rugeley	9 2 22	75 3
Wetherington, Martha	Cheltenham	—	68 10
Whade, William -	Tipton	—	136 18
Whale, Daniel -	Rowley Regis	—	219 -
Whale, Daniel T. -	Tipton	—	23 18
Whale, Thomas -	Rowley Regis	—	32 -
Whalley, A., Trees. of	Firebridge, Stafford	1 - 17	84 5
Whalley, J. G. -	Stoke-upon-Trent	—	466 3
Whalley, Thomas -	(Stafford)	2 - -	185 -

Landowner Records. From one or two fields to extensive estates, the Landowner Records can help you to discover the wealth and prosperity of your ancestor. To own rather than rent land was a huge achievement. No matter how small the area, this was their domain. This example shows the English and Welsh Landowner Records of 1873 and covers the Stafford area. The Return listed by county the owners of all land holdings, in A – acres, R – roods and P – square poles, and estimated the yearly rental income of all holdings over 1 acre. The Wedgwood family are listed a third of the way down the second column. Courtesy of thegenealogist.co.uk.

each decade of the census. Agricultural labourers – sometimes shortened to 'Ag Lab' by the census enumerator – could be hired at country fairs and were often journeymen, working their way around the county, taking employment where they could get it and lodging at the farm as long as each period of work lasted.

Tithe maps and the returns of landowners will highlight the amount of land farmed by the occupier and its location, whilst trade directories usually mention the names of local farmers and their addresses – visit your County Archive to find out more.

Discovering evidence of a trade that has been passed down within your family for generations is quite a find and a great example of the past helping to shape the future. From shopkeepers and steelworkers to blacksmiths and boot makers, recreating your ancestor's working life can be an illuminating experience as you discover their talents and individual abilities and how they may have unconsciously impacted on your life or that of other family members.

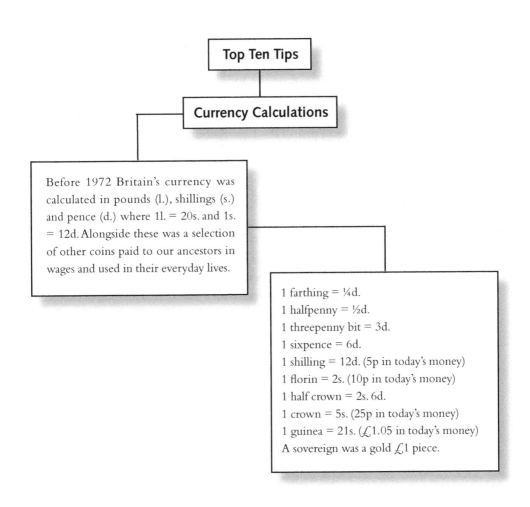

Top Ten Tips

Currency Calculations

Before 1972 Britain's currency was calculated in pounds (l.), shillings (s.) and pence (d.) where 1l. = 20s. and 1s. = 12d. Alongside these was a selection of other coins paid to our ancestors in wages and used in their everyday lives.

1 farthing = ¼d.
1 halfpenny = ½d.
1 threepenny bit = 3d.
1 sixpence = 6d.
1 shilling = 12d. (5p in today's money)
1 florin = 2s. (10p in today's money)
1 half crown = 2s. 6d.
1 crown = 5s. (25p in today's money)
1 guinea = 21s. (£1.05 in today's money)
A sovereign was a gold £1 piece.

What is a Freemason?

Freemasonry is not a religious organisation but is thought to have originated in the seventeenth century and is linked to the trade of stonemasonry. Even today many Masonic symbols derive from the stonemason's tools, clothing and customs. Traditionally open only to men (although today some branches accept women), followers meet together in friendship in divisions known as 'lodges' all over the country which are headed by a master. In 1717, four lodges in London joined together to form the first Grand Lodge in England and continued to strive for better lives for themselves and those within their community through philanthropic works. Early on they tried to show that people had the right to freedom of thought, to worship as they chose, form democratic governments and emphasised the importance of education. As a result, the Freemasons were responsible for founding homes for the aged and orphans, funding medical research and helping people to get through the struggles of everyday life.

Despite the secrecy which surrounds the order and its ceremonial rituals, there are many opportunities to find out about your Freemason forebears. Refer to photographs of your ancestor and look for clues to see if he is wearing any ceremonial regalia, dress or medals.

From 1768 onwards, lodges were required to send annual returns to the Grand Lodge, and these records form part of the Library and Archive at the Freemasons' Hall in Great Queen Street in London. In reality it is necessary for you to know the lodge to which your ancestor belonged for a search to be rewarding. This service is then free but if this detail is unknown a fee is required for each search. The resulting information can include details of the date and age upon joining, any other lodges to which he may have belonged and even his occupation and address at the time – fantastic if you are searching for someone after 1911 when you no longer have a census to rely on for this information (until the release of the 1921 census, of course).

Individual lodge histories may give your ancestor a mention, divulging details of the other members with whom he would have associated, their standing within the community and the charitable work carried out. Do not forget to enquire about the publication of obituaries. The Masonic newspapers – *The Freemason's Chronicle* and *The Freemason* – often mentioned the passing of the higher-ranking officials, especially if they were based in the London area.

Try contacting the Freemasons' Library via their website at www.freemasonry. london.museum where there is an online searchable catalogue and helpful research leaflets available for download. This educational resource explains a great deal about the Masonic history and archives in an easy-to-read and interesting format.

Chapter 7

LOCATION, LOCATION, LOCATION

lthough building a family tree tells us who our ancestors were, it does not tell us about their daily lives and the communities they lived in. To understand their story you often need to use a combination of family history documents and local history resources to follow their trail. As your information begins to grow, a clearer picture should start to appear of the location in which a specific branch of your family lived. Certificates may reveal that they occupied the same house for eighty years, passing the property from generation to generation, or that they moved from town to town – perhaps in search of work – before they finally settled in one locality.

Remember that the period from the mid-eighteenth to the end of the nineteenth century is known as the Industrial Revolution, when Britain's industry and infrastructure changed dramatically, creating jobs and requiring people to move from rural to urban locations for employment. Depending on what you discover, you need to adapt your research skills to hunt your migrating ancestors down.

Maps are an excellent source, enabling you to track down a specific street name or establish the whereabouts of an inherited plot of land. From town plans to tithe maps, you can add extra dimension by discovering more about the highways and byways where your ancestor lived and worked.

Why are maps important?

Maps are essential for giving a real sense of what an area looked like at a particular time. Over the decades places change, as old buildings are demolished and new ones are built in their place. Regions are developed, roads are constructed and what was once an arable area of farmland may have been transformed into a bustling shopping street in the space of 100 years or less. It's therefore vital to compare a variety of maps of the same area to increase your knowledge of what your ancestor would have seen as he went about his daily business.

What information could a map tell me?

Today, we rely on cars, buses and trains to get us from one place to another across land, but in past centuries life was completely different. Horse and cart or pony and trap provided the main form of transport for both passengers and goods, but as canals were constructed and the railways introduced, the face of Britain changed as alternative routes to the bumpy roads, criss-crossed the length and breadth of the country. These routes were gradually incorporated onto county maps making it possible for you to pick out the roads, railways, rivers and waterways which passed closest to the locations where your ancestors lived and enabled them to move around.

Again, bear in mind that in the mid-nineteenth century towns developed, street names changed – which could even affect the numbering of existing housing – and some buildings were pulled down to make way for the new railways. At this point you should try to locate maps for every ten or twenty years over a particular period to see how that area has been affected by this progress. Where possible, compare your findings to the addresses of your ancestors on the census.

Moving forward, why not take advantage of twentieth-century technology and log on to Google maps (http://maps.google.co.uk)? Find your location on the large image of Britain and keep zooming in until you can narrow down your street names and isolate your area of investigation. This is a fabulous tool allowing you to narrow or widen your search over any given area. Industrial, historical and numerous other places of interest are all marked enabling you to compare the information with older maps and chart the changes.

DON'T FORGET!

Not near your computer or out and about on a research trip? Then take advantage of your satellite navigation system to see if a street name or locality still exists.

Have you tried?

The website genuki.org.uk plays host to a huge range of genealogical information on England, Ireland, Scotland, Wales, the Channel Islands and the Isle of Man. From church histories and gazetteers to historical geography and land and property records, Genuki provides links and information which only help to motivate your research and offers alternative resources to consider. If you have an hour spare and are in need of a little inspiration, then grab a cup of coffee and browse the site – you will not be disappointed.

What is a topographic map?

This is a map characterised by large-scale detail, represented in relief using contour lines to show the dimension of the land's surface and the natural and man-made features of the terrain.

In topographical terms, what is a 'hundred'?

By the eleventh century, to aid administration, Britain divided areas of a shire into districts known as 'Hundreds'. In Kent, these were known as 'Lathes', whilst in Yorkshire they were called 'Wapentakes'. Each area was mapped out to show its borders and the towns and villages confined within.

What is an Ordnance Survey map?

The first topographical map of a country – which showed landscape and landmark information – was completed of France in 1789. These topographical surveys were also created to aid the military when preparing for battle to make them aware of the lie of the land, areas of elevation and the best places to build defences, establishing what was to become known in the UK as Ordnance Survey (OS) maps.

During this period, the majority of England and Wales was being re-surveyed to bring about the introduction of the most comprehensive county maps of that time. Parishes, hundreds and Poor Law unions were marked, making Ordnance Survey maps and issues of publications such as *Lewis's Topographical Dictionary of England and Wales* useful aids for the local and family historian.

The first OS map was produced for Kent in 1801 and other counties soon followed using a scale of one inch to one mile. After a number of mistakes and re-surveying, the OS map changed its scale to six inches to the mile in the 1840s. Ask at your local history library and county archive to see what type of maps they hold in their collections.

What effect did the Enclosure Act have on local map-making?

In 1845 the General Enclosure Act was granted, resulting in a further series of acts which enclosed common land and open fields in the country. This meant that the rights which people had once held to graze livestock and make use of the natural resources in these areas were denied. In effect, the wealthy landowners took over the common ground, fencing it off, incorporating it into their own and charging higher rents – beneficial to some but forcing smaller landowners to become labourers and leaving the landless poor without a home.

What is a tithe map and when do they date from?

From as early as Anglo-Saxon times, landholders were expected to give one-tenth of their local produce to the church – this was known as a tithe. By 1836, the Tithe Communication Act was granted which allowed this tithe to be converted to cash payments. This required accurate maps to be drawn up of the parishes to establish how much land was occupied and consequently how much tithe should be paid. Each map was accompanied by a schedule which gave details of the landowner, occupier, description of the land and fields. Over 500 of Cheshire's tithe maps are viewable online at http://maps.cheshire.gov.uk/tithemaps, whilst other counties such as Worcestershire and Yorkshire had their own tithe apportionment projects under way at time of writing.

The tithe commissioner's copies are held in The National Archives although, sadly, many of these holdings were destroyed in the Second World War so always check locally to see what maps are still available. Remember – the Tithe Act did not apply to Scotland and Ireland so surveys do not exist for these countries.

DON'T FORGET!

Take time to brush up on your units of measurement. You may come across some of these terms in texts, documents or on maps so familiarise yourself with their meanings.

Rod	=	5.5 yards
Chain	=	4 rods
Furlong	=	40 rods
Acre	=	4,840 square yards
Square Mile	=	640 acres

What is the difference between a map and a chart?

In general, charts were used to plot out the seas and oceans and were created by marine hydrographers, whilst maps recorded land mass and were produced using the skills of a cartographer.

What is a thematic map?

These are produced to illustrate a theme in relation to a particular geographical area. The subjects can range from agricultural to economic and can show anything from specific health issues in a region to its population density. A prime example of this was the 1854 map created by physician John Snow to work out which of London's city streets were affected by the spread of cholera. By plotting each outbreak and comparing how close they were to the water pumps, he was able to pinpoint which pump – located near a sewer line – was helping to spread the disease.

You can use these types of thematic maps in your own research, perhaps locating where your ancestors lived, whether the area was overcrowded and build a picture of the surrounding habitat. The conditions in which they lived may have been the cause of a death in the family or may have even prompted a move to another area.

What is a poverty map?

Between 1886 and 1903, Charles Booth carried out an investigation *Life and Labour of London*. As part of his research he created poverty maps of the city which recorded the type of people living in the streets and their differing levels of income.

The Booth Collection – an online database – is part of the archives of the London School of Economics, and for those who had ancestors living in the capital during this period research on this site is essential. The abundance of maps available for viewing is staggering and combines Booth's income findings via colour-coding classifications which list every possibility from 'Lowest class: Semi vicious criminal' to 'Upper middle and upper classes; Wealthy'.

Police notebooks and those relating to the Jewish community and their trades of tailoring and bookmaking can also be found with original downloadable descriptions of their employment, conditions and everyday life as explained in Charles Booth's own hand. Step back in time at http://booth.lse.ac.uk.

What other maps could be helpful and where would I start looking for them?

Estate plans and manorial records can give names of landowners, occupiers and tenants. Your local archives library should be able to point you in the right direction, explaining what examples they have in their own collection or where to look if they know of other sources, especially those regarding estate maps which are in private ownership.

Trench maps (held at The National Archives) can give detailed topographical information about areas of the Western Front where your ancestor may have fought during the First World War and are essential for understanding the conditions in which British soldiers lived and died.

DON'T FORGET!

Not all maps have to be officially produced – our ancestors can often leave their own clues. Diaries may provide hand-drawn maps of an area that was important to them, whilst scrapbooks could present a description of their hometown, favourite place or holiday destination with artistic interpretations of the location or printed maps pasted within the pages. Even rough drawings in handwritten journals can give clues as to favourite family walks, whilst sketches of street plans can identify the location of a family business or a property which no longer exists.

Surprisingly, wills can also be a fruitful source if land was left in a bequest. One of my ancestors left a small amount of land to each of his children with all of the fields listed by name. With the aid of a tithe map, I was able to cross-reference this information and find out exactly where this was. Another ancestor had 'made good' by immigrating to America around the time when the railroads were being built. On the inventory attached to his will he had left details of the sections of land he had bought along this stretch in both Nebraska and Kansas and even added co-ordinates to help pinpoint their location.

What is an indenture?

An indenture is a deed and legal contract made out for the sale of land or property, for a commercial debt or even contractual employment. Historically, two copies of the deed were made on one piece of parchment which was cut apart along a torn or indented line with each party involved keeping one half of the document to prevent forgery. You may have inherited one of these fascinating documents which could shed light on the business dealings of your ancestors.

I don't seem to be able to decipher the name of a location on an old map that I've inherited. How can I overcome this?

Initially, find words within the map that you *can* read and compare each letter with the spelling of your 'challenging' location to see if you can decode the problem. Track down a slightly later map and compare the place names to try and establish a match or use the website multimap.com. By typing in a few combinations of the illegible name, the search engine will try to confirm the existence of the place name and show you a modern map of that area.

I've heard that trade directories are ideal for helping to locate an ancestor. What are they and where would I find them?

These directories were the early equivalent of today's Yellow Pages and contain lists of tradesmen and their businesses. Although one of the earliest examples was published in 1781, they became popular during the nineteenth and twentieth centuries after Fredric Kelly took over production of the Post Office London Directory in 1835. Gradually, Kelly began to produce directories relating to various areas across the country and, along with the works of competitors White, Slater and Pigot, these volumes benefited from the

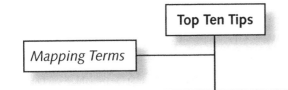

Top Ten Tips

Mapping Terms

Armorial	A decorative symbol used to embellish a map usually in the form of a shield bearing a coat of arms.
Cartouche	A type of frame used as a device for surrounding the title of a map or any additional information. They could vary from being simple in design to being elaborately decorated with scrolls, swirls or even leafy garlands.
Co-ordinates	A set of numbers on a map used to find the distance from a specific place.
Elevation	Describes how high a point or an object is above or below sea level. This can also be described as altitude or height.
Latitude	A term used to describe a location north or south of the equator which is the earth's base line and point of its widest circumference.
Linear Feature	This refers to the lines on a map such as roads, rivers, railways and boundaries.
Longitude	Used in cartography as an east to west measurement recorded in degrees.
Meridian	These are the lines running vertically around the globe from pole to pole.
Recto/Verso	'Recto' refers to the front of the map; 'Verso' to the reverse.
True North	This is the direction of the northern rotational axis of the earth and refers to the upper part of the map.

inclusion of additional local information which now provides an essential resource for the family historian.

County directories included historical details about the towns and villages within each county, as well as recording the local churches, schools, public houses and mail coach times alongside a list of prominent people in the area, the main businesses and residents. Successive additions show how a locality has changed and developed, and by comparing

BIRMINGHAM ALPHABETICAL LIST.

Butler Thomas, last and boot tree maker, 17, Park street, Bull ring

Butler Thomas & William, snuffer mnfrs., Brueton's mill

Butler Thomas, dairyman, Farm street

Butler Wm., dairyman, Park rd. Nechells gn

Butler William, snuffer manufacturer; h. court 10, Aston road

Butler William, shoe maker, 28, Gt. Barr st

Butler William, gun barrel browner, court 8, Loveday street

Butler William, pearl button manufacturer, 2, Summer hill terrace

Butler Wm., blacksmith, ct. 21, Gt. Lister st

Butler William, scabbard maker; h. 240, Great Colmore street

Butt Mrs. Frances, 142, Bloomsbury, South

Butterwick Thomas, news agent, 73, Stafford street

Butterworth Mrs. Sarah, Richard street

Butts John, wood turner, 2, Moore's row

Buxton Steph., green grocer, 249, Sherlock st

Bynner Jeremiah, lamp mkr. 86, Green lns.

Bynner William Warner, assistant overseer, 1, Princes street

Byrne Michael, carpenter, 31½, Dale end

Byrne Patrick, pig and cattle dealer, 1, Allison street

Bywater Harvey, broker, 1, Tonk street

Bywater Joseph, fruiterer and shopkeeper, 3, Ludgate hill

Cadbury Brothers, tea dealers and coffee roasters, 93, Bull street, and wholesale tea dealers and coffee merchants, Bridge street, Broad street

Cadbury Benjamin Head, tea and coffee merchant; h. 114, Broad st., Islington

Cadbury John, tea and coffee merchant; h. 34, Calthorpe street

Cadbury Richard, gent., 39, Calthorpe st.

Cadby George, shopkeeper, 10, Tanter st.

Cadby James Edward, metal ingot caster, 39, Mount street

Cade Charles, pump maker and well sinker, 10, Manchester street

Cade Graham, green grocer, 261, Bradford st

Cain Isaac, currier; h. 14, Francis st. Ashted

Cain & Maxwell, curriers, 11½, Prospect row

Cairns Ann, register office for servants, 36, Colmore row

Cairns Benj., relieving officer, fifth district, 57, Kenion st.; h. 44, Lower Camden st.

Cairns Mary, clothes broker, 11, Lichfield st

Caldecutt Edward, beerhouse, 32, Hatchett st

Caldecutt Henry, coach harness plater and beer house, 48, Price street

Calder Edwin, corn and seed merchant, &c.; h. 149, Lancaster street

Calder E. & Co., corn millers, Lancaster street corn mill, and corn and seed merts. 149, Lancaster street, and 2, Easy row

Caldicott Alfred Millwater, shorthand writer, Lee Crescent

Caldicott John, printer and publisher, *Aris's Birmingham Gazette*, (Monday,) 71, High street; h. Camp hill

Caldicott Leonard, land surveyor, &c.; h. Edgbaston

Caldicott Oswald, coffin furniture manufacturer, George st. Parade; h. Reservoir rd

Caldicutt Mrs. Sarah, Gradigan terrace, Frederick street, Edgbaston

Callow Ann, school, 282, Ashted row

Callow Martin, upholsterer, 52, Broad st. Islington

Callum William, (late Beardsworth,) Midland Counties horse and carriage Repository, 1, Cheapside; land agent, auctioneer, appraiser, and broker to the Bankruptcy court, 14, Bennett's hill

Cameron Mary Ann, milliner and dress maker, Blakemore terrace

Cameron Thomas, shoemaker, 30, Tonk st.

Camm James, master, St. Mark's school, St. Mark's street; h. Springfield place, Springfield street

Cammerer Henry, pork butcher, 66, Aston st.

Campbell Donald McDonald, (from London) general dyer, 54, Great Hampton street

Campbell Elizabeth, Lancasterian schoolmistress, 102, Tennant street; house, 150,' Broad street, Islington

Campbell James, Esq., Vicarage road

Campbell Robert, brass founder, fender and fire brass manufr., 39, Bartholomew st.

Campbell William Inness, seal and stone engraver, 54½, Great Hampton st.

Campbell William Knight, solicitor, 3, St. Mary's row

Campion Maria, dress & straw hat maker, 27, Cherry street

Camwell George, dairyman, 79, Essington st.

Canning Charles, coal mstr., 34 Islington rw

Canning Charles Henry, draper, silk mercer, hosier, haberdasher, laceman, and straw bonnet warehouse, 180, High st. Deritend

Canning J. Samuel, attorney's clk., Grant st

Canning William, grocer and druggist, 1, Prospect row, and 137, Great Hampton st.

Cannon John, chimney sweep, Brickkiln street, Lancaster street

Canter Benjamin, coal dlr., 4, St. James's pl.

Cantrill Ann, pawnbroker, 126, Moor st.

Cantrill John, clerk, Grant street

Cantrill Joseph, cork cutter, 158, Moor st.

Cantrill Thomas, spectacle maker, court, 1, Sherlock street

Capell James, gold watch hand maker, 43, Hurst street

Capella Michael, carver and gilder, 104, Digbeth, and 53, Edgbaston street

Capenhurst Elizabeth, milk seller, 19, Brearley street, West

Capewell James, wholesale boot and shoe manufacturer, 31 Exeter row

1849 Birmingham White's Directory. This example shows the Cadbury Brothers – John and Benjamin – when they were still tea dealers and coffee merchants at 93 Bull Street, and their other Birmingham addresses. Courtesy of thegenealogist.co.uk. See the website's coverage for the related records which help to chart the Cadbury story.

DISTRICT OF YORKSHIRE.

HANGING HEATON, see Heatons, (P.) Dewsbury.

HARTSHEAD, (Vil.) in the (P.) of Dewsbury, 4 m. N. of Huddersfield.

** Thus * attend the White Swan, Call lane, Leeds, & White Horse, Huddersfield.

Hodgson Geo. cattle dealer
Pearson John, gardener
Roberts John, shoemaker

Stott John, wire drawer
Webster Wm. joiner

*Wilby Henry, sen. general merchant
*Wilby Jph. woollen mfr.

CARD MAKERS.
Kitson Jonathan
*Wilby Henry, jun.
FARMERS.
Barker Benjamin
Birkhead Joseph
Brook Aaron M.

Clayton George and Charles
Crossley Robert
Fitton Joseph and Robert
Normington Chas.
Pearson Joseph

Pearson Samuel
Thornton John

SHOPKEEPERS.
Armitage Richard
Hirst Joseph

Horsfall Elizabeth
Ramsden George
STONEMASONS.
Horsfall Richd.
Jackson George
Jackson Wm.

For Carriers—*See* Clifton.

HAWORTH (Chp.) in the (P.) and 10 m. W. of Bradford.

** Letters arrive at Haworth from Bradford by a Foot Post daily, at 9 mng. and are despatched ¼ p. 10 mng.

Those marked 1, reside at Oxenhope—2, at Far Oxenhope ; 3, Stanbury ; & the remainder at Haworth.
Andrew Thos. surgeon
Barraclough John, clock and watch maker
2 Barstow Saml. corn miller
Binns Joseph, wood turner
Bowcock Wm. plasterer
Bronte Rev. Patrick, A.B. incumbent of Haworth
Brown Wm. sexton & stone letterer
1 Butterfield Henry, master of the Free school
1 Carlill John, gent.
Constantine James, painter
Craven Hiram & Jph. Murgatroyd, corn millers
Eccles Wm. woolstapler
Firth Joseph, cooper
Foster John, librarian
1 Greenwood Wm. sen. gent.
Hardaker Joseph, druggist
Hartley Wm. iron & tin plate worker, & Post office

2 Heaton Michl. heald yarn manufacturer
3 Heaton, Robert, gent.
2 Horsfall Heaton, gent.
1 Horsfall Jones, gent.
Jennings Starkey, painter
Jowett Mr. John
3 Lister Thos. cotton spinr.
3 Moore John, gent.
Newell John, linen draper
3 Newsom Wm. and Sons, cotton spinners
Oddy Rev. Miles, Baptist min.
3 Ogden Jas. day school
2 Ogden John, assistant overseer
1 Pepperlow Samuel, Excise officer
3 Pickles Thos. gent.
Ramsden John, plasterer
3 Robinson James, gent.
1 Rushworth Wm. gent.
Saunders Rev. Moses, Baptist minster
Slugg Rev. Thos. Meth. min.
3 Taylor Steph. woolstapler
Thomas Wm. spirit mercht.

Thompson Saml. bookkpr.
1 Townend John, top mkr.
Townend Robt. W. spinner, Ebor
Winterbottom Rev. John, assistant Baptist min. & schoolmaster
Wood John, plumber and glazier
INNS AND PUBLIC HOUSES.
2 Bay Horse, Wm. Greenwood
Black Bull, Abraham Wilkinson
3 Board, Joshua Sunderland
3 Cross, Joseph Wignall
Fleece, Dan, Brearley
King's Arms, John Gledhill
2 Lamb & Butcher, James Roberts
1 New Inn, John Fawthrop
2 Shoulder of Mutton, Wm. Pollard
Sun, Thos. Aykroyd
3 Waggon & Horses, Ogden Sunderland
White Lion, Wm. Garnett

BLACKSMITHS.
Foulds Thomas
Hutley Jonathan
1 Rushworth Yates
Scarborough David
Wright Nathan
BOOT AND SHOE MAKERS.
Aykroyd Jonathan
Aykroyd Joshua
Barraclough Francis
Hudson Henry

Hudson Isaac
Hudson Joseph
Varley Thomas
BUTCHERS.
Bramley John
Feather John
Garnett Wm.
Holmes Joseph
Midgley Robert
3 Story Robert
Thomas John
Thomas Enoch

Thomas Wm.
CLOG & PATTEN MAKERS.
Hartley John
Robertshaw Benj.
GROCERS.
*Marked * are Dprs. and † Ironmongers.*
*Atkinson Henry
†Barraclough John
*Driver James
Hartley Timothy

*Hartley John
Hudson John
Lambert Tobias
†Moore John
Roper Wm.
Thomas John
Wood John
Wright James
JOINERS.
*Marked * are Cabinet Makers.*
1 Ogden Nathan

R 2

1830 Parson and White's Directory of Leeds. This example shows a page detailing the inhabitants of the village of Haworth. From the proprietors of inns and public houses to cabinet makers, grocers and blacksmiths, most notable is the name of Reverend Patrick Brontë, incumbent of the local church and father of the famous Brontë sisters. Was your ancestor one of his parishioners? Courtesy of thegenealogist.co.uk.

a series of directories over a number of years you can establish how long a person resided in a particular area or a tradesman was in business. They are essential for filling the gaps in the years between each census and may help you to flesh out the story of your ancestors' lives in the intervening decades.

If your interests lie in the local history of the town/village/hamlet in which your family lived then these volumes are indispensable. You could create a whole back story with the information gleaned – ideal if your ultimate goal is to write a book or article based on your findings.

You will usually find copies at your local archives library and can even purchase your own CD Rom versions from specialists such as S&N Genealogy, genealogysupplies.com and parishchest.com, or search online at historicaldirectories.org or ancestry.co.uk.

Production of town directories continued into the 1970s whilst the last Kelly's London Post Office Directory was published in 1991.

Our family occupied the same property for over 100 years. How do I find out more about the history of this house and are there any specific documents that are likely to relate to my family?

Researching your house history can be a hobby in itself and although some documents that you use in genealogical research will be of great help, there are other records that you can call upon.

First, get organised and write down everything you already know about your house – the location, its name, number and street, the parish it falls within, etc. Try to find out who has the old title deeds of the property – start with the solicitor or estate agent – and talk to neighbours, or where possible, past residents to uncover any stories which surround the building or the families who lived within it. If possible, dig out old mortgage agreements, indentures or even wills which list your property by name and may have been part of a bequest within your family. If death duties were payable on a property over a certain value then these registers can help you find a place of probate and, in turn, a will. Contact The National Archives to discover how you can access these records.

Compare your property to others in the street – was it built as a 'one off' or as part of a series of similar houses? Look at the architectural differences – was it built during a different period to the surrounding properties and has it had additions or renovations that are noticeable from both inside and out?

At your local archive, try to pinpoint the house in historical directories and the census. Follow its trail back through the decades making notes about the people who lived there at certain times and if the building was used for any specific purposes, i.e. perhaps as a shop, post office or even a pub, and also if there has been a name change to the property or the street in which it is located. Depending on the age, size and historical importance of your house, there may even be documents relating to its past held in the archive collection so it is always worth making a quick enquiry.

Old wills and probate documents can give details about your ancestor's life that you may not be able to find anywhere else.

Armed with a list of owners and occupiers over key dates you can now take your research further; land surveys should be your first port of call. If your property is rural and in England or Wales try the National Farm Survey from 1943 – ideal for tracking occupants after the census years. Tithe apportionments (*see* above) will help you to see how much land came with the property during different periods. Each plot of land is accompanied by a number which can be cross-referenced with a schedule explaining the name of the owner and the tenant, a description of the land, its size, its state of cultivation and the amount of rent charged.

The list of documents which may be able to help you include local rate books, taxation records (such as hearth and window tax depending on the age of the building) and electoral registers, whilst the Valuation Office Survey could provide more clues from 1910 onwards. Accessing some of these records may require you to search further afield so try contacting The National Archives at nationalarchives.gov.uk/a2a to see where the records important to you are based. If you're serious about pursuing this 'architectural' side of your family history, consider investing in specific publications that can cover this subject in more detail. Nick Barratt's *Tracing the History of Your House: The Building, the People, the Past* ISBN-13: 978-1903365908 is a great place to start, or Pamela Brooks' *How to Research Your House: Every Home Tells a Story...* ISBN-13: 978-1845281656.

DON'T FORGET!

In the past, the first place where you would look for information – of any kind – would be in a book. Family historians are detectives of the past so why not use the resources which were – and still are – primary sources and seek out the old volumes which could help you in your mission? Specialist companies like parishchest.com combine twenty-first-century technology with early books, maps and manuscripts to provide access to information which in some cases is not recorded anywhere else.

If you find a reference or historical book particularly useful at your local archive library, take a note of the title, name of the author, publisher and date of publication – you may wish to try and source a copy for yourself. Locate volumes that are now out of print at sites such as the Advanced Book Exchange (abe.com) which has contacts worldwide, or at second-hand bookshops and antiquarian book fairs. Some dealers provide a book search service to track down that illusive title.

Chapter 8

EMIGRATION

In all of us there is a hunger, marrow deep, to know our heritage – to know who we are and where we came from.

Alex Haley, *Roots*

Although this book deals mainly with following our ancestors who lived in Britain, we cannot forget that there have been numerous occasions throughout our history when events have prompted people to leave our shores – often forever – in the hope of creating a new life overseas. Perhaps a particular branch of your family has suddenly gone missing from the census and no matter where you look they seem to have disappeared. Why not do a little historical research of your own? Cross-reference the period in which they have gone missing and see what was happening in the world at that time. Perhaps you already know that great-uncle Joseph was a bit of a pioneer and took off to America in the 1870s, but you do not know how to track him down? This chapter should help to shed some light on our ancestors' travels overseas as our research goes global.

If you take a look at any British history books for this period, most of the events which affected the country also had a knock-on effect on its inhabitants. Escaping poverty and famine with hopes for a better future and steady employment have all played their part. Fleeing the persecution of their nationalities and beliefs, taking the opportunity to acquire cheap land alongside the newly built railroads of America or to prospect for gold in locations around the globe could have influenced the life you now lead today. Below are just some of the reasons for mass migration.

Highland Clearances

The suppression of the Jacobite Rebellion of 1745 saw an end to Highland society as the Government began to destroy the basis of Highland life. Landowners had previously shared their land with their clan folk but now were investigating new farming methods to make profits for themselves – their only obstacle to making more money was their tenants. The introduction of large numbers of sheep which could be farmed for their high-quality wool brought about mass evictions known as the Highland Clearances.

Nineteenth-century captain's log book detailing information about each crew member and the voyage.

Those tenants that failed to leave by appointment were forced to flee as their crofts were burnt or destroyed in front of them. Some sought resettlement in other areas of Scotland but many others chose to emigrate in search of opportunities overseas.

There are some fabulous books on the Clearances to be found, whilst numerous websites can describe this time in more detail. One of the most comprehensive yet easy-to-follow sites regarding the timeline of events has been compiled by the Cauldeen Primary School and can be found at highlandclearances.info. Don't forget to visit theclearances.org where you will find numerous articles on everything from writs of removal to the emigration influx to Canada. Armed with this knowledge, visit the Rootsweb Highland Clearance Mailing List at http://lists.rootsweb.ancestry.com/index/intl/SCT/SCT-HIGHLAND-CLEARANCES.html for help in weaving your story into the past.

Religious Recruitment

Life for the working classes in Victorian Britain could be extremely hard and although the Industrial Revolution brought with it regular employment, the hours were long and the work was tough, even hazardous. There were very few health and safety regulations and exposure to dangerous substances and working conditions resulted in many lives being lost. Coal mining, quarrying and iron smelting were just some of the jobs in which employees took their lives in to their own hands. When Mormon missionaries visited specific areas of Britain – some polluted by industry, others with little in the way of opportunity for betterment – their promise of a new life in America following the trail of early pioneers was all that was needed to persuade some believers to leave their homeland for good.

Recruited into the Church of the Latter-day Saints (LDS), hundreds immigrated with their families to Utah. The journey would not be an easy one. The LDS movement established the Perpetual Emigration Fund to enable the poor to emigrate and even set up a system of handcart companies allowing them to travel more cheaply, pulling their belongings behind them. The vessels on which they crossed the Atlantic could reach 120 degrees farenheit between decks. There were water shortages and even outbreaks of cholera but despite this, and the perilous wagon trail across the American Plains where they were vulnerable to attack by Native Americans, the draw of a better life was strong.

Now recognised as the world's foremost authority on genealogical studies, the LDS Church has a vast holding of records, ensuring that at some point in our research we will all refer to information available on the LDS online databases at familysearch.org. If you can travel to the United States you may even be able to visit their archives in person.

Perhaps your ancestor was one of the early Mormon pioneers, trading a life in Britain for one overseas? The LDS 'housekeeping' and organisation has meant that even early records regarding Mormon immigration have been kept. For those who took the long journey by sea, visit xmission.com/~nelsonb/ship_list.htm and expect to find details of the ships, where they were bound, ports of departure and arrival and how long the passage took.

Between 1847 and 1868, 60,000 Latter-day Saints of varying nationalities followed the overland Mormon Trail with the help of over 250 'travel companies'. Use the library resources at lds.org to find out more. To establish the truth about your ancestor's settlement in the New World, consider subscribing to ancestry.com to gain access to their US census records taken every decade from 1790.

Irish instability

During the 1840s, England saw an influx of migrants arriving from Ireland who wished to settle on the mainland. The possibility of fleeing the poor social and economic conditions in Ireland and the promise of work and the ability to escape famine made a new life seem all the more tempting, whatever the cost. Although some decided to leave the shores of Britain for good by embarking on the long journey to the Americas, others were quite happy with the prospect of a new start across the Irish Sea. For many of these migrants, Liverpool was their port of entry.

The industrial city of Manchester, with its cotton and textile mills, links to the canal network and railways, brought a huge amount of work to the area, and this in turn was a magnet for large numbers of Irish immigrants who congregated in districts such as Chorlton cum Medlock and Ancoats. In 1841, 10 per cent of the inhabitants were Irish. It is important to remember that these families came with nothing but the clothes on their backs and very few, if any, personal possessions. As a result, these areas were poverty stricken; houses were overcrowded, and a lack of ventilation and sanitation made them an ideal breeding place for disease.

Many of the immigrants were of Roman Catholic persuasion, although some did change their faith to Church of England as soon as they set foot on English soil, believing this could give them a better chance at integrating into life on the mainland. Roman

Catholic records can be found at the Lancashire Records Office which is the official reserve for the church registers of this region. Go to lancashire.gov.uk/education/record_office. Also consider Manchester city library archives at manchester.gov.uk/libraries/arls for census returns, rate books, school records and cemetery registers and the Greater Manchester County Record Office at gmcro.co.uk.

You are likely to find the Manchester and Lancashire Family History Society (mlfhs.org.uk) extremely helpful. The interests of its 3,500 worldwide members are dominated by Irish and Anglo-Scottish ancestry branches. By joining, you will have access to specialist data sets such as the city's asylum admissions and police records, as well as the opportunity to get involved in active transcription projects.

We often hear of those migrants who left Ireland after the potato famine, but are there any resources which give details of those left behind?

Try getting access to the Griffiths Primary Valuation which was published between 1847 and 1864 and gives details of land and property owner/occupiers across Ireland during this period, listing almost every head of the household for each county. The National Archives of Ireland at nationalarchives.ie provides guidelines to this resource, whilst the website irishorigins.com includes access to the Griffiths Valuation and survey maps when you subscribe.

Australian emigration

Since the start of European settlement in Australia in 1788, more migrants have travelled there from the UK than any other country. Although some of the first settlers were

Diary entries are not only fascinating reading but tell the story from your ancestor's perspective.

convicts, the nineteenth century saw a growing influx of volunteers leaving the shores of Britain for this new destination. Over 60 per cent of migrants embarked from the port of Liverpool, making this city and its archive an essential place for those trying to trace their emigrant ancestors. Go to liverpool.gov.uk to get started.

In 1851, gold was discovered just outside Bathurst and the Australian Gold Rush began in earnest as people fought to stake their claim. The following decade saw 600,000 immigrants arrive, many settling for good, starting families and increasing the population. Another million arrived between 1860 and 1900, so to control and maintain the high numbers of newcomers, assistance schemes and immigration policies were introduced.

The National Archives of Australia is very similar to our own, but a lot of civil records are held by individual states so do not expect to find records on immigration, convicts or details of birth, marriages or deaths here. It does, however, have a vast collection of twentieth-century records begun by the federal government in 1901, including military records, citizenship and migrational records and an image bank of over 200,000 photographs. Use this site as your starting point, read their guidelines on how to research your Australian ancestry and then follow their links to the repositories which hold the information you require. On many occasions you can download copies of documents for a fee online or take advantage of the research services they have on offer.

My ancestor immigrated to New Zealand in the early 1900s. Once I have located them on the passenger lists, how do I go about establishing their lives in their new home?

Try searching the online index of birth, marriages and deaths in New Zealand to follow their story and that of their next generation. This can be found at bdmonline.dia.govt.nz and enables you to order certified copies or printouts. Family historians connected to the New Zealand Society of Genealogists (genealogy.org.nz) may be able to help you tighten the net, whilst The National Archives of New Zealand at archives.govt.nz could help you to establish if your ancestors left a will.

What is a passenger list?

A passenger list is a register of travellers who were onboard a ship during a particular voyage. Most available records date from the latter part of the nineteenth century when the master of a vessel was required to present the officer at the port of departure and the immigration authorities at the port of arrival with an inventory of their passengers. The information provided grew from simply a name, age and occupation to include their address, how much money they were taking with them and even a description of their appearance. With over 24 million records of ships sailing to worldwide destinations between 1890 and 1960, start your search for outbound passengers at ancestorsonboard.com.

Passenger List. A page from the *Titanic*'s passenger list showing what details a passenger had to provide to be allowed to travel. (Courtesy of BT27/780 The National Archives UK.)

What was the difference between assisted and unassisted passengers?

Voluntary settlers had two ways in which they could travel, either as assisted passengers – who had all or part of their passage paid for them – or unassisted passengers, who funded their own trip.

It was taken into consideration that those wishing to emigrate, who could offer skills but had little money, faced the prospect of not earning wages for the length of the journey and the period of settlement once they reached their destination. As a result some form of grant had to be found. Incentives to farm land and help populate Australia and New Zealand were offered in the form of an assisted passage. Sadly, in many cases, life aboard ship was far from pleasant with poor sanitation, ventilation and crowded dormitories which bred disease in the form of typhoid and cholera. The Passenger Act of 1855 improved facilities and sanitation.

For a comprehensive guide to searching for passengers who arrived in New South Wales between 1788–1922 (both assisted and unassisted across different time frames between this period), start your search at records.nsw.gov.au. Dates of embarkation, ports of arrival and names of the vessels are listed on these indexes, and information concerning how to access the records or employing a researcher to help is also covered. Immigration indexes and records for Sydney disembarkations can be found here, whilst mariners' and ships' records for vessels in Australian waters are the ideal starting point for unassisted passengers.

The State Library of New South Wales at sl.nsw.gov.au holds copies of newspapers from this period which often reported the arrival of a ship and listed the passengers aboard. For unassisted passengers to Victoria between 1852 and 1923, visit the online site of the Public Records of Victoria and search by name or ship at proarchives.imagineering.com.au.

Surprisingly, no official application was required to emigrate from Britain and Ireland in the mid-nineteenth century. Permission in the form of a completed request was only necessary when the passenger needed financial assistance. Sadly, these application forms do not seem to have survived except those for the New Zealand Company between 1839 and 1850. After 1922, immigration became the responsibility of the Commonwealth Government and the records are held by The National Archives of Australia at naa.gov.au.

What is meant by 'steerage'?

Steerage – also known as 'between decks' – was the area below the main deck on a sailing ship. In the early years of emigration, passengers were transported to their new homes in cargo ships with temporary accommodation set up in what had previously been the cargo hold. These furnishings were cheap and designed to be discarded once the passengers had been dropped off so that the vessels could make a return journey with a profitable cargo. As a result, conditions in the steerage area were poor with little in the way of sanitation and comfort. Steamships also used the term 'steerage' to apply to those passengers who had paid the cheapest fares, who were without a cabin and usually accommodated in the lower decks of the ship.

CABIN PASSENGER LIST

OF THE

IMPERIAL GERMAN & U. S. MAIL STEAMSHIP

"E M S"

A. HARRASSOWITZ, Commander

SAILING FROM GENOA FOR NEW YORK

VIA NAPLES AND GIBRALTAR

Thursday, May 25th, 1899

FOR NEW YORK.

Mr. Paolo Adrino	Ivrea
Rev. Joseph Amrhein	Hoboken, N. J.
Mr. H. C. Butler	New York.
Miss Margaret Benevantano del Bosco	Naples.
Rev. John Baudinelli	West Hoboken, N. J.
The Right Rev. Courtney Bishop of Nova Scotia	Nova Scotia.
Mrs. Courtney	Nova Scotia.
Mr. Andrew C. Coddington	Capri.
Mrs. Andrew C. Coddington	Capri.
Miss Elsie Coddington	Capri.
Mr. H. W. G. Dieck	Baltimore, Md.

Miss Olive B. Gilchrist	Melrose, Mass.
Mr. Wm W. Hubbard	New York.
Mrs. Wm W. Hubbard	New York.
Mr. Joaquin Marquez	Madrid.
Mr. Frank C. Moodey	Painesville, O.
Mrs. Frank C. Moodey	Painesville, O.
Mr. C. E. Rice	Watertown, N. J.
Mr. Joseph Lindon-Smith	Boston, Mass.
Miss Lucia G. Swett	Boston, Mass.
Miss M. C. Swett	Boston, Mass.
Dr. H. W. Joung	New York.

FOR GIBRALTAR.

Mr. I. H. Heer	Glarus.
Mr. Kerl Swidom	Breslau.

FOR NAPLES.

Mr. D. F. Kellogg	New York.
Mrs. D. F. Kellogg	New York.

Miss J. E. Corne ⎱ *Cambridge Mass.*
Miss A. B. Corne ⎰
Mr. José Dunipe *Seville Spain*
Miss Carmela Marino
Mr. Dr. A. Per Lee Pease *Massillon Ohio*
Miss M. Aster Woodcock

Documentation kept from a special voyage can shed light on the destination, date travelled and fellow passengers.

Labels and tickets can give clues to journeys taken.

S H ——————— S J.

Name of the Bearer of the Passport.		Number of the Passport.	Date of the Passport.		OBSERVATIONS.
Sheldon	Edward, Junior	6716	July 17	1851	
Sheppard	Miss Caroline	4166	April 4	.	
Sheppard	Joseph B.	9398	Sept 15	.	
Sheridan	Richard B.	6823	July 19	.	
Sheridan	Geoffrey John	9788	Oct 3	.	
Sherwood	W. E. Madox	7255	July 29	.	
Sherwood	Joseph	7256	. .	.	
Shields	James	5229	June 9	.	
Shillibeer		4478	May 2	.	
Shirreff	Mrs	5461	June 17	.	
Shoppee	Charles John	8637	Aug 25	.	with C. Roke
Shore	Hon: Charlotte	9775	Oct 3	.	
Shortridge	George Y	5689	June 24	.	
Shuckburgh	Captain George	8017	Aug 12	.	
Shuttleworth	John, Junior	7203	July 29	.	
Shuttleworth	Sir James Kay, Bart	7666	Aug 6	.	
Shuttleworth	Robert James	9498	Sept 18	.	
Sidebotham	Samuel	4395	April 25	.	
Sidey	Duncan	5628	June 21	.	
Siebe	Frederick	4557	May 7	.	
Siebe	A	4558	. .	.	
Sillifant	John	9100	Sept 5	.	
Siltzer	John Ludwig	8891	Aug 30	.	A Naturalized British Subje
Silver	Dr Ebenezer David	8026	. 12	.	
Silvester	H. E.	4923	May 26	.	
Sim	John Craysgarne	7947	Aug 11	.	
Sim	William	9834	Oct 6	.	
Simeon	John	10228	. 30	.	
Simmons	Capt. J. L. A.	7300	July 30	.	
Simms	John	10412	Nov 19	.	
Simon	Julius	4786	May 20	.	A Naturalized British Subject
Simon	Mrs Julius	5190	June 6	.	
Simon	John	7099	July 25	.	
Simons	William	9824	Oct 6	.	
Simpson	Maxwell	4434	April 29	.	

77

Passport Application Index. This shows a list of passport applications from 1851. It gives the name of the passport holder, the date of issue, the passport number and any remarks or observations. Image courtesy of findmypast.co.uk.

When were passports introduced, where are related documents held and what information could I expect to find on them?

It was not until in the 1850s that the early passport – issued in a pre-printed format displaying the Royal coat of arms – came into force. This stayed largely unchanged until the introduction of the blue booklet in July 1921, before being replaced by the current red design in the 1990s.

Previously, travel with this documentation was extremely hit and miss. For every person travelling abroad with a passport there were hundreds visiting the same destinations without one. You will be exceptionally lucky if you discover a passport owned by your ancestor that has been validated in each country he visited, but are just as likely to have had a well-travelled ancestor who left no documentary trace.

Sadly, no description or photograph of the holder was put on the passports until 1915 when the outbreak of the First World War required a worldwide revision of passport procedure. But do not raise your hopes of discovering a photo and detailed narrative of your ancestor's distinguishing features as the original applications were not retained – so unless you actually possess the passport within your family you could well be out of luck. That said, you may be able to search a register which recorded the issuing of passports by the Foreign Office. Each ledger displays the information in columns and states the date of issue, passport number, the name of the holder, the destination to which they were bound as well as the name of a referee who would recommend the traveller for a passport – this was usually someone of standing such as a solicitor or doctor. By looking through the registered names on either side of your ancestor you may also be able to establish a link with other passengers who could be related and have applied for a passport at the same time.

If you are fortunate enough to own your ancestor's passport, take a closer look at the visa and entry stamps that were used at border control upon entry and exit of a country and you may be able to trace their journey by plotting their travels on a map.

Where would I find documents relating to someone who was buried at sea?

Burials of British passengers at sea can be found at The National Archives. You will need to know the person's name, approximate date of death and, if possible, a geographical location of where to focus your search. By subscribing to findmypast.co.uk you will be able to search online records covering deaths at sea between 1854 and 1890, as well as births and marriages at sea between 1854 and 1887.

My ancestors immigrated to America and I'm led to believe they entered the country via Ellis Island. How can I find out more?

From 1892 to 1954, Ellis Island was the main point of entry into the United States. Over 22 million immigrant passengers and crew passed through this way and one of them could well have been your ancestor. Every ship's company kept a detailed list of

Deaths at sea. This list from 1873 includes the name of the deceased, their sex, age, cause and date of death, as well as the name of the ship and the date when the list was received. (1) Bear in mind that the name of the deceased may not be completely accurate. (2) Treat ages with caution. These figures would have been taken off the passenger list when the individual bought their tickets. (3) The cause of death is a useful piece of information as it may not have been recorded anywhere else. (4) All ships registered with Lloyds were given an official number; this can be extremely helpful when trying to identify a ship with a common name. (5) The date of receipt by the ship column was used to record the date when the information was officially entered in the records. Image courtesy of findmypast.co.uk.

passengers known as a manifest, and it is these manifests that have now been transcribed and digitally stored in an archive allowing you to track down an individual at the website ellisisland.org. With hints and tips on how to get the most out of your searches and the opportunity to see images of not only the passenger lists but also of the actual vessels themselves, this site is an important resource for anyone with ancestors who chose to travel to or settle in the New World.

Although Ellis Island was a gateway for immigrants during this period, what if your ancestor arrived here before the construction of the immigration station? The website castlegarden.org is a rapidly expanding (and free) database featuring over 11 million people who arrived at this New York port between 1820 and 1892.

Castle Garden – now known as Castle Clinton National Monument – is the major landmark within the 25-acre waterfront park at the tip of Manhattan known as The Battery. From 1855 to 1890, the castle was America's first official immigration centre before the construction of Ellis Island.

Is it true that Ellis Island officials changed many immigrants' names upon entering the US?

No. When a passenger bought a ticket at their port of departure they were required to provide their name so that the passenger lists could be created. On entering Ellis Island, the official would simply check that the names provided matched the passenger list. If names were changed it was down to the passengers themselves, who would sometimes modify their names either to make them easier to spell or to sound more American, perhaps in the belief that this would enable them to fit in and give them a fresh start in their new lives.

DON'T FORGET!

If your ancestors settled in America then a subscription to the world's largest online resource for family historians is a must; ancestry.com gives you access to 4 billion records and if you have even the slightest doubts about subscribing then why not try out their 14-day free trial? Access to their US census data will help you follow your ancestor's trail from the moment they set foot on American soil. Taken every ten years, there is coverage from 1790 to 1930 ,and if your forebears travelled over the border into Canada you can also find Canadian returns from 1861 to 1911 and border-crossing statistics.

These records are just the tip of the iceberg, with new databases added all the time covering everything from US Phone and City Directories to First World War draft registration cards. Perhaps you have a whole branch of living relatives just waiting to be found and by visiting other members' trees, uploading your own and sharing your data, you could make some fascinating links with your American cousins. (For more about social networking see Chapter 15).

I believe my ancestor was a child migrant. How would I find out more?

Child migration from Britain first began in 1618 when 100 children from London were sent to Richmond, Virginia to supply labour to plantation owners. The practice continued in earnest from the 1800s and it was only after the Second World War that numbers started to decline.

Back in the mid-Victorian era, British cities absorbed a huge influx of people from rural areas and Ireland, and the economy began to buckle under the strain. When there were not enough jobs to go around and unemployment figures rose, housing and food became scarce and many families lived in squalid conditions of overcrowded tenements and courtyards where diseases like cholera, TB and smallpox were rife. The situation prompted some parents to take drastic action, abandoning their offspring, whilst others forced their youngsters into a life of crime in order to survive. Increasing numbers of children lived on the streets and gradually, officials realised they had to find a way to protect these youngsters from the hardship. Poor Law Unions were already sending some adults overseas as a way of populating the new colonies, so it was not long before the idea was extended to include children.

Despite the process being thought of as a way to give underprivileged youngsters a better start in life, for many this was not the case. The system was plagued by scandals with reports of physical and sexual abuse, child labour and lack of education. It has to be said that not all children suffered the same fate but the system did not live up to the promises that it had made. In Canada, most children were housed with farmers and thought of as cheap agricultural labour, carrying out tasks without training or preparation and with little supervision. In Rhodesia, their arrival was thought to be a way of preserving the 'elite' white, race whilst later, in Australia, they would boost their diminished post-war population.

Barnado's and many other church organisations and charities sent orphans all over the British Empire in the hope that it would provide them with a better future. Banardo's (www.barnardos.org.uk/who_we_are/history/child_migration.htm) has comprehensive online resources with details of the charity's involvement with the scheme and contact details of how to receive assistance in investigating your case.

Between 1865 and 1935, 100,000 children arrived in Canada, so if this was where your ancestor ended up then try visiting the online site of The National Archives of Canada at collectionscanada.gc.ca to find out more. The British Isles Family History Society of Greater Ottawa (bifhsgo.ca) has a work in progress locating and indexing the names of these children from a variety of records, and at present have over 118,000 references which may hold the key to your ancestor's past.

Check outbound voyages from Britain between 1890 and 1960 available for viewing at findmypast.co.uk, or visit ancestry.ca for indexed Canadian passenger lists. Read on to find just some of the useful addresses and web links, essential for following this sensitive area of research.

Perhaps you have found gaps in your own family tree with young relatives seemingly untraceable. Investigate their parents and any other siblings, then consider that they too may have been part of Britain's child migration programmes. Remember, if you do make contact with a relative who has been directly involved, always tread with caution and consider that feelings may be very raw. Tact and diplomacy is needed and be prepared to accept that not everyone will want to talk about this part of their past.

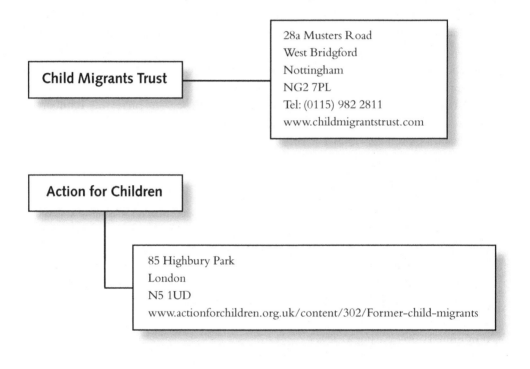

Child Migrants Trust

28a Musters Road
West Bridgford
Nottingham
NG2 7PL
Tel: (0115) 982 2811
www.childmigrantstrust.com

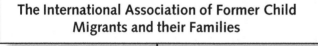

Action for Children

85 Highbury Park
London
N5 1UD
www.actionforchildren.org.uk/content/302/Former-child-migrants

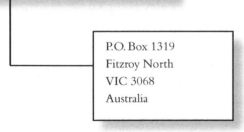

The International Association of Former Child Migrants and their Families

P.O. Box 1319
Fitzroy North
VIC 3068
Australia

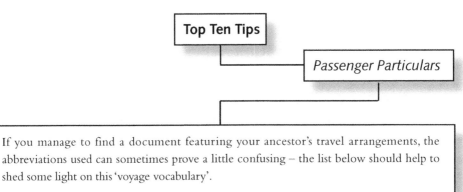

Top Ten Tips

Passenger Particulars

If you manage to find a document featuring your ancestor's travel arrangements, the abbreviations used can sometimes prove a little confusing – the list below should help to shed some light on this 'voyage vocabulary'.

Pob	Parents onboard but listed separately
Cob	Children onboard but listed separately
Inft	Describes an infant
Bv	Born on the voyage
B&dv	Born and died on the voyage
Tw	Travelling with…
Sf	Used to denote a stepfather
Nat	Naturalised
LCD	Loathsome Contagious Disease (mental or physical defectiveness)
Stow	Stowaway

Chapter 9

A CULTURAL MIX

We are the children of many sires, and every drop of blood in us, in its turn …
betrays its ancestor.

Ralph Waldo Emerson

Today, the United Kingdom is described as a multicultural society but, in reality, this was already the case in the late eighteenth, nineteenth and early twentieth centuries. Events overseas resulted in foreign nationals seeing Britain as a safe haven and they fled here to take refuge and make their homes. They had a great impact on our communities, bringing with them traditions and customs to integrate with our own. Your investigations may have led you to discover that you too have foreign connections which have inspired you to want to find out more. Begin with the basics and examine the origins of your surname before you spread your net too wide.

What should I consider when studying the history behind my family surname?

Britain has had a long history interspersed with frequent periods of migration both from and to the country, bringing with it an assortment of naming conventions. The majority of our British ancestors did not acquire a surname until around the fourteenth century, although noblemen did start using them much earlier with some examples recorded around the time of the Norman Conquest in 1066.

Very few people could read or write so they spelt their words phonetically, resulting in changes with every dialect across the country. For example, the surname Taylor could be spelt Tailor, Tayler, Tailer or Taylur so it is important to be reasonably circumspect when trying to find family members who are connected to your tree. Do not be too quick to dismiss a possible ancestor just because of a slight variation in spelling. Say your name aloud and write down as many spelling variants as you can think of.

In the majority of cases, our surnames derived from one of four basic roots – a first name, a nickname, an occupation or a place name.

First-name related surnames often had the addition of 'son', resulting in 'Richard' becoming 'Richardson' or 'John' becoming 'Johnson', which also give clues to a previous relationship, i.e. Robertson meaning 'son of Robert'.

Nicknames usually developed from distinguishing features or personal descriptions, resulting in unusual surnames such as 'Eyeball', 'Lightfoot' or 'Redhead'.

Occupational surnames often end with 'man' or 'er' such as 'Woodman', 'Baker' or 'Archer'; 'Smith' – as in Whitesmith – describes someone who worked with white metals. Bear in mind that occupations change and become obsolete, so do a little research and you may be surprised at what job roles your name is connected to.

Place-related surnames can range from using the whole word, such as 'Coventry' or 'Durham', to the description of a location such as 'Underhill'. Check through gazetteers at your local archive library or online at gazetteer.co.uk to find a connection.

The less common your surname the easier it will be to discover its origins. Whatever your family moniker, consider acquiring the help of organisations who have already compiled research on name studies. The Guild of One Name Studies at one-name.org is a great place to start and as the world's foremost authority in this field, there is a likelihood that they will be able to advise who may have knowledge of your surname and the research which has already been carried out on it.

CENSUS SURNAME CONCENTRATIONS WITHIN ENGLAND AND WALES

Surname | Bayley

○ 1841   ○ 1851   ○ 1861
○ 1871   ○ 1891   ◉ 1901

AGY	BDF	BKM	BRE	BRK	CAE	CAM	CGN
0	3	16	2	21	2	0	1
CHI	CHS	CMN	CON	CUL	DBY	DEN	DEV
0	581	1	20	9	27	15	123
DOR	DUR	ESS	FLN	GLA	GLS	HAM	HEF
30	15	96	0	18	72	63	46
HRT	HUN	IOM	KEN	LAN	LEI	LIN	LND
2	0	0	159	669	32	14	691
MDX	MER	MGY	MON	NBL	NFK	NTH	NTT
116	1	2	9	24	19	19	43
OXF	PEM	RAD	SAL	SFK	SOM	SRY	SSX
8	3	0	117	21	29	116	125
STS	WAR	WES	WIL	WOR	YKS		
939	260	13	8	104	165		

Number of matches:

| 0 | 1-49 | 50+ | 100+ | 250+ | 500+ | 1000+ | 2500+ | 5000+ | 10000+ |

Surname Mapping. This is an example of the kind of data you can discover if you use the Surname Mapping facility at www.thegenealogist.co.uk. The name Bayley was used for illustration focusing on the census year of 1901. The selection of boxes to the left shows the concentration of the name across the various counties, whilst the map gives a colour chart of the number of matches in each area. This is a fabulous tool to follow the spread of your family names by completing the search across all of the census years. Courtesy of thegenealogist.co.uk.

Get hold of a dictionary of old trades and occupations by searching booksellers, such as amazon.co.uk or the Advanced Book Exchange at abebooks.co.uk, to see if your surname is linked to the common occupations of the past; or use an online search engine to establish any connections with place names and locations around the country.

Distribution maps compiled from various censuses can help you to pinpoint in which areas your surname was most popular during a particular decade. The best facility I have found is at thegenealogist.co.uk where their clever Mapping Tool allows you to see the concentrations of your surname on the British mainland in the census years of 1841, 1851, 1861, 1871, 1891 and 1901 – it is as easy as inputting your surname and selecting the census year. The data found is displayed on a map showing the areas most populated by your name, whilst alongside is a chart that gives the actual number of people that share the surname broken down into counties. It is a great gizmo and also a lot of fun. Introduce your children or grandchildren to family history using this – their surname makes the whole procedure very personal to them and will soon have them hooked and wanting to find out more. If you find you get a taste for these 'Family History Calculators', consider giving the *Life Expectancy Age Maps* a go over at www.familyrelatives.com. These are searchable by surname and region and cover the years 1866–1920 and 1984–2005.

Exploring surname origins can be an addictive hobby in itself, but if time is limited and you still wish to pursue this area of your family history, then consider hiring the skills and services of a professional surname researcher to help.

Have you tried?

Now you are well on the way to establishing your surname origins, why not visit the website movinghere.org.uk – a graphically illustrated resource which explains why people have moved to England over the last 200 years. You can search migration histories of the Caribbean, Irish, South Asian and Jewish communities, get advice on where to locate related records, maps, documents and photographs or even share your own story with their online community.

THE CELTIC NATIONS

Although there are many similarities to English research techniques when investigating Irish, Welsh and Scottish ancestry, there are also many differences. Despite being part of the United Kingdom, it is worth looking out for resources specific to the individual countries of England, Scotland, Wales and Northern Ireland which make up our sovereign state. Languages, traditions, cultures and events have all had an impact on their history so consider narrowing your search to find out detailed information when researching those nationalities which are on our doorstep.

I've just discovered Scottish forebears in my tree. Is there a book you would recommend which would give me a good overview of this area of research?

For an easy-to-follow guide which is packed with good advice then Chris Paton's *Researching Scottish Family History* is a great place to start. At 120 pages long it offers a relaxed approach to the subject and points you in the right direction to get the most out of the archives, records and resources available.

Where is the best place to start my online investigations into my Scottish branch?

It's impossible to carry out online Scottish family history research without paying a visit to the pay-per-view website scotlandspeople.gov.uk, hosted at present by the company Brightsolid. With a wealth of records and enhanced features available, from the General Register Office censuses to wills, heraldry records and Roman Catholic parish registers, there are plans under way to add new resources, such as kirk sessions and valuation rolls, helping to add flesh to the bones of our ancestors in the years between the censuses.

The 1911 census records for Scotland are also well on the way to completion and although the household schedules did not survive like those of England and Wales, these digitalised records will show the enumerators' returns – essential for those of us waiting to find out more about our early twentieth-century families.

When trying to track down a particular location then scotlandsplaces.gov.uk may provide just the help you need. The site enables you to view digital copies of plans, maps, photographs and other documents from a whole host of national institutions. Easy to use and searchable by county or place name, you can compare Scotland's past and present using road and canal maps, plans of churches, private houses, farms, schools and quarries, as well as viewing photographs of the built environment in conjunction with The Royal Commission on the Ancient and Historical Monuments of Scotland (rcahms.gov.uk).

Launched in 2003, the website www.scottishdocuments.com from The National Archives of Scotland (NAS) began a project to digitalise and preserve over 520,000 Scottish wills and testaments. After a hugely successful response, they are currently digitising other historical documents including kirk sessions, records of presbyteries, synods and the General Assembly of the Church of Scotland. Contact them online to find out more about their latest work in preserving Scotland's written heritage and how to access their records.

I have Welsh ancestors in my tree and have heard that their naming systems are notoriously difficult. Is there anything I should take into consideration?

Genealogical research uses many of the same techniques in whichever part of Britain you wish to investigate, but there are some areas which need extra attention and Wales is one of them. As well as the use of common surnames such as Jones, Evans and Williams, making distinguishing between families and generations a sometimes frustrating task, there's the additional hurdle of what is known as the patronymic system: giving a child the father's forename as a surname, resulting in the surname changing in successive generations. This can create difficulties for newcomers and experienced historians alike.

The patronymic system began in Wales with the wealthy classes during the fifteenth century, and the procedure spread to those in the middle and lower classes before slowly evolving into the natural inheritance of family names in the mid-eighteenth century. If your Welsh research eventually takes you this far back, this is where you may start to hit problems and really have to use your wiles to confirm your family line.

You will discover this family association when the term 'ap' or 'ab' from the Welsh word 'mab' meaning 'son' starts to appear. For example, Rhodri ap Dafydd can be translated to Rhodri, son of Dafydd. Names such as Pritchard and Powell have been anglicised from 'ap Richard' and 'ap Hywel'.

The main centre for Welsh research is at The National Library of Wales (llgc.org.uk).

Why is it that various members of my Welsh ancestral families all had similar occupations?

Rural or coastal, village or town dweller, like many Brits our Welsh ancestors made use of their natural surroundings in order to get by. Many of the occupations they chose or were

Occupational Images.
Collect period postcards
to illustrate your
ancestor's occupation

Occupational Images.
Some of these can be long
forgotten trades.

born to were steeped in history and tradition, and the skills and methods required passed down from generation to generation.

With a large proportion of Wales bordered by the sea and its accompanying river tributaries, it is not surprising that many people made use of these aquatic resources. Mussel-fishing, cockle-picking and seaweed-gathering were occupations which could be carried out by both men and women and put food on the table as well as providing a surplus for selling on. Coracle-makers were proficient in the art of fashioning small one- or two-man craft by hand which were light enough to be carried on a man's shoulders. They could be used as ferries, for transporting goods and fished from.

You may have been intrigued to find your ancestor listed on the census as practising one of these trades, yet disappointed that you own no images to show them at work. Postcards produced in the early 1900s depicted many of these trades, showing those involved in traditional Welsh outfits adapted to suit the role and weather conditions endured when working by the sea. You will also be able to get an idea of the type of basic equipment they used, the traditional baskets or donkeys and carts required for carrying their harvests.

Those further inland took employment in the wealth of coal mines and slate quarries that brought income to Wales when these commodities and products were shipped around the country or further afield. Visiting a dedicated museum can help you visualise the hardships faced in these occupations. The National Slate Museum at Llanberis (museumwales.ac.uk/en/slate) is one of the best examples of its kind, whilst the Big Pit Museum in Blaenavon (museumwales.ac.uk/en/bigpit) provides a great day out and can open your eyes to the harsh realities of life down the mine.

Why did many Welsh immigrants congregate in Patagonia?

Previously, Welsh immigrants who had travelled to America had begun to lose their identity and language when they realised that they had to learn English in order to fit in. To overcome this, a colony was founded in Patagonia, Argentina, in order to re-establish the language and customs, with the first group of 150 settlers arriving from Liverpool in 1865. Their task was a hard one – requiring them to fight floods, bad harvests and settle disputes before they were officially granted the land and able to encourage other colonists to join them.

It was not only in Argentina that the Welsh founded new colonies but North America and Australia, with miners, foundrymen and other skilled workers using their talents and knowledge to find employment in the expanding industrial areas of these countries.

Are there any tips you can give for tackling an Irish branch of my family tree?

As touched upon in previous chapters, Irish research can sometimes be overshadowed by the loss of much of the nineteenth-century census returns and the 'late start' of the civil registration records in 1864, but there are other options.

In talking to relatives, first try to establish the parish or townland from where your ancestors originated and, if possible, their religious denomination. Townland indexes were compiled during the nineteenth and early twentieth centuries and can often be found in Ireland's major libraries and archives. These invaluable records give the names of land divisions in each townland in the form of county, parish and Poor Law Unions, whilst later indexes include an Ordnance Survey map reference so that you can isolate an exact location. Consider getting back to basics and take a fresh look at your ancestor's surname. Identify its origins and see if you can tie it to areas where your ancestors may have lived.

Perhaps you know when and where an individual died; if so, attempt to track down their place of burial. A gravestone can be a real find, not only for the information it may include about family members, but it gives you a definite link to an event which can be followed up with enquiries at the church and the hunt for possible details of a funeral in the local newspaper. For those with Northern Irish roots, visit historyfromheadstones.com, which contains 50,000 inscriptions from over 800 graveyards and explains more about the location of the churches and their religious denominations.

Over 70 million people around the world can claim Irish ancestry giving you a wealth of potential links to swap information. The IrelandGenWeb project (irelandgenweb.com) is supported by volunteers and is a great place to learn more about Ireland's topographical layout, with links to various province and county information – essential in helping you to locate records and resources and make connections. Its surname registry is regularly updated and its links to query boards and mailing lists help you to make contact with like-minded researchers. Irish Origins (irishorigins.com) also holds a wealth of information that can help you to plug the gaps between the census years or before the start of Irish civil registration. Their index of pre-1858 wills may help uncover lines of research of which you had not previously thought.

Make use of emails and postal enquires to nearby Family History Societies if you're unable to visit in person – you may be able to enlist their help for the small fee of annual membership – which is well worth the investment for their experience and knowledge of surviving records alone.

Read, read and read some more on everything you can find relating to Irish genealogy – it is a massive subject and often requires expert advice to point you in the direction of documentation which could open up a possible gold mine of information about this area of your family tree. Consider trying *Your Irish Ancestors* by Ian Maxwell, published by Pen and Sword. This practical guide will lead you through the maze of resources available whilst its no-nonsense approach can help you overcome any brick walls.

Why might my ancestors have emigrated from their birth country to Britain?

A little historical research needs to be done to understand your ancestor's particular plight. Read up on what was happening in their birth country and in Britain around the time of their migration to help you discover more. Religious persecution, famine, political upheaval, lack of work and recession are just some of the reasons why people made the decision to leave. Despite the passing of time, today's immigrants face very similar problems to those of our ancestors 2–300 years ago.

Are there any specific documents which may record their new citizenship?

From 1851 onwards, the census would often indicate the origins of individuals born outside Britain so this might be where you will find your first clues. Naturalised British citizens were regularly recorded with the initials 'BS', meaning British Subject.

It was not until the mid-nineteenth century that restrictions were put on immigrants arriving from the Commonwealth – previously, those from the British Empire were automatically classed as citizens and did not have to apply for the right to live in Britain. Others were required to apply for either a 'patent of denization' which, once granted by the sovereign, allowed the applicant to live in Britain, or for 'naturalisation', which gave foreign nationals the same rights as a native-born resident. The Naturalisation Act was introduced in 1844 and stated that anyone wishing to stay in Britain should declare their age, trade and residence, as well as swearing an oath of allegiance to the country, before they were granted permission in the form of a certificate and allowed to stay.

Before this date the acquisition of these documents was not obligatory, so those from the poorer classes who were desperate to flee their homelands often didn't bother. A completed application can prove very useful to the family historian giving details about the hopeful candidate and their family – documents produced from 1800 onwards have been indexed at The National Archives. Successful naturalisation documents can reveal the name and address of the applicant, their country and place of birth alongside their profession and marital status.

During your investigation, it is worth remembering that women were able to become naturalised through marriage to a natural-born or naturalised British citizen – this ruling did not apply to men.

By 1870, these regulations changed again with consideration only given to those applicants who had served the Crown or lived in Britain for at least five years. Many of the accepted immigrants decided to change their names by deed poll to an anglicised version of their original, in the belief that this would give them a better chance of integrating into the community.

What is the difference between an immigrant and an alien?

An immigrant moves to a foreign country in order to settle and make a new life for themselves and their families, whilst an alien moves to a foreign country but does not intend to settle there. Over the centuries, a number of concerns have been felt by British people about these 'newcomers' which have resulted in the compiling of records that may be of help to today's genealogists in their quest to find out more about their immigrant ancestor. Concerns raised included anything from the possibility of foreigners working for less money and taking jobs in times of economic crisis, to the chance that they may be potential spies and pose a threat to the country.

From the sixteenth century regular surveys were produced which documented the number of strangers in the capital; by the seventeenth century quarter and borough sessions recorded immigrants and those that employed them, whilst in the eighteenth and nineteenth centuries, foreign arrivals were obliged to register themselves at port and to the local Justice of the Peace to notify them of their presence. Masters of ships were required to fill out certificates relating to any alien passengers they brought into the country and, although these certificates no longer survive before 1836, an index to them can be searched at The National Archives.

Bear in mind when trying to establish a person's nationality that certificates of arrival completed between 1826 and 1905 usually state the last port from which a person sailed, but as journeys were often taken in stages this does not necessarily mean that this was the country from which they originated.

If your ancestor arrived after the start of the First World War then they would have been required to register with the police. Those documents which have survived should be held at the County Record Office for that area, while London records are likely to have been deposited at The National Archives. These Registers of Aliens can hold quite comprehensive information – expect to find the person's name, nationality and place of birth, their residential address with details of the type of tenancy, their occupation (even if they were not actually practising the trade at the time), their employer's address as well as information about the individual's spouse and children who accompanied them.

Who were the Huguenots?

The term 'Huguenot' is alleged to be the Gallicised version of a combined Flemish and German word which became the 'badge' used to describe those whose faith in the Protestant religion brought them into conflict with the king of France and with the Catholic Church, who saw their beliefs as heretical.

During the sixteenth and seventeenth centuries, over 250,000 French Protestants fled their homeland to escape Catholic persecution and extermination, settling in Germany and Switzerland or making their way further afield to South Africa or America. But with France on our doorstep, it is perhaps not surprising that the majority took refuge in Britain, greatly increasing the population and resulting in later claims that a large percentage of Britons have Huguenot blood.

Many early immigrants headed to the London areas of Spitalfields and Soho. They sought employment in trades in which they excelled, such as hat- and felt-making, gold and silversmithing, silk weaving and cabinet making. They brought with them new skills and design styles influenced by their French roots.

Where could I find more about my Huguenot ancestors?

Following the trail of French Protestant ancestors can be a daunting task but not impossible. Look for unusual names, name changes or references to foreign places of birth on birth certificates and censuses back to the start of civil registration in 1837. Establish where your ancestors settled – they would often try to re-establish their own communities, attempting to integrate while upholding their own traditions and customs as well as finding the means to support themselves. The French Protestant Church of London (egliseprotestantelondres.org.uk) was once a place of worship for these early settlers, while churchyards across this region became the final resting place for many who adopted this country as their own. It is said that most people with London ancestry will eventually discover a Huguenot ancestor.

Founded in 1885 and renamed a year later, The Huguenot Society of Great Britain and Ireland is the ideal place to advance your search. All the registers that are known to exist in England and Ireland have been published by the society, but by becoming a member you will also have free access to their extensive library as well as journals devoted to Huguenot genealogy and the opportunity to attend informative meetings held throughout the year. Visit their website at huguenotsociety.org.uk. The National Huguenot Society (huguenot.netnation.com) provides more information on the history of these refugees and offers useful advice on how to track those who settled in other countries besides Britain. As always, The National Archives may prove fruitful with naturalisation records available for viewing as well as records of baptisms and marriages from Huguenot churches which will help to establish a person's place of origin.

With the aid of a search engine you can find Huguenot museums not only in France but in various locations around the globe, including the Huguenot Museum in Franschhoek, South Africa, which documents the lives of those who arrived at the Cape of Good Hope in the late seventeenth and early eighteenth centuries, and the Huguenot Street Historic District in New York where buildings have been preserved to tell the tale of their migration and settlement in the US. An unrestored Huguenot silk-weaver's house has been preserved at 19 Princelet Street in east London, but is sadly under threat from a lack of funds. Visit 19princeletstreet.org.uk for more information.

What does the term 'Walloon' mean?

Often when researching Huguenot ancestry you will come across the term 'Walloon'. Wallonia is a French-speaking area of southern Belgium – traditionally Protestant – whose refugees came to England in the late 1500s. The records for Belgian Walloons are often mixed with those of the Huguenots.

How would I find out more about my Quaker ancestry?

The Religious Society of Friends – also known as the Quakers – formed in England in the 1650s and believe that there is something of God in everyone. They profess to value all individuals equally, and as a result oppose any harm that may threaten them. They integrate their religion into their everyday lives, worshipping and working actively to try to bring peace, equality and social freedom for all.

The Quaker Family History Society was formed in 1993 and concentrates on assisting those with British or Irish Quaker ancestry. Contact details and information on access to records can be found via their Ancestry Rootsweb link at rootsweb.ancestry.com/~engqfhs.

Many Quakers held monthly meetings and some of the minute books have survived, which record issues discussed, decisions made and the individuals involved. Registers of Quaker births, marriages and burials were also kept but ceased in 1837 upon the introduction of civil registration. By 1840, along with all other Nonconformists, they were required to surrender these original records to the Registrar General. Those that still exist are held at The National Archives.

Initially, Quakerism was prevalent in Yorkshire and from here spread across the country. The University Library of Leeds holds a special collection of Quaker archives and although staff are unable to undertake research for you, you can arrange to visit in person or make use of their extensive online digitalised database. To find out more visit bei.leeds.ac.uk/FreeSearch/LIBSPCOL/Quakers or make an appointment by contacting the Special Collections department.

For one of the largest Quaker resources in the world, try the library at the Quaker headquarters of Friends' House in London (friendshouse.co.uk). Founded in 1673, it boasts a collection of thousands of books, manuscripts, photographs and documents relating to their meetings and members.

On the census my ancestor's birthplace is listed as India. How would I find out more?

You may find a reference on the International Genealogical Index (IGI) at familysearch. org but perhaps start your search at the India Office Family History Search database at indiafamily.bl.uk/UI which contains 300,000 records of British and European people in the country between 1600 and 1949, as well as biographical notes from a number of sources. There is a very useful Dictionary and Glossary of Terms included on the site relating to the various abbreviations which are used within these records.

Consider joining the Family in British India Society at fibis.org, essential for anyone who has European or Anglo-Indian ancestors that lived or worked in India or South Asia between 1600 and 1947. Their holdings include transcribed information from ecclesiastical, maritime and military records from the India office and East India Company. Although based in England, membership is open worldwide and gives access to over 580,000 records, a members' area where you can contact others interested in this line of research, as well as a biannual journal to keep you up to date with the latest data and findings.

I have Jewish ancestry; how can I trace my roots?

Jewish migration to Britain goes back a long way. In 1290 the Edict of Expulsion was proclaimed by King Edward I banishing the entire Jewish population from our shores. It would be another four centuries before the readmission of these families was allowed, under the rule of Oliver Cromwell.

Towards the end of the nineteenth century, large numbers of Jewish families began to settle in countries such as Holland, Germany, Poland and the UK to avoid the difficult conditions they were experiencing elsewhere in Europe and Russia. In Britain, they quickly established communities, incorporating their own worship in synagogues alongside that of Reform, United and Independent churches.

In general, you will need to employ the same research techniques as if you were trying to locate anyone else who lived in Britain. Gather together any old documents, ask family members for their recollections, jot down name variations and try to establish their approximate date of arrival.

Why not consider joining a Jewish group or society whose knowledge of specific records and experience of deciphering old Hebrew documents or memorial inscriptions will be an advantage. The Jewish Genealogical Society of Great Britain (jgsgb.org.uk) promotes and encourages the study of Jewish genealogy – if you have the time and are able to travel, think about enrolling on a beginner's workshop or attending one of their talks. In early 2010 they released the 1851 Anglo-Jewry Database – a collection of approximately 29,000 records covering the lives of more than 90 per cent of the Jewish population of the British Isles in the mid-nineteenth century. Searchable by non-members, this resource is just one of the important databases relating to this area of research. The online aids to understanding synagogue marriage authorisations can be a great help to the novice family historian, whilst the library of Jewish genealogical books is unrivalled by any other in Europe.

If you prefer to do your research online visit JewishGen (jewishgen.org), a discussion group for genealogists offering searchable resources from a Holocaust database listing over 2 million victims and survivors of this terrible time, alongside access to the family trees containing the details of over 4 million people with Jewish ancestry worldwide. Consider using online translation aids to decipher Hebrew, Russian, Yiddish and other languages; translatorbar.com allows free translation to and from any language and enables you to download a 'translator toolbar' to your computer for future use.

The International Jewish Cemetery Project (iajgsjewishcemeteryproject.org) aims to catalogue every Jewish cemetery or burial site listed here by town or city, country and geographic region around the world.

If your Jewish ancestors settled in the capital, why not visit London's Museum of Jewish Life in Finchley? Their archive includes many artefacts and photographs of Jewish social history in the London area and reflects the origins and traditions of emigrants from Eastern Europe and the Middle East, including refugees from Nazism. Why not combine your visit by enrolling on one of their family history workshops which are held periodically throughout the year. Find out more at jewishmuseum.org.uk.

DON'T FORGET!

To ensure that official records were made, many Jews were registered in the Church of England parish registers so don't limit yourself purely to Jewish records when trying to find your forebears.

What is an 'Ashkenazi' Jew?

The term derives from the word 'Ashkenaz', which is the Hebrew word for Germany. These Jews were of central or eastern European descent and approximately 120,000 arrived in Britain between 1880 and 1914.

What is a 'Sephardi' Jew?

This term derives from the word 'Sepharad' meaning Spain, and referred to those families of Spanish or Portuguese origin. Today, many Sephardi Jews are from North Africa or the Middle East.

My Jewish ancestor came here as a refugee in the Second World War but ended up in an internment camp – why was this?

After the Nazis came to power in Germany in 1933, the Jewish community was subject to increasing persecution. In order to escape their anti-Semitic laws, many chose to flee to Britain. As a result, over 13,000 people (10,000 of them children) had arrived here by 1939 and the Government feared this sudden 'invasion' would create a huge unemployment problem. They looked for ways to repatriate the newcomers. Temporary shelters were erected in existing Jewish communities but, as many had come from enemy territory, they were initially treated with caution – and sometimes hostility – and placed in internment camps alongside those who had persecuted them.

The National Archives has an excellent online help guide to enable you to track down any existing records relating to interns during both the First and Second World Wars.

My ancestor was a member of the Polish Army who settled here during the Second World War – how can I find out more about this period of his life?

During this wartime era thousands of Poles took refuge in Britain when Germany invaded Poland, and London became the seat of the exiled government. Over 160,000 of these were members of the Polish Army who, in turn, were attached to the British Army. To assist their transition, the Polish Resettlement Corps was founded to demobilise the troops and help them to integrate into civilian life. The records that they created can be searched at The National Archives as well as any applications for citizenship. The Ministry of Defence would be the best place to make enquiries about your ancestor's military career. Your regional archive library may be able to help out with any general local history information regarding the Polish communities which were created during this time.

Chapter 10

IN THE FORCES

When you do genealogy, you do history by accident.

Deanna Fisher

Over the centuries Britain has been involved in numerous wars and conflicts so, whatever period you are researching, it is highly likely that military service will arise at some point.

Below is a list of just some of the major campaigns in which our armed forces were involved. This is not exhaustive but focuses on the main military actions from 1800 to the latter part of the twentieth century. It is important to consider that if one of your ancestors was untraceable on the census during any period when conflicts were taking place, they may well have been posted overseas or been caught up in combat defending their country.

1775–83	American War of Independence
1793–1802	French Revolutionary War
1803–15	Napoleonic Wars
1853–56	Crimean War
1857–58	Indian Mutiny
1879	Zulu War
1880–81	1st Boer War (Transvaal War)
1899–1902	2nd Boer War
1914–18	First World War
1936–39	Arab Revolt in Palestine
1939–45	Second World War
1950–53	Korean War
1956	Suez crisis
1969–2007	'The Troubles'
1982	Falklands Conflict

This is a fascinating and highly specialised area of research. Each stage of a person's career would have generated records – it is just a case of knowing where to look.

World War I Army memorabilia. Diaries, photographs of battalions and units and other ephemera may have been passed down in your family and could help shed light on your ancestor's war years.

World War I postcards can help to illustrate uniforms, thoughts and feelings of those on the front line and those left waiting at home.

THE VICTORIA CROSS

THE VICTORIA CROSS.

CHRONOLOGICAL LIST OF OFFICERS AND MEN OF THE ROYAL NAVY, ROYAL MARINES, ROYAL NAVAL RESERVE AND ROYAL NAVAL VOLUNTEER RESERVE UPON WHOM THE DECORATION HAS BEEN CONFERRED.

Name.	Rank.	Place where Act of Gallantry was performed.	Date of Act of Gallantry, and Rank at the time.	Date of *London Gazette* in which the Act of Gallantry is detailed.
Sir L. S. T. Halliday, K.C.B., D.L.	General, R.M.	Pekin, China	June 24, 1900 (Captain, R.M.).	January 1, 1901.
Basil J. D. Guy, D.S.O.	Commander	Tientsin, China	July 13, 1900 (Midshipman).	January 1, 1901.
N. D. Holbrook	Commander	The Dardanelles	December 13, 1914 (Lieutenant).	December 22, 1914.
H. P. Ritchie	Captain	Dar-es-Salaam	November 28, 1914 (Commander).	April 10, 1915.
E. C. Boyle	Vice-Admiral	The Dardanelles	April 27, 1915 (Lieut.-Com.).	May 21, 1915.
Sir Martin E. Dunbar-Nasmith, K.C.B.	Admiral	Sea of Marmora	June, 1915 (Lieut.-Com.).	June 24, 1915.
E. Unwin, C.B., C.M.G.	Captain	The Dardanelles	April 25, 1915 (Commander).	August 16, 1915.
W. St. A. Malleson	Lieut.-Com.	The Dardanelles	April 25, 1915 (Midshipman).	August 16, 1915.
E. G. Robinson, O.B.E.	Rear-Admiral	The Dardanelles	February 26, 1915 (Lieut.-Com.).	January 1, 1916.
R. B. Davies, D.S.O., A.F.C.	Captain	Bulgaria	November 19, 1915 (Squad.-Com., R.N.A.S.).	March 31, 1916.
G. Campbell, D.S.O.	Vice-Admiral	The Atlantic	February 17, 1917 (Commander).	April 21, 1917.
J. Watt	Skipper, R.N.R.	Straits of Otranto	May 15, 1917	August 29, 1917.
R. N. Stuart, D.S.O.	Captain, R.N.R.	The Atlantic	June 7, 1917 (Lieut., R.N.R.).	July 20, 1917.
W. Williams, D.S.M.	Seaman, R.N.R.	The Atlantic	June 7, 1917	July 20, 1917.
C. G. Bonner, D.S.C.	Lieutenant (late R.N.R.).	The Atlantic	August 8, 1917 (Lieut., R.N.R.).	November 2, 1917.
E. Pitcher, D.S.M.	Petty Officer	The Atlantic	August 8, 1917	November 2, 1917.
A. F. B. Carpenter	Vice-Admiral	Zeebrugge and Ostend.	April 22–23, 1918 (Act. Captain).	July 23, 1918.
N. A. Finch	Q.M. Sergt., R.M.	Zeebrugge and Ostend.	April 22–23, 1918 (Sergt., R.M.).	July 23, 1918.
R. Bourke, D.S.O.	Lieut.-Com. (late R.N.V.R.).	Ostend	May 9, 10, 1918 (Lieut., R.N.V.R.).	August 28, 1918.
V. A. C. Crutchley, D.S.C.	Captain	Ostend	May 9, 10, 1918 (Lieutenant).	August 28, 1918.
H. Auten, D.S.C.	Lieut.-Com., R.N.R.	The Atlantic	July 30, 1918 (Lieut., R.N.R.).	September 14, 1918.
D. M. W. Beak, D.S.O., M.C.	Commander (late R.N.V.R.).	Longeast Wood, France.	August 21–25, 1918	November 15, 1918.
A. W. S. Agar, D.S.O.	Captain	The Baltic	June 17, 1919 (Lieutenant).	August 22, 1919.
G. C. Steele	Commander	Kronstadt Harbour	August 18, 1919 (Lieutenant).	November 11, 1919.
R. B. Stannard	Lieut.-Com., R.N.R.	Namsos	May, 1940. (Lieut., R.N.R.).	August 16, 1940.
P. S. W. Roberts	Lieutenant	Mediterranean	February 16, 1942 (Lieutenant).	June 10, 1942.
T. Gould	Petty Officer	Mediterranean	February 16, 1942 (Petty Officer).	June 10, 1942.
R. E. D. Ryder	Commander	St. Nazaire	March 28, 1942 (Commander).	May 21, 1942.
S. H. Beattie	Lieutenant-Commander	St. Nazaire	March 28, 1942 (Lieut.-Com.).	May 21, 1942.
A. C. C. Miers, D.S.O.	Commander	Mediterranean	March 4, 1942 (Commander).	July 7, 1942.
R. St. V. Sherbrooke, D.S.O.	Captain	North Cape	December 31, 1942 (Captain).	January 12, 1943.
B. C. G. Place, D.S.C.	Lieutenant	Kaafiord, North Norway.	September 22, 1943 (Lieutenant).	February 22, 1944.
D. Cameron	Lieutenant, R.N.R.	Kaafiord, North Norway.	September 22, 1943 (Lieut., R.N.R.).	February 22, 1944.

1944 Navy List showing recipients of the Victoria Cross. Entries supply the name and rank of all personnel along with the date, place and act of gallantry, their rank at the time and the issue date of the *London Gazette* where the event was detailed. Courtesy of thegenealogist.co.uk.

I've heard that The National Archives is the best place to look for any military related records, is this true?

Without a doubt TNA holds the largest collection of documents connected with all three branches of the armed forces – the Army, Royal Navy and Royal Air Force. They produce detailed leaflets of their holdings which cover everything from conscription,

[1842]
Local Rank.

LIEUTENANT-GENERALS.

☒—Rt. Hon. Sir Edw. Blakeney, KCB. GCH.	26 Aug. 1836		Ireland.
Lambert Loveday	10 Jan.	37	East Indies.
Sir John Doveton, GCB.	do		do
Nathaniel Forbes	do		do
John William Morris	do		do
Thomas Marriott	do		do
George Dick	do		do
John Cuninghame	28 June	38	do
Sir Hugh Gough, KCB.	18 June	41	do and China.
James Price	23 Nov.		East Indies.
Thomas Boles	do		do
Sir Hugh Fraser, KCB.	do		do
Sir Hopetoun Stratford Scott, KCB.	do		do
Sir John Sinclair, Bt.	do		do

MAJOR-GENERALS.

Sir James Cockburn, Bt. GCH.	22 Feb. 1831		Late Insp. Gen. of R. Mar.
◎-✠-Sir S. Remnant Chapman, KCH.	28 Oct.		Bermuda.
Sir Henry Lindsay Bethune, Bt.	21 Dec.	35	Asia.
Hugh Stacey Osborne	10 Jan.	37	East Indies.
George Carpenter	do		do
William Roome	do		do
John Luther Richardson	do		do
Sir David Leighton, KCB.	do		do
Sir Charles Deacon, KCB.	do		do
James Welsh	do		do
Sir Thomas Corsellis, KCB.	do		do
John Nicholas Smith	do		do
Charles Farran	do		do
Sir James Russell, KCB.	do		do
Sir Donald Macleod, KCB.	do		do
Sir Jos. O'Halloran, KCB.	do		do
Martin White	do		do
Edward Boardman	do		do
George Wahab	do		do
David Courtney Kenny	do		do

Josiah

1842 Army List. This example shows the ranks of lieutenant general and major general. Courtesy of thegenealogist.co.uk.

In the List of General and Field Officers, the names printed in *Italic* are those of Officers retired from the Army, which are specially allowed to be retained in the Army List.

The words subscribed under the Titles of Regiments denote the Honorary Distinctions permitted to be borne by such Regiments on their Colours and Appointments, in commemoration of their Services.

Officers who have no Date in the Column of Rank in the Army take Rank according to their Regimental Commissions.

Officers having the * before their Names have *Temporary Rank only.*

The following denote the Honorary Distinctions of individual Officers, viz.

KG.	Knight of the Order of the Garter.
KT.	———————— the Thistle.
KP.	———————— St. Patrick.
GCB.	Knight *Grand Cross* of the Order of the Bath.
KCB.	Knight *Commander* of do
✠ before the Name, *Companion* of do
GCMG.	{ Knight *Grand Cross* of the Order of St. Michael and St. George.
KCMG.	Knight *Commander* of do
CMG.	*Companion* of do
GCH.	{ Knight *Grand Cross* of the Royal Hanoverian Guelphic Order.
KCH.	Knight *Commander* of do
KH.	Knight do
☒☒☒ Crosses with Clasps ☒ Cross only ◎-◎ Medals with Clasps ◎ Medal only	} Vide Page 77.
Waterloo Medal	{ Officers *actually* present in either of the Actions of the 16th, 17th, or 18th June, 1815.

N.B.—All communications regarding Deaths (*more particularly of those Field Officers who have retired from the Army, but whose names are specially allowed to be retained, and of Officers having Local Rank*), Errors, or Omissions, which may be discovered in this, or in the MONTHLY Army List (which is also published by Authority), verified by real Signature, should be addressed to "The Right Honourable the Secretary at War," marking the words "*Army List*" on the corner of the Cover.

1842 Army List cover page. This explains how the Army Lists were compiled and the abbreviations used to denote the honorary distinctions of individual officers. Courtesy of thegenealogist.co.uk.

commissions and promotions to being taken prisoner, dying in service and acquiring a pension for those who survived or their widows and children. If related records are held in another repository then they will happily help point you in the right direction. Start your search at nationalarchives.gov.uk.

But do not stop there – read up on your subject and use the internet to find other databases, museums and exhibitions of relevance. Consider visiting thegenealogist.co.uk, which has a wide selection of Army and Navy Lists from between 1806 and 1944, as well as roll of honour records which cover both world wars and have biographies with portraits and personal information. The site also has some notifications of deaths of members of the British forces from the Second World War, as well as records of those made prisoner of war, civilian internees and deaths during air travel. Spread your net wide and see what you can find.

I'm unable to visit the TNA in person. Does this mean that this area of research is closed to me?

Definitely not. There are private researchers available who are prepared to undertake specific searches on your behalf, for a fee. They usually live within travelling distance of the archives and you can contact them by phone or email to discuss your request. Often the researcher specialises in one branch of the services although there are those who generalise. My advice would be to seek out the specialist who will often have a greater knowledge of their particular field. The National Archives provides their own search service – you can choose an independent researcher from a list on their site at nationalarchives.gov.uk/irlist or seek out someone that appeals to you from the many advertisements in any of the family history magazines.

How is the British Army structured?

As a result of the varying origins and pedigrees of its constituent parts, the British Army is complex, and its structure can be difficult to understand. Leaving aside smaller tactical formations for the sake of simplicity, the basic building block of the Army is the **regiment**, which in the infantry and some supporting arms may be comprised of one or more **battalions**. These regiments and battalions are permanent units that are assigned to temporary formations according to operational requirements. Such formations include **brigades**, two or three of which may be grouped into a **division**. Two or more divisions make a **corps**, but this kind of very large formation is now a rarity.

Which records will best help me to identify a military ancestor from the First World War and the campaigns in which he took part?

The key is to discover the regiment he was serving with and his army number. The best place to find these are on his Medal Index Card (MIC), a series of records created by the War Office to establish which medals were to be given to each soldier. Medals were issued to those who survived the war and to the families of those who did not. At first glance the MICs seem to contain a variety of confusing abbreviations used to record the theatres of war in which each individual was involved, but enlist the help of websites such as 1914–1918.net for easy explanations and help in deciphering these codes. Search online at ancestry.co.uk or nationalarchives.gov.uk.

What were the main medals issued during the First World War?

Every soldier who fought was entitled to a War Medal and Victory Medal, which covers the period from 1914–1920, as well as service in Russia between 1919 and 1920. Approximately 6.5 million of these medals were issued. The goddess Victory was the image used on the Victory Medal given to each allied nationality between 1914 and 1919.

Men who served overseas in the first year of war were entitled to the 1914 Star Medal, whilst the 1914–15 Star was given to those who had fought in the first two years of war but not received the 1914 Star.

Did You Know?

These three medals (the 1914 or 1914–15 Star, the British War Medal and Victory Medal) became affectionately known as 'Pip, Squeak and Wilfred'. Try to discover more about their recipients by contacting the museum of the regiment or service shown on the back of the medal.

France and Belgium awarded the Croix de Guerre to allied servicemen who had performed acts of extreme bravery and heroism. If your ancestor received this honour why not search through newspapers of the time or at gazettes-online.co.uk to see if any details were given as to why he received the award. Allow a wide search period around the event as often there could be a long time delay between the actual occasion and the published report of gallantry. There is also likely to be more information in the archives of the battalion in which he served – consider contacting the local military museum for help in trying to track it down.

Although not technically a medal, the Silver War Badge – circular in shape with a crown in the middle – was given to all those who had retired or been discharged through wounds or sickness since the start of the war. It also served to prevent mistaken accusations of cowardice for those no longer in military uniform.

I have a photo of my ancestor in Army uniform taken during the First World War. There are two stripes on the left arm of his jacket and chevrons stitched on the right arm – what do they signify?

The stripes on his left arm are likely to be 'wound stripes' worn by officers and men to denote the number of times they had been wounded in action (although being gassed did not count). The chevrons on his right arm were used during the First World War to show the number of years that each man had spent in active service abroad.

What is a service record?

These are the papers filled out by the individual when they first enlisted. Expect to find a whole host of details including their name, age, date and place of birth and even their civilian occupation, alongside height, weight, hair colour and a description of any distinguishing features such as tattoos and scars. The papers would then record whether the person had served in the forces before – perhaps opening up a whole new area of research – and their length and place of service at home and overseas. Sadly, a large proportion of First World War documents now known as the 'burnt records' were lost to German bombing in the Second World War, and many others did not survive or are now in poor condition. But do not be disheartened – your ancestor's records may have survived and be available for viewing at ancestry.co.uk. It is always worth following the trail once you have established your ancestor's military links via the Medal Index Cards.

Where would I search online for an ancestor who survived the First World War?

The records of non-commissioned officers and other ranks can be searched in person at TNA or online at ancestry.co.uk. A fee is payable depending upon the length of subscription but will give you access to the 1914–20 British Army First World War service records, pension records – which will enable you to establish whether your ancestor was discharged because of wounds or entitled to a pension after the war was over – as well as war diaries which give a fascinating insight into the day-to-day activities of the men, listing casualties, battles fought and acts of bravery undertaken.

Where would I get a deeper insight into the conflicts and campaigns that were taking place during a particular period?

Newspaper reports of the day provide detailed accounts of battles, the movement of regiments and battalions and the heroics of individual soldiers. During the Boer, First and Second World Wars, campaigns were summarised in the press, with details of gallantry awards as well as weekly casualty lists, obituaries and memorandum notices.

The British Library website allows you to search through forty-nine local and national newspapers from between 1800 and 1913. Some viewings are without charge whilst others require a small subscription, but check with your local library who may allow access for free. Go to newspapers.bl.uk/blcs.

Those looking solely for information on the First World War should visit The Long, Long Trail at 1914-1918.net. Packed with content, it will help answer all your questions relating to the British Army during this period, giving advice on how to search for a soldier, numerous unit histories alongside details of theatres of war and the battlefields upon which they were fought.

The War Illustrated. These pictorial magazines help to visually explain the events of the time.

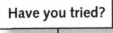

Have you tried?

Keen to find out about the Second World War? Check out ww2history.com, where you will find an encyclopedia of information in varying formats, from video and audio to text and images. Written by some of the world's experts combined with eyewitness accounts, this is the ideal place to expand your knowledge and understanding of this period.

Newspapers reported events as they unfolded and are a prime source of announcements, advertisements and obituaries.

Is there anywhere I can search for Second World War soldiers who were held as prisoners of war (POWs)?

Under the 1929 Geneva Convention, opposing forces were required to notify each other of captured combatants. As a result, ancestry.com was able to release details of more than 100,000 POWs to mark the seventieth anniversary of the Second World War, which includes records (compiled by the German military authorities) of all British Army personnel who were held in Germany, Austria and Poland. Canadian and Australian troops are also included. The thousands of air force personnel who were shot down over Europe at this time are not included in this database.

Base camps were known as 'stalags' and housed the general personnel, whilst 'oflags' held the officers. Conditions and treatment in a given camp varied depending on where it was situated; food was scarce, and although British officers were generally not required to work, soldiers were compensated if they did.

Records of POWs were also compiled by the Red Cross and are now held centrally at

Archives Division and Research Service,
International Committee of the Red Cross,
19 Avenue de la Paix,
CH-1202 Geneva, Switzerland

Paid searches are available for First World War information as these records are not open to the public, but they are free for prisoners of the Second World War or later. The more information you can provide about your relative will help in the search but find out more by visiting icrc.org and following the links to their archives.

If you had ancestors interned in the Far East, why not try the COFEPOW database (Children and Families of Far East Prisoners of War)? Liberation questionnaires were completed by British POWs held by the Japanese and the site aims to ensure that their story is never forgotten. Find out more at cofepowdb.org.uk.

Do not forget to visit the National Ex-Prisoner of War Association at prisonerofwar. org.uk. The wealth of information, from a detailed record of the individual camps to a comprehensive list of links to related sites and prisoner experiences, is guaranteed to help you understand the experiences of your ancestor.

What is the Commonwealth War Graves Commission?

It is a sad fact that it is easier to search for an ancestor who died during the world wars than it is for someone who survived, and this is thanks to the fantastic work carried out by the Commonwealth War Graves Commission (CWGC).

The CWGC was established by Royal Charter in 1917 and pays tribute to the 1,700,000 men and women of the Commonwealth forces who died in the two world wars. The commission's tireless work has enabled them to compile a 'Debt of Honour

Register', listing the people who died during these conflicts and the 23,000 cemeteries, memorials and other locations worldwide where they are commemorated. The register can also be searched for details of the 67,000 Commonwealth civilians who died as a result of enemy action in the Second World War, whilst the 'Histories' section gives you an insight into some of the major campaigns that took place during both world wars, in which your ancestor may well have taken part. Start your search now at cwgc.org.

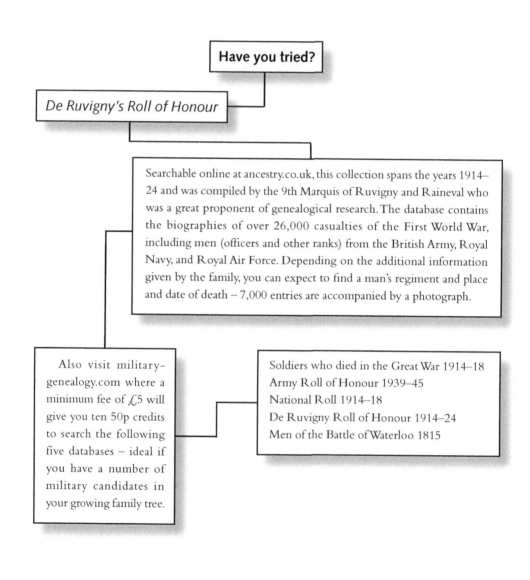

Have you tried?

De Ruvigny's Roll of Honour

Searchable online at ancestry.co.uk, this collection spans the years 1914–24 and was compiled by the 9th Marquis of Ruvigny and Raineval who was a great proponent of genealogical research. The database contains the biographies of over 26,000 casualties of the First World War, including men (officers and other ranks) from the British Army, Royal Navy, and Royal Air Force. Depending on the additional information given by the family, you can expect to find a man's regiment and place and date of death – 7,000 entries are accompanied by a photograph.

Also visit military-genealogy.com where a minimum fee of £5 will give you ten 50p credits to search the following five databases – ideal if you have a number of military candidates in your growing family tree.

Soldiers who died in the Great War 1914–18
Army Roll of Honour 1939–45
National Roll 1914–18
De Ruvigny Roll of Honour 1914–24
Men of the Battle of Waterloo 1815

The Roll of Honour

DARNILL, WILLIAM ALFRED, Private, No. 8/358, 8th Southland Regt., Otago Infantry, New Zealand Expeditionary Force, *s.* of the late Francis William Darnill, of 218, Crinan Street, Invercargill, Southland, New Zealand, formerly of Richmond, co. Surrey, by his wife, Jane, dau. of Thomson McNatty; *b.* Otatara Bush, Southland, New Zealand, 25 March, 1882; educ. Otatara School; volunteered on the outbreak of war and joined the New Zealand Expeditionary Force about 10 Aug. 1914, left for Egypt in Oct., and died of wounds, 25 April, 1915, received in the landing at the Dardanelles; *unm.*

William A. Darnill.

DARROCH, ALEXANDER, Private, No. 2866, 2nd Battn. Royal Scots (Lothian Regt.); served with the Expeditionary Force in France, etc.; killed in action near Kemmel, 21 April, 1915.

DART, GEORGE WILLIAM, A.B. (R.F.R., B. 2788), 214135, H.M.S. Good Hope; lost in action off Coronel, on the coast of Chili, 1 Nov. 1914.

DARTON, HENRY THEODORE, Corpl., No. 929, 1st Battn. Australian Imperial Force; killed in action at the Dardanelles, 17 May, 1915.

DARTY, EDWARD, Private, No. G. 63, 3rd Battn. Middlesex Regt.; served with the Expeditionary Force in France, etc.; died 20 April, 1915, of wounds received in action; *m.*

DARVILL, PERCY HENRY, Leading Seaman, 184384, H.M.S. Hogue; lost in action in the North Sea, 22 Sept. 1914.

DARWIN, ERASMUS, 2nd Lieut., 4th Battn. Alexandra, Princess of Wales' Own Yorkshire Regt. (T.F.), only *s.* of Horace Darwin, F.R.S., Chairman of Cambridge Scientific Instrument Co., by his wife, the Hon. Emma Cecilla (Ida) née Farrer, only dau. of Thomas Henry, 1st Lord Farrer, and grandson of Charles Darwin; *b.* Cambridge, 7 Dec. 1881; educ. at Horris Hill and Marlborough (Cotton House), and gained an exhibition for mathematics at Trinity College, Cambridge. He went up to Trinity in Oct. 1901, and took the Mathematical Tripos in his second year, being placed among the Senior Optimes. Afterwards he took the Mechanical Sciences Tripos, and was placed in the second class in 1905. On leaving Cambridge, he went through the shops at Messrs. Mather and Platt's at Manchester. After this he worked for some little while with the Cambridge Scientific Instrument Co., of which he was a director, and then became assistant secretary of Bolckow, Vaughan and Co., Ltd., at Middlesbrough. Here he stayed for seven years, and at the outbreak of war occupied the position of secretary to the company. As soon as war broke out he decided to join the army and on 12 Sept. 1914, was gazetted 2nd Lieut. in the 4th (Territorial) Battn. of the Yorkshires, which after training at Darlington and Newcastle crossed to France, as part of the Northumbrian Division, on 17 April, 1915, and was within a week called upon to take part in the second battle of Ypres. Here these Territorial troops fresh from home and tried at the very outset almost as highly as men could be tried, behaved with a steadiness and coolness which gained for them the congratulations of the Generals commanding respectively their Division and their Army Corps. Early in the afternoon of 24 April the Battn. was ordered to attack the village of Fortuin, close to St. Julien where the Germans had broken through. This attack they successfully carried out in the face of terrific shell fire, before being ordered to retire at dusk. By driving the enemy back a mile or more they had attained their object which was to prevent a breach in the line; and they had made good their front with the Canadians and Royal Irish on their right. It was during this advance that Darwin fell, killed instantaneously. His Commanding officer, Colonel Bell, wrote of him: "Loyalty, courage, and devotion to duty—he had them all. . . . He died in an attack which gained many compliments to the Battn. He was right in front. It was a man's death." Corpl. Wearmouth, who was in his platoon, wrote: "I am a section leader in his platoon, and when we got the order to advance he proved himself a hero. He nursed us men; in fact, the comment was, 'You would say we were on a field-day.' We had got to within twenty yards of our halting place when he turned to our platoon to say something. As he turned he fell, and I am sure he never spoke. As soon as I could I went to him but he was beyond human aid. Our platoon sadly miss him, as he could not do enough for us, and we are all extremely sorry for you in your great loss"; and Private Wood wrote to a friend in Middlesbrough: "I expect you would know poor Mr. Darwin . . . I was in his platoon, and I can tell you he died a hero. He led us absolutely regardless of the bullets from the German Maxim guns and snipers that whistled all round him." Just before he left England, when his Battn. was under orders for the Front, he was summoned to the War Office and offered a Staff appointment at home in connection with muntions of war. This would have given great scope to his capabilities. "It would have been interesting and important work," he wrote, "but, of course, there are plenty of older men who can do it just as well as I can." He felt that at that moment his place should be with his regt., and made, in the words of one present at the interview, a "fine appeal" to be allowed to go with his men. It was granted, and he went gladly and with no looking back. The Times (30 April, 1915) said of him: "Erasmus Darwin would, if he had lived, have added fresh distinction to the name of his family in a walk of life in which it has never before figured. Between Cambridge and a great iron works in the North there is something of a gulf fixed and one who knew Darwin only in his Cambridge home cannot say anything more than that all those who met him in business conceived a very high opinion of his grasp of his subject, his acuteness and administrative ability. It was, indeed, impossible to know him without realising that he combined with intellectual ability a calm, sound, and practical judgment, and a general capacity for doing things well and thoroughly. He had, too, what must have been invaluable to him in his work, a most genuine sympathy with and affection for working men, and this quality, which, amongst so many other things, had made him love his work at Middlesbrough, gave him intense pleasure when soldiering came to him as a wholly new and unlooked-for experience. He delighted in the men, and especially in long expeditions across the moors with his scouts. There is one more quality as to which all his friends would agree, namely, a conscientiousness that was eminently sane and wide-minded and completely unswerving. No one in the world was more certain to do what he believed to be right."

Erasmus Darwin.

DASH, FREDERICK JOHN, Officer's Cook, 1st Class, 363215 (Ports.), H.M.S. Pathfinder; lost when that ship was sunk by a mine, about 20 miles off the East Coast, 5 Sept. 1914.

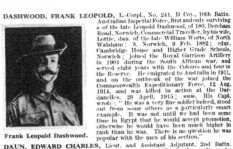

DASHWOOD, FRANK LEOPOLD, L.-Corpl., No. 241, D Coy., 10th Battn. Australian Imperial Force, first and only surviving *s.* of the late Leopold Dashwood, of 180, Dereham Road, Norwich, Commercial Traveller, by his wife, Lottie, dau. of the late William Worts, of North Walsham; *b.* Norwich, 9 Feb. 1882; educ. Cambridge House and Higher Grade Schools, Norwich; joined the Royal Garrison Artillery in 1901 during the South African war, and served eight years with the Colours and four in the Reserve. He emigrated to Australia in 1911, and on the outbreak of the war joined the Commonwealth Expeditionary Force, 12 Aug. 1914, and was killed in action at the Dardanelles, 26 April, 1915; *unm.* His Capt. wrote: "He was a very fine soldier indeed, stood out from some others as a particularly smart example. It was not until we had been some time in Egypt that he would accept promotion, otherwise he would have been much higher in rank than he was. There is no question he was popular with the men of his section."

Frank Leopold Dashwood.

DAUN, EDWARD CHARLES, Lieut. and Assistant Adjutant, 2nd Battn. Royal Sussex Regt., 2nd Infantry Brigade, only *s.* of Charles James Daun, by his wife, Ada Margaret, dau. of Lieut.-Gen. Edward Arthur Williams, C.B., Colonel Commandant R.A., and great-grandson of Col. Henry Williams, R.A., who served at Waterloo; *b.* Streatham, Surrey, 15 June, 1885; educ. Sunningdale School and Harrow; joined the 3rd Battn. Royal Sussex Regt. 27 Feb. 1904; gazetted 2nd Lieut. in the 2nd Battn. 29 Nov. 1905, and promoted Lieut. 10 Nov. 1909. On the outbreak of war he left Woking for the Front, 12 Aug. 1914; was present in the fighting at, and retreat from, Mons, and was killed near Troyon at the Battle of the Aisne, 14 Sept. 1914; *unm.* A comrade wrote: "We were in the same company. I was unfortunately sent home with an injured leg, but last saw your son on 4 Sept. At that time he was in splendid health and in such good spirits. He was a splendid officer, and worked night and day for the good of his regt. and his company, and had a great future before him. He was to have been our next Adjutant, and will be a great loss to the regt." The Colonel, senior Major and Adjutant all fell the same day. Lieut. Daun was a fine rifle shot, and won the Officers' Cup at the Aldershot Command Meeting in 1912 and 1913, and was second in 1914. Of his uncles, Lieut.-Col. H. F. Williams, Royal Munster Fusiliers, and Lieut.-Col. E. G. Williams, C.M.G., commanding 1st Battn. Devonshire Regt., are at the Front; and Capt. A. L. Williams, Royal Scots (died 24 May, 1906) served with the Bechuanaland Expedition, 1884-85; while of his great-uncles, Lieut.-Gen. Sir H. F. Williams, K.C.B., 60th Rifles, served through the Mutiny and Lieut.-Col. the Hon. H. R. Handcock, 97th Regt., was killed at the storming of the Redan in the Crimean war; and his great-great-uncle, Admiral Sir William Pierson, K.C.B., was wounded as a Midshipman in the Belleisle at Trafalgar.

Edward Charles Daun.

DAVEY, ARTHUR JOHN, Private, No. 11483, 1st Battn. Coldstream Guards, *s.* of Richard Soper Davey, of Broadway, Woodbury, Exeter, by his wife, Emily, dau. of Samuel Litten; *b.* Woodbury, co. Devon, 23 May, 1897; educ. Woodbury Council School; enlisted 31 Aug. 1914; went to France, 11 Dec., and was killed in action at Givenchy, 22 Dec. 1914; *unm.*

DAVEY, WILLIAM ALFRED GEORGE, Rifleman, No. 2080, 1/18th Battn. (London Irish) The London Regt. (T.F.), *s.* of James Best Davey, Sergt. 15th Middlesex Regt., by his wife, Sarah Elizabeth (42, Pretoria Avenue, Walthamstow), dau. of William Thomas Warner; *b.* Willesden, 18 May, 1894; was a student at the International Correspondence Schools, Kingsway, and had been employed for many years on the clerical staff of the Stores Department of the London County Council. After the outbreak of war he joined the London Irish on 31 Aug. 1914; went to the Front, 9 March, 1915, and was killed in action at the Battle of Loos, 25 Sept. 1915; *unm.* He was in the first line of German trenches binding up wounds sustained by a comrade, when he must have been observed by a German sniper, for, as he was advancing towards the second line of trenches, he was shot in the head by a rifle bullet. Lieut. G. M. Slattery wrote: "The Capt. of your son's company was struck by a shell, and your son was seen at once to make for him. On his way he was struck in the head and killed. He was a good lad and liked by everybody, and the action which led to his death was characteristic of him He never seemed to trouble about himself, but was always the first to help others." He was buried in a village just outside Loos.

William Alfred G. Davey.

DAVID, CHARLIE, Stoker, 1st Class, 311578, H.M.S. Good Hope; lost in action off Coronel, on the coast of Chili, 1 Nov. 1914.

DAVID, JAMES STANLEY, L.-Corpl., No. 30737, 1st Battn. Welsh Regt., *s.* of Walter David, of Uplands, Swansea; served with the Expeditionary Force in France, etc.; killed in action, being buried in a trench on the night of 3 Aug. 1915, aged 23; *unm.*

DAVIDSON, ALEXANDER BISSETT, Private, No. 16166, 2nd Battn. (Queen's Own) Cameron Highlanders, *s.* of James Brown David son, of 15, High Street, Portobello, near Edinburgh, an employee on the N.B. Ry., by his wife, Margaret, dau. of Alexander Bissett; *b.* Portobello, 12 Jan. 1891; educ. Tower Bank Public School there; enlisted 7 Dec. 1914; and was killed in action at the Battle of Hill 60, 29 April, 1915; *unm.*

DAVIDSON, ALEXANDER MURRAY STUART, A.B. (R.F.R., B. 6689), 185747, H.M.S. Hawke; lost when that ship was torpedoed in the North Sea, 15 Oct. 1914; *m.*

Alexander B. Davidson.

De Ruvigny's Roll of Honour 1914–1918: an example of how much information can be attained from this fantastic resource. Here, one of those mentioned is 2nd Lieutenant Erasmus Darwin – grandson of Charles Darwin. It gives details of his education, marriage and occupation before enlisting. It also explains his final battle and the cause of his death. Could you use this Roll of Honour to find details of your ancestor's military career? Courtesy of thegenealogist.co.uk.

DON'T FORGET!

Keep your eyes peeled during visits to the churchyards. War memorials can often form a focal point in the churchyard layout and one of your ancestors may well have been listed amongst the fatalities.

What is a Chelsea Pensioner and where could I find related records?

This term refers to a soldier who had been pensioned out of the Army and whose allowance was administered through the Royal Hospital at Chelsea; the majority were 'out-pensioners' who did not reside on the premises. Soldiers were eligible for a pension after twelve years of service, earlier if wounded, so these records can refer to men of all ages.

Service records from 1883 to 1900 can be searched online at findmypast.com and offer a fascinating insight into the lives of 'ordinary' soldiers who were in receipt of a pension (rather than merely those of officer class). Providing details of the regiment in which they served, as well as personal information such as chest size and even descriptions of any tattoos, each document is at least four pages long and not only covers those servicemen from the UK but also those born as far away as India and the Caribbean. The records list individuals who completed full service or who were wounded in action and received a pension but not those who deserted or were killed in action. This first release comprises 285,000 records and it is hoped that the remaining documents, dating from 1760 to 1913, will be made available for viewing in the near future.

Opposite and following eight pages: Chelsea Pensioners British Army Service Record for Joseph Grandy. All of the following details about Joseph Grandy are recorded in his service record:

Born: Gibraltar
Trade: Wheelwright
Joined: 28th January 1870, aged 19 years and 3 months at Aldershot
Discharged: 21st June 1899
Description: 5'10", 35 inch chest, 'fresh' complexion, hazel eyes, dark brown hair, Church of England
Corps: 4th Battalion Rifle Brigade
Career: Private – Corporal – Sergeant. Received a good conduct medal and also a medal for service in Afghanistan during the Second Afghan War (the 'Ali Musjid')
Medical history: suffered from Tonsillitis, Bronchitis, Muscular Rheumatism, Dysentery and the Fracture of his Clavicle after a fall from a horse while serving in the Army
Married: Catherine Louisa Taylor, Dublin, on 16th September 1873. Catherine lived with the battalion.
(Courtesy of WO97/2920/106 The National Archives UK.)

ATTESTATION OF

(late W. O. Form 39).

No. 1799 Name *Joseph Grandy*

Corps *4th Batt. Rifle Brigade*

Joined at *Aldershot*

on *H gr Recruit*

A

For Twelve Years Army Service.

Questions to be put to the Recruit before Enlistment.

1. What is your Name? — *Joseph Grandy*

2. In or near what Parish or Town were you born? — In the Parish of *C* in or near the Town of *C* in the County of *Hants*

3. What is your Age? — *19* Years *3* Months.

4. What is your Trade or Calling? — *Wheelwright*

5. Are you, or have you been, an Apprentice? if so, where? to whom? and for what period? — *No*

6. Have you resided out of your Father's house, and paid rates and taxes of £10 a year, and if so, where? — *No*

7. Are you Married? — *No*

Do you now belong to the Militia, or Army or Militia Reserve, to the Volunteers, or to the Naval Coast Volunteers? or to the Royal Naval Reserve Force? — *No*

Do you belong to any Regiment, Brigade or Corps in Her Majesty's Army? — *No*

Have you ever served in the Army? — *No*

Have you ever served in the Marines? — *No*

Have you ever served in the Militia? — *No*

Have you ever served in the Royal Navy? — *No*

If so, the Recruit is to state the particulars of his former Service, and the cause of his Discharge, and is to produce his Parchment Certificate of Discharge.

Have you truly stated the whole, if any, of your previous Service? — *Yes*

Have you ever been rejected as unfit for Her Majesty's Service? — *No*

15. For what Corps are you willing to be enlisted, or are you willing to be enlisted for General Service? — For *Rifle Brigade at Aldershot*

16. Did you receive a Notice, and do you understand its meaning? — *Yes*

17. Who gave you the Notice? —

18. Are you willing to serve for the term of twelve Years, provided Her Majesty should so long require your services? — *Yes*

19. Are you willing to serve for a further term of twelve months if abroad, or if a state of War exists between Her Majesty and any Foreign power, if you should be directed so to serve by the Secretary of State for War, or by the Commanding Officer on any Foreign, Colonial, or Indian Station? — *Yes*

Signature of Recruit *Sgd. Joseph Grandy*   Witness *Sgd. J Thom Corpl*

DECLARATION TO BE MADE BY RECRUIT ON ATTESTATION.

Joseph Grandy do solemnly and sincerely declare, That to the best of my Knowledge and Belief the above answers to the foregoing questions made and signed by me, are true; and that I am willing to be attested for the Term of Twelve Years provided Her Majesty should so long require my Services, and also, if I am on service beyond the seas, or if a state of War exists between Her Majesty and any Foreign Power, for such further term, not exceeding Twelve Months, as shall be directed by the Competent Military Authority.

Sgd. Joseph Grandy {Signature of Recruit.}   *Sgd Geo Harvey Corpl* {Signature of Witness} *4 B RB*

OATH TO BE TAKEN BY RECRUIT ON ATTESTATION.

I, *Joseph Grandy* do make Oath, that I will be faithful and bear true Allegiance to Her Majesty, Her Heirs, and Successors, and that I will, as in duty bound, honestly and faithfully defend Her Majesty, Her Heirs, and Successors, in Person, Crown, and Dignity, against all enemies, and will observe and obey all orders of Her Majesty, Her Heirs, and Successors, and of the Generals and Officers set over me. So help me God.

Witness my hand.

Signature of Recruit *Sgd. Joseph Grandy*

Witness present *Sgd. Geo Harvey 4th B RB*

The above questions were asked of the said *Joseph Grandy* and answered by him in my presence, as herein recorded; and the said *Joseph Grandy* made the above Declaration and Oath before me at *Aldershot* this *28th* day of *January* One Thousand eight hundred and *Seventy* at *12 o'clock noon*

Signature of the Justice *Sgd. George W. Smith J.P. for Hants*

The Recruit should, if he require it, receive a copy of the Declaration.

Description of *Joseph Trevart*

Distinctive Marks.

Age apparently ___19___ years ___3___ months.

Height ___5___ feet ___10 7/8___ inches.

Chest Measurement ___ inches.

Complexion ___Irish___

Eyes ___Hazel___

Hair ___Dk Brown___

Religious denomination ___Ch of E___

MEDICAL CERTIFICATE ON ENLISTMENT.

I have examined the above-named Recruit and find that he does not present any of the following conditions, viz. :—Scrofula ; phthisis ; syphilis ; impaired constitution ; defective intelligence ; defects of vision, voice, or hearing ; hernia ; hæmorrhoids ; varicose veins beyond a limited extent ; inveterate cutaneous disease ; chronic ulcers ; traces of corporal punishment, or evidence of having been marked with the letters D., or B.C. ; contracted or deformed chest ; abnormal curvature of spine ; or any other disease or physical defect calculated to unfit him for the duties of a soldier.

He can see at the required distance with either eye, and he declares he is not subject to fits of any description. I consider him fit for Her Majesty's Service.

Dated at ___Aldershot___

this ___24th___ day of ___January___ 18_70_.   Signature of Surgeon ___Sgd. J L Scott M D___ ___Surgeon Major___

MILITARY MEDICAL CERTIFICATE—ON APPROVAL.

Re-examined by me at ___Aldershot___ on the ___29th___ day of ___January___

18_70_, and finally approved as fit for Service. ___Sgd. J L Scott M D___ Surgeon,

Recruiting District, Brigade Depôt, or B. ___Regime___

NOTE.—Should the approving Surgeon consider the Recruit unfit, he will leave this Certificate unsigned, and report the case on W. O. Form 584, Sub-Districts to the Officer Commanding the Brigade Depôt, and in Regiments or attached Depots to the Officer Commanding, after obtaining the concurrence of the Principal Medical Officer, should there be one at the Station.

Certificate of Superintending Officer or Adjutant.

I hereby certify that the above-named recruit ___

was inspected by me, and I consider him in every respect fit (or unfit, as the case may be) for Her Majesty's Service, and that I have examined this attestation and find it properly filled up.

Superintending Officer,
Recruiting Service.

Certificate of Approving Field Officer.

I certify that this Attestation of the above-named recruit ___Joseph Graudy___

is correct, and that the required forms appear to have been complied with. I accordingly approve, and appoint him to ___Rifle Brigade___ for the period of his Army Service.

Date ___Aldershot___   ___Sgd A J Nixon B Co___ Signature of Approving Field Officer.

___January 18 70___

		Description on Discharge.
Service Abroad .. { *True Extract*		Age ___ years ___ months
Wounded........ {		Height ___ feet ___ inches
		Complexion ___
Effect of Wounds	___ Major	Eyes ___
		Hair ___
Distinguished himself	*Staff Paymaster Rifle Depôt*	Trade ___
		Marks or scars ___
Married		
Passed Classes of Instruction .. {		Intended place of residence }

STATEMENT of the SERVICES of No. *1799* Name *Joseph Grandy*

Corps in which served	Battn. or Depôt	Promotions, Reductions, Casualties, &c.	Army Rank	Dates	Service not allowed to reckon for fixing the rate of Pension		Service in Reserve not allowed to reckon towards G. C. Pay.		Signature of Officer certifying correctness of Entries
					years	days	years	days	
		Service towards limited engagement reckons from 28 Jan: 76							*Adjutant 4th Bn Rifle Brigade.*
Rifle Bde	4th	Permitted to serve after 21 years subly a a 9th Southern district dt 16.1.91							H. G. Majendies Lieut Act Adjutant 4th Bn Rifle Brigade
		Reserved deferred Pay on Completion of 2 years service 28.1.91							Adjutant 4th Bn. Rifle Brigade
	"	Elect to serve under the new rules of messing vide Special A.O.d. 2.4.98		1. 4. 98					H Vernon Capt. Adjutant, 4th Bn. Rifle Brigade
		J Grandy	Sergt.						
	4th	Discharged Having completed over 19 years service under para. 1805. xxiii Q. Rgn. 1898	Sgt.	21. 6. 99					H Vernon Capt Adjt 4th Bn RB
		W Pemberton Commd 4th Bn Rifle Bde	Lt Col.						

					years	days
Total amount of Service forfeited towards pension, and not allowed to reckon towards G. C. Pay brought forward from the old Record ...						
Total Service forfeited as above					—	—
Total Service towards Engagement to 21/6/99 (date of discharge)					29	145
" " " Pension " (")					—	—

H Vernon Capt Adjt 4th Bn R Bde

F & T 80,000 1—90   Forms Miscellaneous 89

(Form F.)

MEDICAL HISTORY.

W. O. Form 1143.

Regiment,
or Corps
Battalion,
or Brigade } *Rifle Brigade*

Regimental Number *1799*   Name *Joseph Grandy*

Enlisted { on *26 January 1870*
{ at *Aldershot*

Birthplace { Parish *Gibraltar* } Country *Spain*
{ County

Age (last Birthday) *19*

Former Trade or Occupation *Wheelwright*

GENERAL REMARKS
On his Habits and Conduct in the Service,
Temperance, &c.

Height ... ... *5 10 5/8* inches
Circumference of Chest (over the Nipple) *35* inches
Spirometer ... ... inches
Weight ... ... lbs.
Dynamometer ... ... lbs.

Small Pox Marks ... ... *none*
Vaccination Marks ... ... *distinct*
When Vaccinated ... *Infancy & Janry*
Hair ... ... *Dark Brown*
Pulse (regular) ... ... *74* beats
Respiration ... ... *18* inspirations
Muscular Development ... *good*

Rank and Dates of Promotion; also Dates of Transfer to other Regiments.

Dates of Punishment; and whether Corporal or by Imprisonment.

The above was his state

when examined on the *29* day of *January* 18 *70*

(Signature)
(Rank) *Rifle Brigade*

Station, Garrison, Barrack, General Hospital, &c., with Date of Arrival.*	No. in Admission and Discharge Book.	Date of						Diseases. (a) Primary. (b) Secondary.	Duration of Diseases. Days.	Completed Years of		Treatment. Class of Remedies.	Observations. Circumstances in or by which Disease was induced.
		Attack.			Recovery.					Age.	Service.		
		Year.	Month.	Day.	Year.	Month.	Day.						
Aldershot 29 Jan 70	82	71	Feb	16	71	Feb	23	Sprain	8	20	1	local	of ankle
Shorncliffe 31 Aug 70	323	71	July	6	71	July	12	Tonsillitis	7	20	1	local	cold
Chatham Aug 71 Dublin 16 Sept 72	457	72	Oct	10	72	Oct	15	Bronchitis	6	22	2	at Rifle Practice at Curragh	
Umballa Oct 14 73	1088	Arrival in India 23-11-73						febricula	6	24	4	Seraph: climate	
	463	75	7	2	75	7	22	Muscular Rheumatism	20	25	6	local general	cold & exposure

In addition to the record of sickness, the date of the following events should be recorded:—(1) Death and Cause of Death in the Service. (2) Discharge on Pension or Temporary Allowance for Life or for a Term of Years. (3) Discharge by Purchase or other cause of the kind. (4) Promotion to the rank of Commissioned Officer. (5) Capture, Desertion, &c.

* This column should be filled up in all cases when the Soldier remains any length of time at the Station, even if he has no attack of sickness while there.

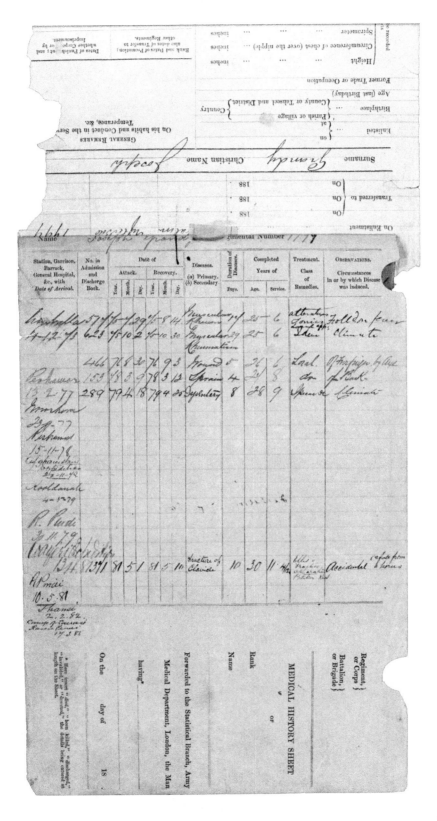

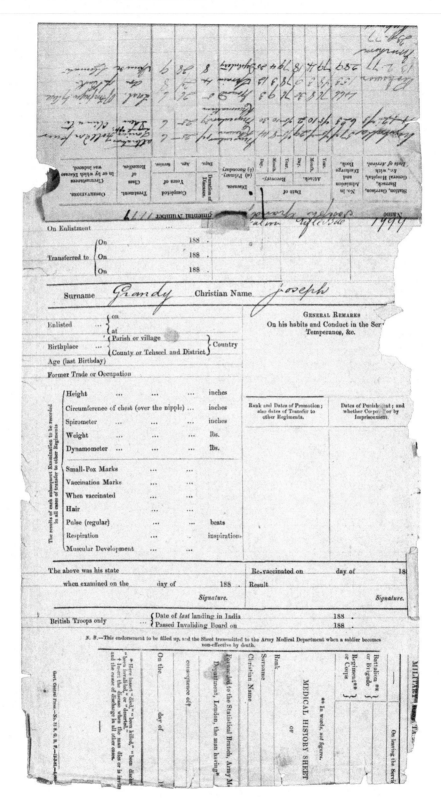

MEDICAL HISTORY —continued

Christian Name   Joseph

Surname

Station, Gart- ment, Barrack, General Hos- pital, &c.	Date of arrival at the Station.	No. in Admission and Discharge Book.	Admission to Hospital			Discharge from Hospital			Disease. (a) Primary. (b) Secondary.	Duration of Disease. Days.	Treatment. Class of Remedies.	OBSERVATIONS. Circumstances in or by which Disease was induced.
			Year	Mo.	Day	Year	Mo.	Day				
Chatham 24.5.85												

ARMY FORM B 266.
4th page.

1499 Joseph Grandy
MILITARY HISTORY SHEET.

Service at Home and Abroad.

COUNTRY.	FROM	TO	Years	Days	
Home	28 Jan. 1870	20 Oct. '73	3	266	The country only to be shown —it is not neces- sary to show sep- arately the ser- vice in the differ- ent stations of same country.
India	21 Oct. '73	4 Sept. 88	15	45	
Burma	5 Sept. 88	28 Jany. 90	1	55	
Home	29 Jany. 90	21 June 1899	9	144	

Next of kin — wife - Catherine Louisa - with Battalion

NOTE.—For mode of computing Foreign Service, see G. O. 56 of 1874.

		Initials of Officer making the Entry.
Campaigns ...	Afghan Campaign 1878-79 Waziri Expedition 1881	
Wounded ...	nil	
Effects of Wounds	nil	
Special instances of gal- lant conduct.		
Medals and decorations...	Medal for Afghanistan 1878-79 Ali Musgid Good Conduct Medal Army Order 308 of 1888	
Injuries in or by the Service.	nil	
Married { To whom	Catherine Louisa Taylor	
{ Place and date	Dublin - 16th September 1873	
Passed Classes of Instruc- tion.	nil	
Certificates of Education {	2d class Certificate (13.11.72)	
Character on being passed to Reserve. {		
Character on being Dis- charged. {		
Place of Discharge ...		
Cause of Discharge ... {		
Pension awarded ...		
Died ...		

NOTE.—These entries are to be made from time to time as they occur, and initialled by the Officer making the entry.

153

1799

Joseph Graney

Description extracted from his Attestation.

———

Born in the Parish of *Gibralter* in or near the Town of *Gibralter*

in the County of *Gibralter*

Age, *19* Years and *3* Months.

Trade or Calling, *Wheelwright*

Size, *5* Feet *10* *⅝* Inches.

Complexion, *Fresh* Eyes, *Hazel* Hair. *Dk. Brown*

Distinctive Mark or Scar,

———

Service Abroad   *Embarked for India 21 October 1875.*

Wounded

Distinguished Himself

Married

Discharged on the

Character—Reported by the Regimental Board to be

Pension awarded

Died

Nan.   W. O. Form 738.

1499 Joseph Gandy

ENLISTED for the *Rifle* Regiment of *Brigade* on the *26 January 1870*
at *Aldershot*   ATTESTED for the said Regiment *at Aldershot*
On *28 January 1870* at the Age of *19* Years and *3* Months.   Service towards G.C. Pay

Regiment	Promotions, Reductions, Casualties, &c.	Rank	Period of Service in each Rank		Amount of Service towards &c. Rupee Pension		Amount of Service towards completion of limited engagement		Service towards G.C. Pay	
			From	To	Years	Days	Years	Days	Yrs	Days
2/8588		Private	28 Jany 1870	17 May 71	1	110	1	110	1	110
	Promoted Corporal	Corporal	18 May 71	31 Jany 75	1	259	1	259	1	259
	Granted G.C.P. at 1d. 28 Sept 1871									
	Promoted Sergeant	Sergeant	1 Feby 75	12 Decr 73	"	315	"	315	"	315
	Appointed Sergeant	Sergeant	13 Decr 73	31 Mar 76	2	110	2	110	2	110
					6	64	6	64	6	64
	Reverted	Sergeant	1 April 1876	31 Mar 77	1	"	1	"	1	"
	Reverts to Sergeant	Sergeant	1 April 1877	30 June 81	4	91	4	91	4	91
	G.C. Pay at 2d. 28 Jany 1876									
					11	155	11	155	11	155
	Continued	Sergeant	1 July 81	9 Nov 81		132		132		132
	Reengaged to complete 21			10 Nov 81		11	287	11	287	11	287
	years service									
	Entitled G.C. Pay at 3d. 28 Jany 1882									
	Continued	Sergeant	10 Nov 81	9.1.91	9	61	9	61	9	61

Reengaged on the 10th Novr 1881 and thereby
Consented to the application to him of the
full provisions of part II of the Army
Discipline and Regulation Act 1879

    2 Recruit hunt us .   J. Gandy Sergt

Commg 4th Batt Rifle Brigade
entitled to G.C. Pay at 4d. 28 Jany 96

U.R. Pemberton Lt Colonel
Commdg 4 Bn Rifle Bde

Granted Medal for Long Service & Good Conduct Army Order 355 of 1871

The Discharge of the above named man is hereby confirmed.
(Station)
(Date)   188

155

I'm trying to locate a site which would help me find a list of military museums, which do you suggest?

Without doubt, ukmfh.org.uk is a brilliant research and resource tool brought to us by the creators of UKBMD (births, marriages and deaths) and UKGDL (trade directories and electoral rolls). Here, there are links to army, navy and air force museums but this is only a tiny portion of what this site can do to advance your knowledge. With a huge selection of records accessible, from militia rolls and war diaries to discharge papers and training records, this link provider is free to search by county but may direct you to other sites which require a small fee or subscription – another one-stop shop for the military historian's arsenal.

Similarly, you cannot go far wrong if you visit the Ogilby Trust's guide to over 136 military museums at armymuseums.org.uk. Their search engine allows you to locate specific museums of interest by collection, regiment or region – ideal for pinpointing your particular area of research.

I believe my ancestor received a 'gift from the Queen' for his service during Christmas time. Which Queen would this have been and why was the gift awarded?

To lift the spirits of the men caught up in various military campaigns, there have been two specific occasions when a member of the Royal household has awarded the troops with a gift at Christmas time in recognition of their services, and as an acknowledgement of the sacrifices they were making. This gift is thought to have first been given in 1899 during the Boer War, when Queen Victoria decided to give each of her soldiers fighting in South Africa a tin of chocolates as a commemorative Christmas present. Despite having Quaker origins and strong moral opposition to warfare, the three major chocolate companies of Fry, Rowntree and Cadbury rallied together to produce in excess of 40,000 tins of chocolate. Decorated with a patriotic logo and the queen's medallion, each bar was embossed with the company name.

By 1914, when Britain became caught up in its biggest conflict to date, the general public were eager to support those in the forces who would experience their first Christmas at war. Shops carried advertisements in their windows appealing for money, gifts and food parcels to bring comfort and cheer to those who served their country. By October 1914 the appeal had resulted in the production of the embossed brass Princess Mary Gift Box. Inside was one ounce of tobacco, a pipe, twenty cigarettes and a tinder lighter, as well as a Christmas card and photo of the princess. For non-smokers, the tobacco and cigarettes could be exchanged for acid tablets and a khaki writing case containing a pencil, paper and envelopes. The religious and dietary requirements of the Indian troops were also taken into consideration, with the Sikhs receiving a box of candy, a tin of spices and a Christmas card – some Indian troops also received cigarettes. Nurses serving in the front-line hospitals of France were also included and given a chocolate-filled box. A surplus of funds eventually allowed the scheme to be extended to bestow on all servicemen a simple present.

It should also be noted that a message printed on a specially designed postcard sent by Princess Alexandra – president of the Queen Alexandra's Imperial Military Nursing Service (QAIMNS) – was given to those nurses spending their first wartime Christmas in France. The image used – alongside a photo of the princess – was of an angel looking over the shoulder of a nurse caring for a wounded soldier. The angel became known as the Angel of Pity. Each nurse was sent a canvas bag containing acid drops, chocolates, notepaper, and a fur-lined cape, hood and muff.

By the third Christmas of the war, every sick or wounded soldier in every hospital, casualty clearing station, hospital ship or train abroad or at home was sent a message of thanks from George V inscribed in gold letters on embossed white card with the Windsor crest.

For many troops, this gift from home made all the difference and although the cigarettes and tobacco were smoked, the little brass tin was carefully kept as a memento of the war and sent back home to their wives and sweethearts and possibly handed down to someone in your family. Visit the website of the Imperial War Museum to find out more about Princess Mary's gift to the troops. The site details the work involved and problems faced in getting a large quantity of items to the forces on the front line in time for Christmas Day. Photographs also provide illustrations of the completed boxes which are extremely sought after by collectors today.

I come from a long line of Army ancestors and would like to research the lives of those who saw service prior to the twentieth century. Where do I start?

The National Army Museum (national-army-museum.ac.uk) has information on military history from 1485 to the present day. Their massive collection includes private, regimental and business papers illustrating more than five centuries of British and Commonwealth military history, from a muster roll of some of the men who served in the Hundred Years War (1337–1453) to the order that launched the Charge of the Light Brigade in 1854. The museum is well worth a visit in person if you want to add to your knowledge of early campaigns. An extensive archive of over half a million photographic images can help you understand the types of uniform worn, the equipment used and the conditions endured from the 1840s onwards.

The Imperial War Museum has a large collection of regimental histories which, if you are successful, could prove a real boon to finding out about the manoeuvres and procedures of the unit in which your ancestors served.

If you want to increase your understanding of early campaigns then The National Archives is the place to find commanders' dispatches from the Crimean War, Napoleonic and Boer War correspondence and a whole host of fascinating records relating to Britain's history of military conflict. Bear in mind that much of this information is not yet available online and would require you to visit the archives in person. Use the online catalogues viewable at a2a. org.uk to help you plan your visit to one of the country's archives. Each time you visit a repository – not just TNA – collect copies of their printed and digital leaflets and help guides which give hints and tips on how to use and get the most from their holdings.

Where would I locate a Royal Navy service record and what information could I expect to find?

In early 2010, the records of 600,000 men who joined the Royal Navy as ratings between 1853 and 1923 went online at The National Archives, from where they can be downloaded for £3.50 each. You can expect to find details such as a rating's date and place of birth, physical appearance and occupation before joining. The names of the ships on which they served will also be listed, enabling you to seek out the relevant log books or vessel information to embellish the story of your ancestor's life. The seaman's number on the ship's register would be indicated, as well as the 'rating' or capacity in which they served, and length of service – allowing you to track their career with a degree of precision. Information about badges awarded for good conduct was added while a discharge column tells their reason for leaving the navy which could have included injury, disability or even death.

The National Archives has a series of research guides available from their website, helping you to plan your navy research and discover where specific registers and returns are located. These are also available from the National Maritime Museum at nmm.ac.uk.

For ancestors who joined between 1928 and 1938, next of kin can contact:

> The Directorate of Personnel Support (Navy)
> Navy Search TNT Archive Services
> Tetron Point
> William Nadin Way
> Swadlincote
> Derbyshire, DE11 0BB
> Tel: 01283 227913 or email navysearchpgrc@tnt.co.uk

Royal Navy Service Records after 1938 can be found at:

> Data Protection Cell (Navy)
> Victory View Building 1/152
> HM Naval Base
> Portsmouth PO1 3PX

What were the main medals awarded to naval personnel?

During the world wars, Royal Navy officers and ratings were entitled to the same campaign medals as their Army and RAF comrades, as well as the Victoria Cross, the George Cross and the Distinguished Service Order. Alongside these were the specific gallantry medals such as the Distinguished Service Medal, introduced for junior naval officers in 1901 but extended to the Merchant Navy from 1931 and to Army and RAF officers serving aboard ship from 1940.

The Atlantic Star was given mainly to Royal and Merchant Navy personnel who served in the Atlantic between 1939 and 1945.

My ancestor was a Royal Marine. Are there any specific records I can search to find out more?

The website findmypast.co.uk provides access to the records of 75,000 officers, NCOs and other ranks on their Royal Marine Medal Roll of 1914–20 so this should be your first port of call. With both transcripts and images of the original records, these documents not only list the medals each marine received, but also their service number and a description of where and when the medals were issued and extra details of those who were killed in action or died of wounds during the First World War.

My great-great-grandfather served in the Napoleonic Wars. Where would I find out more?

There is a huge range of coverage of the Napoleonic Wars online. Alongside The National Archives' extensive holdings of everything from pay lists and muster rolls to ratings service and discharge papers, are Napoleonic military guides to aid you in your research. Below is my 'Fab Five' selection of other sites which you may find useful.

napoleon-series.org The material on this site was gathered after the First World War when Captain Lionel Challis trawled through gazettes, Army Lists and regimental histories to create this extensive compilation, including his Peninsula Roll Call of over 9,600 men who served in the British Army in the Peninsula War.

nationalarchives.gov.uk/aboutapps/trafalgarancestors It's back to TNA if you want to search their online database for those who served in the Royal Navy at the Battle of Trafalgar. The clever search facility allows you to pinpoint your query by name, age, birthplace, rank, rating or ship.

hms.org.uk/nelsonsnavymain.htm For everything you wanted to know about what life was like serving in Nelson's Navy during the Napoleonic Wars, visit the Historical Maritime Society. This is a fascinating site and could help to answer all your questions about life for the ordinary rating aboard ship.

Napoleon's defeat at Waterloo in 1815 means the Waterloo Roll Call is the ideal place to find those involved in this final bloody battle. Visit **findmypast.co.uk** where you'll find details of all ranks who received the first military award by fighting in the Battle of Waterloo and the preceding conflicts at Ligny and Quatre Bras. The Waterloo Medal was the British Army's first campaign medal and was awarded to nearly 37,000 veterans.

napoleonguide.com/armyind.htm From the artillery and tactics, manpower and manoeuvres used, to the uniforms of each country's troops, this online guide to the armies of the Napoleonic Wars could tell you all you ever wanted to know.

My great-great-grandfather is listed as a Greenwich Pensioner on the census. What was a Greenwich Pensioner and how could I find out more?

On 25 October 1694, a charter was granted by William III which aimed to provide relief and support for the seamen who had served onboard ships belonging to the Royal Navy who, due to their age, wounds or other disabilities, were incapable of further service or were unable maintain themselves, at the Royal Naval Hospital at Greenwich. This ruling also proposed to support the widows of seamen and maintain and educate their children.

By 1705 the first pensioners were admitted. To benefit from this facility, seamen were required to contribute sixpence per month from their pay towards the upkeep of the hospital. Clothing was provided in the form of a uniform – forty years before the navy even had one – making the pensioners instantly recognisable in their dark-grey apparel complete with blue linings and brass buttons. Later, the colour changed to a brown outfit before a final change to blue.

By 1815, when the Napoleonic Wars had taken their toll, there were 2,710 residents. Governors were appointed to oversee the institution and included distinguished naval figures such as Admiral Hardy, the captain of Nelson's flagship *Victory* at the Battle of Trafalgar. After the end of the Napoleonic Wars, the number of admittances gradually started to decline and a new idea was devised which meant the men would be paid pensions to live outside. This was found to be more economical and, by 1869, the Royal Naval Hospital closed its doors for the last time to its residential pensioners.

The National Archives online catalogue features the *Records of Royal Greenwich Hospital and the Chatham Chest* – consider starting your search here. You can expect to find anything from the injuries the naval pensioner suffered and the pension amount paid, alongside the dates they were admitted and the ships on which they once served.

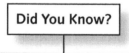

Did You Know?

In 1753, James Lind published his findings that scurvy – a disease caused by the lack of vitamin C which can result in open wounds and loss of teeth – could be cured by taking orange or lemon juice. Although scurvy had plagued the navy for decades due to the shortage of fruit and vegetables on long sea voyages, it was over forty years until the Admiralty agreed to issue lemon juice in the rations of its sailors. Almost at once, the citrus had the desired effect and scurvy was banished from the fleet. Could scurvy have been the cause of death of one of your ancestors? Remember, this disease not only affected those in the maritime profession but also those living in poorer areas with little access to fresh fruit and vegetables. Small children were particularly prone, with the lack of vitamins causing problems with their bone development.

The National Maritime Museum is an ideal place to visit in person, with its displays and exhibitions helping to bring to life what naval conditions were like through the ages. The library holds a vast array of records, including crew lists, staff registers, ships and company lists.

My ancestor was an officer in the RAF. Where is the best place to start my search?

It helps if you know the squadrons in which your ancestor served, but try consulting the Royal Air Force Lists at The National Archives. These registers start from 1 April 1918 when the Royal Flying Corps (RFC) and the Royal Naval Air Service (RNAS) merged to form the RAF. RFC service records from 1914–18 can also be found here. For those who served after 1920 try writing to:

> RAF Disclosures
> Room 221B Trenchard Hall
> RAF Cranwell
> Sleaford
> Lincolnshire NG34 8HB

There is usually a fee of £30 for this service, which is available only to next of kin, but the information you may discover could prove well worth it.

A valuable resource which could help you familiarise yourself with the type of related archives available is the Imperial War Museum. Although they do not hold any personal service records, they have a wealth of letters, diaries, film and photograph archives which can help transport you back in time to the period in which your ancestor served. They offer a wide range of leaflets to aid your research, including 'Tracing your RFC and RAF Ancestry', downloadable from their site at iwm.org.uk.

How did RAF medals differ from those of other services?

RAF personnel were entitled to the same campaign medals as those in the Army, although those who flew over occupied Europe between 1939 and June 1944 would have been awarded the Air Crew Europe Star. Officers who performed acts of valour whilst flying in operations against the enemy may have received the Distinguished Flying Cross or the Air Force Cross for recognised gallantry on non-operational flights, whilst other ranks would have received the Distinguished Flying Medal.

The RAF Museum at Hendon (rafmuseum.org.uk) holds medal citations for RAF servicemen in their Air Ministry Bulletins where you might find details of the individual and their career, but a trip to The National Archives would enable you to search Second World War award recommendations. These are separated into two holdings – one for individual acts of gallantry in the 'Immediate' category, and the other for extended periods of bravery in the 'Non Immediate' category.

What role did women play in the RAF?

The RAF Nursing Service was established in 1918, changing its name in 1923 to become the Princess Mary's RAF Nursing Service. Visit pmrafns.org for an excellent overview of RAF nursing history.

Women also had their own 'division' known as the Women's Royal Air Force (WRAF) but this was abolished in 1920. By 1939, the Women's Auxiliary Air Force (WAAF) was set up and, although during the First World War they had been confined to administration duties, by the outbreak of the Second World War they were employed in mechanical and technical activities (although not as aircrew). Their work became essential to the service, so much so that by 1994 the WAAF had been integrated into the RAF, enabling men and women to work alongside each other doing the same job. Find out more at waafassociation.org.uk.

There are very few records which have survived relating to women in the service during the First World War. What does remain can generally be found at TNA, including an index of personnel and their service numbers.

Chapter 11

SERVING THE NATION

The subject of defending our country is, undoubtedly, a massive topic. Over the decades, our success has been put down to the combined forces of our troops in the field and those at home who have ensured that up and coming recruits are trained, our manufacturing industries continue to operate and that the remaining men, women and children can step into the roles left by those at the front line. This unity in the face of adversity has ultimately led us to victory. Have you ever considered the contributions that your ancestors may have made in preparation for and during these times of conflict?

What was National Service?

First established in 1939, National Service was a recruiting campaign to attract men to the new Civil Defence services created in preparation for war. Compulsory military service in peacetime was also launched for Britain's young men, just before the scheme was introduced for all when war broke out a few months later.

The National Service Act came properly into force on 1 January 1949 and with the exception of some trades, such as farmers and coalminers, all fit and able-bodied men between the ages of 18 and 25 were called upon to serve in the armed forces for one year. The majority of conscripts passed through the Army ranks with fewer going into the Royal Navy and RAF. The period of service soon extended to eighteen months before increasing to two years – with three and a half years in the reserves – from 1950 onwards. Men from Northern Ireland were exempt from National Service, as were women – although the latter had the option of volunteering for the new peacetime women's services.

The Army was grateful for the boost in numbers but slightly hesitant about the continual training of new batches of recruits, which took precious time away from the regular soldiers. The aim was to make the new servicemen work as one unit and, initially, some had difficulties adjusting to the way of life. Repetitive routines, harsh criticism and strict authority forged teamwork when the poor standards of one man would reflect on the group. Eventually, every man would raise his standards, each helping and relying on the other, and with basic training complete, they would be posted to support various units throughout the world. These included policing areas of Egypt, Malaya and Kenya as well as being involved in front-line operations in the Korean campaign.

The diminishing size of the British Empire meant that the need for a large army to police it was in turn diminished. The final conscripts were recruited in 1960 and the last National Serviceman was demobbed in 1963.

Did National Servicemen receive medals?

Yes, if they took part in a campaign. If a former National Serviceman did not claim his medals then you can apply for these from the Ministry of Defence Medal Office. This site also applies to the next of kin of deceased regular serving personnel who did not claim medals from the Second World War.

In 1991 the Armed Forces Veterans' Badge was introduced as a way of demonstrating that all veterans, including National Servicemen, had served their country even if they had not been involved in a campaign. Funds raised go to the Poppy Appeal and National Service Memorial Fund. Find out more at awardmedals.com.

Where can I find records relating to National Servicemen and their army careers?

Former servicemen, their widows and next of kin can apply for official service records from the UK Veterans Agency at veterans-uk.info. An application form can be downloaded from the site and there is no fee for the record.

BRITAIN AT WAR

It is virtually guaranteed that each one of us will have a relative or ancestor who experienced the triumphs and tragedies of the Second World War. Not everyone may have seen active service, but all will have been concerned with the problems of a country 'held to ransom', the limitations and restrictions imposed by war and its effect on their everyday lives.

What is meant by the 'Home Front' and what was rationing?

The outbreak of war in 1939 brought with it some of the hardest times that Britain had ever experienced and with the majority of menfolk called up to fight, it was often left to the women, children and older generations to keep the home fires burning. The 'Home Front' was a term used to describe the civilian population as an active support to the nation's military, vital in its efforts to ensure the survival of those in Britain and provide a constant supply of essential materials for those on the front line.

Rationing was introduced in 1940 and made everyone's task even more challenging when products were removed from the shops which had previously been taken for granted. Butter, sugar and meat were rationed early on but by the end of the war virtually half of Britain's food, as well as its clothing, and fuel were limited by the system. Ration books tightly controlled the consumption or use of certain products which were in high demand. Inside were an allotted amount of coupons which were handed to the retailer when purchasing goods, helping to restrict the amount that each individual could buy and allowing a fair and even distribution.

In the country, people were used to growing their own fruit and vegetables which helped to supplement their meagre rations. In agricultural areas open land could be ploughed and replanted, ensuring that locals could be self-sufficient in food production. The Ministry of Agriculture introduced the 'Dig for Victory' campaign, and the growing of produce and staple ingredients was encouraged on all available land in towns and cities with allotments sprouting up in parklands and even alongside railway lines.

Ration Books and Coupons – personal wartime memorabilia from the Home Front.

At this time the Government was trying to save ships for military purposes, rather than importing food when alternatives could be grown at home. Surprisingly, much of our wheat came from Canada so 'Food Flashes' at the cinema used characters such as 'Potato Pete' to encourage people to eat more potatoes instead of bread. By 1940, the Government had lifted some restrictions on livestock, allowing people to keep rabbits and poultry in domestic gardens in support of those who would breed animals for food.

'Make Do and Mend' became one of the wartime slogans and when clothes rationing began in June 1941, alternative ways had to be found to recycle and restyle clothing and household items. Due to the air raids, blackout curtains were made from thin white curtains or sheeting which was dyed black to block out any light. Lack of street lighting meant that torches were an essential item if you were out after dark, whilst any lights fitted to pushbikes had to be shaded.

Many local museums have an area dedicated to the effects of war in their particular location, so do your research and pop along to see ration books, gas masks and an array of wartime memorabilia on display. Dedicated venues such as Llandudno's Home Front Museum transport you back in time with newsreels, audio/visual displays and ephemera, enabling you to envisage the era whilst prompting you to ask older relatives to dig out their period photos, documents, identity cards and memories to aid your investigations.

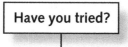

Have you tried?

The War Illustrated was a series of British pictorial magazines produced during the First and Second World Wars. The illustrations were initially hand-drawn, but photographic images were later added which, along with the journalistic reports, gave the reader a real insight into what battles were taking place and what events were occurring. Although printed on poor-quality paper, many copies stood the test of time and single and bound versions can be picked up at antique, book and ephemera fairs – and if you're lucky – even at car boot sales. A boxed set of *The War Illustrated* on CD is a fabulous investment from genealogysupplies. com. Containing nine volumes in the shape of 234 issues, you're certain to find something of interest that will help you better understand this turbulent period of our history.

What was the Home Guard?

With the fall of France in June 1940, Britain set about organising patrols of the countryside in preparation for invasion. An announcement was made for 'men of all ages who wish to do something for the defence of their country to take the opportunity for which so many of you have been waiting'.

Volunteers from reserved occupations such as munitions workers and farmers, veterans of the First World War and those who were over the age of 41 and considered too old or physically unfit to join the regular Army took up the challenge and helped create the Local Defence Volunteers (LDV), later officially renamed the Home Guard. Although at first they were poorly equipped, lacking uniforms and weapons, by 1941 they were a properly equipped and organised force that operated under military discipline. Made up of local detachments, their role was to guard nearby key points and hold or delay the enemy on the beaches or on inland defensive lines in the event of an invasion. Fortunately, the nation's defences were not fully tested against Hitler's armies who never attempted to land on the British mainland.

Visit the local archive library in the area where your Home Guard ancestor was likely to have been based and they should be able to point you in the right direction to aid your search. Home Guard Lists were published and certain local history books often record those men of a village who enrolled in the local battalion. Consider tracking down military historians within the community who may be able to shed some light on Home Guard operations in your particular district, or place an advert for information on the records office notice board or even in the regional newspaper – you may be surprised by the helpful responses that you receive.

What was a VAD nurse and where would I find more information about individuals and their work?

Before the outbreak of the First World War there was no Ministry of Health, and the War Office soon realised that in the outbreak of war their medical arrangements to deal with injured personnel would be totally inadequate. As a result, the British Red Cross Society linked up with the Order of St John of Jerusalem and formed the organisation known as the Voluntary Aid Detachment (VAD). By August 1914, thousands of women had volunteered, training was given and emergency hospitals were set up across the country. A dedicated history of Oakwood Sanatorium – the location of one of Britain's VAD hospitals – can be found at micklebring.com/oakwood/index.htm, but for detailed advice on how to research the indexes to find an individual volunteer, visit redcross.org.uk.

What was the role of a Land Girl?

'Land Girl' is a term used to describe a recruit of the Women's Land Army (WLA) who worked on the farms and fields of Britain to help keep the nation fed during the Second World War. First formed in 1917, the WLA recruited women to don trousers and take over the working roles of their menfolk whilst they fought in the trenches. Despite being disbanded in 1919, its services were called upon once again in August 1939. The realisation that Britain imported 70 per cent of its food, and the impending shortage of farm labourers, brought about the need for a united force of women to perform a whole host of essential agricultural duties from ploughing and harvesting to milking and lambing.

Government recruitment campaigns were implemented and although this civilian organisation was initially voluntary, compulsory call-up for women was introduced in

1941. Most young women were only too happy to volunteer as it heralded a new era of independence and a chance to do 'their bit' for the war effort. Those from the towns and cities jumped at the chance to leave home and work outdoors.

Their uniform of corduroy jodhpurs, green v-necked jumpers and brown hats marked the Land Girls out and they earned respect for the back-breaking work that they undertook. Felling trees and digging ditches was all in a day's work, which could often last from the early hours of the morning to as late as 9pm during haymaking – all for very little pay.

Although they faced criticism and opposition from some farmers, who thought they would not be able to complete the work or could even eventually drive the wages down for their male counterparts, the Land Girls persevered and gradually they gained admiration for their gritty determination. Such was their impact that they were required by the Government to continue after the war to help with food production, until they were finally disbanded in 1950.

Despite this, the WLA never received the recognition and welfare benefits that their female counterparts in the armed services were given and, although they took their rightful place in victory parades, it was not until 2000 that they were invited to march past the Cenotaph. Eight years later, all surviving members were to receive a special badge as a form of commendation, and although this was accepted, it is thought by many to be a case of too little, too late.

How can I find out if my ancestor was a Land Girl?

Family photos and letters could hold the key, whilst the unearthing of an original discharge or release certificate (given when an individual left the Land Army) could tell you their years of service and unique WLA number. Contact the Imperial War Museum by email at docs@iwm.org.uk or ring their archive at 020 7416 5222 to enquire about their large collection of WLA service cards, donated correspondence and diaries which may pertain to your relative. They also hold a complete set of *The Land Girl* magazine, issued monthly from April 1940 to March 1947, enabling you to immerse yourself in the daily lives, activities and experiences of its members.

DON'T FORGET!

Scour the local newspaper in the areas in which your Land Girl was based for related adverts, details of billeting officers or their involvement in rural issues.

What was an evacuee?

The outbreak of war meant that not only were husbands, fathers, brothers and sons called up to fight, but also that children were to be sent away to protect them from the threat of enemy bombing. There were three main periods of evacuation during the Second World War: first at the declaration of war in 1939; again in 1940, when Britain was under threat of German invasion; and finally in 1944 when V1 and V2 attacks took place.

The evacuation programme was codenamed 'Operation Pied Piper'. Although the Government sponsored schemes to promote evacuation, many parents made their own arrangements privately in order to keep their children safe. Others were evacuated with their schools, billeted with volunteers in specific areas and educated with the local children to become part of the rural communities. Everyone's experiences were different – some children were homesick, returning home after a few weeks, whilst others stayed with host families for the full six years of war, forming strong bonds with their guardians. If your ancestor was an evacuee, start your search at your local archive or in the area in which they were billeted – on some occasions the education authorities in the child's original location and the reception area may be able to help with your quest.

What was a conscientious objector?

Conscientious objectors (COs) refused to fight, either on religious grounds or through a belief in freedom of thought or conscience.

The introduction of the Military Service Act in 1916 imposed service on all single men between the ages of 18 and 41; previously, soldiers had all been volunteers. These compulsory measures brought the views of the COs to the fore and, to enable their objections to be heard, each man had to appear before a tribunal to apply for exemption. If their application was not granted they could be arrested and imprisoned for being AWOL (absent without leave).

COs' beliefs were not encouraged by the Government and were looked down upon by men who did serve; as a result, harsh prison sentences were handed down in an attempt to make them see the error of their ways. This punishment could be given in the form of approximately 112 days of hard labour, including one month of solitary confinement on a meagre diet of bread and water.

Despite some COs having genuine moral objections to conscription, there were many who suffered mentally and physically from the treatment they received both in and out of prison. The values of the Quaker religion prompted many of their faith to become COs. Today, the Quaker Library in London (quaker.org.uk/library) holds a wealth of extremely useful information on this subject. Tribunals and hearings were often reported in the local newspapers, and some records relating to individual cases may well be held at your local records office.

Chapter 12

FAME AND FORTUNE

It is a desirable thing to be well-descended, but the glory belongs to our ancestors.

Plutarch

B̲e honest: we all crave a little fame and fortune, and perhaps wish that our tree held a drop or two of noble blood. After all, if you do find that you have aristocratic connections, then the discovery of what is known as a 'gateway' ancestor could link you into Britain's finest pedigrees where the work of compiling family histories has already been done for you. Perhaps you've not set your sights quite so high and instead want to follow up a hunch that your ancestor was a star of the music halls, a pioneer in the field of medicine or shared the same surname with someone in the public eye. Whatever your aim, keep an open mind and who knows where family hearsay might lead you.

What is the likelihood of being related to someone famous?

This depends on what you determine to be 'famous'. If you are looking for a Hollywood movie star in your tree then you may have a fruitless search, but if it is someone who used to 'tread the boards' and experienced theatrical fame, or was perhaps an inventor or local celebrity, then the odds are greater.

If you have a direct link to a figure who led his or her life in the spotlight, there's normally someone within your family who knows something about it – but obviously, this is not always the case, and if you are prepared to reassess your perception of 'fame' then you can come across some very interesting surprises. If your sole aim is to find this type of ancestral link then you could end up being very disappointed, but if you treat your investigations as a bit of fun and accept that any related findings are a bonus, then who knows who could be sitting in your tree just waiting to be discovered.

With regard to research, in this case it is often not how far back you go but how much you are able to branch out. Distant cousins or people who have married into your tree may provide a link even if it is a tenuous one. Increasing the amount of connected surnames could provide associations that you had not thought of. Whilst the discovery of a connection to a Nightingale or Churchill family could start lights flashing, be warned:

many ordinary mortals share surnames with such luminaries, so know when to quit or you may set off on a wild goose chase.

Do not become obsessed with the 'famous forebear' quest. All your ancestors have a story to tell – famous or not.

There's talk within our family that we have aristocratic links. How do I go about researching this?

If you have a particular ancestor in mind which links you to this claim consider starting at the end of their lives and working backwards. They may well have been important enough to warrant an obituary in a local, regional or national newspaper from which you could glean a variety of details about their life, title, rank and achievements, giving you valuable avenues of research to follow. Titled males may well have had military careers; follow any leads you discover regarding this to regimental archives or museums, which usually hold records such as diaries, paintings and even photographs that could help give you your first visual link to the ancestor in question.

Knights of England. Perhaps your hopes of fame and fortune have paid off and you've discovered aristocratic or noble roots within your tree. The Knights of England records were compiled for the period between 1127 and 1904 and our example documents the 1581 knighthood of Francis Drake by Elizabeth I, on board the *Golden Hind*, after becoming the first English explorer to sail around the world. Courtesy of thegenealogist.co.uk.

KNIGHTS BACHELORS

1580. WILLIAM CAVENDISH.

1580, Nov. 30. JOHN DAWNAY, of Yorkshire (at Richmond, on Wednesday, being St. Andrew's day).

1580-1, Feb. 5. JOHN BRANCHE, lord mayor of London [in 1580] (at Westminster, on Shrove Sunday).

1581, Apr. 4. FRANCIS DRAKE (at Deptford, near Greenwich, on Tuesday, by the Queen's Majesty, being on the ship the "Golden Hind," wherewith he had travelled about the world).

1581, Apr. 4. GEORGE HART, son and heir of Sir Percival Hart, of Kent (at St. James's, near Westminster).

1581. THOMAS HUMFREY.

1581. JAMES HALES, of Kent.

1581, Sept. 10. WILLIAM RUSSELL (at St. Patrick's Church, Dublin, by lord Grey de Wilton, lord deputy of Ireland).

1581, Sept. 16. McWILLIAM BOURKE (RICHARD AN IARAIN) (by same in Dublin Castle).

1581, Nov. 17. ROBERT DILLON, of Riverston, chief justice of Common Pleas (by same on Coronation day, an erratum for Accession day).

1581 (? 1583), Dec. 31. CHARLES FRAMLINGHAM, of Suffolk (at Westminster on Sunday).

1582, May 3. EDMOND ANDERSON, chief justice of Common Pleas (at the Court at Greenwich on Thursday).

1582, May 6. JAMES HERVY, lord mayor of London [in 1581] (at the Court at Greenwich on Sunday).

1582, May 22. EDWARD HOBBY (at Somerset Place in London on Tuesday, the day after his marriage with the baron of Hunsdon's daughter).

1582, July. JOHN SELBY, knight porter of Berwick (at Nonsuch).

1582, Sept. 6 or 7. ANTHONY COLCLOUGH, of Tinterne, Co. Wexford (in Ireland by the lords justices).

1582. CHARLES CAVENDISH, of Derby.

1582. CLOPTON GARGRAVE.

1582-3, Feb. 11 (12). THOMAS (ANTHONY) SANDES (SANDE), of Throwley, Kent (at Barn Elmes, near Fulham, at Shrovetide).

[? after 1582-3, Feb. 12.] FRANCIS WILLOUGHBY, of Walterton.

1583, May 6. THOMAS BLANKE, lord mayor of London [in 1582] (at Greenwich on Sunday).

1583, May 5. JOHN BOURKE, baron of Leitrim (by the lords justices of Ireland in St. Patrick's Church on Rogation Sunday).

As always, family papers, bibles, correspondence and documents may unlock a few doors but consider the possibility that biographical histories may well have already been published on the individual; search the internet or ask for assistance at your local history library. Depending on the status and achievements of the individual in question, these biographies may have been written by professionals or like-minded historians who could also be related, and as such could be part of your extended family tree. Get access to a copy of *Burke's Peerage and Gentry* and see if you can find any obvious links. First published in 1826, this book lists the aristocracy and their antecedents. Their website, burkes-peerage. net, allows you to dip your toe in the water with a 'Free Noble Family Search'; enter your surname and its variants to seek out any potential gentrified genes lurking within your tree. Although this is more of a fun exercise, if family stories of noble ties have been passed down, this may be the place to get a little more background knowledge about the surname and the location where the main families bearing that name were based.

Equally, why not try one of the more 'unusual' data sets held at familyrelatives.com, which features records such as the 1906 edition of *Burke's Peerage and Landed Gentry*. This resource can provide details of those families who are not quite noble but still own significant amounts of land.

Debrett's Peerage and Baronetage was first published in 1769 and its website concisely explains the term 'Peerage' as 'the hierarchy of titles of various ranks conferred by the Sovereign upon his or her subjects, which has its roots in feudal time', whilst 'Baronetage' is 'a hereditary knighthood created by James I in 1611'. If you're fascinated by the dizzy heights of aristocracy and its ranking in your tree, then visit debretts.com for a detailed description about the titles bestowed and the customs and traditions surrounding each role.

Although for many of us royal or aristocratic links may just be a dream, there are thousands of others who are unaware of their connections to the royal family of Britain and, by association, to the royal families of Europe. Perhaps it is time for a little regal research into *your* family claims?

What is heraldry?

In Medieval times very few people – even members of the aristocracy – could read. In order to distinguish between individuals, a pictorial representation had to be found so as to make them instantly recognisable. The images and icons used formed a seal to be used on letters instead of a signature or in a tournament or battle when the importance of differentiating between one armour-clad soldier and the next was paramount. These 'armorial bearings', painted on shields for identification or embroidered onto a surcoat which covered a knight's armour, coined the description 'coat of arms'. A sign of allegiance was shown by their servants or followers who also wore a badge depicting the same motif. The heraldic coat of arms is made up of a number of components:

At the top of the arms is the **Crest** which sits atop the helm and was originally associated with men of tournament rank. Usually related to other elements of the arms or its supporters, the image could take the shape of a lion, eagle, boar or bear, or one of any number of mythical beasts including griffins, dragons or phoenixes. Whether rampant, couchant or passant in pose, these heraldic beasts were always very fierce.

Below the crest is a decorative wreath known as a **Torse**, whilst the **Helm** is derived from the helmets worn in battle and the shape of it usually signifies the individual's rank – from this, a piece of cloth called the **Mantle** is depicted in a series of flourishes. The shield, coat of arms or **Armorial** is individual in design to the person to whom it was granted and decorated with heraldic beasts, plants, birds and symbolic flowers, whilst the **Motto** below was chosen to express their feelings, beliefs or ideals.

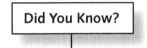

Did You Know?

A coat of arms belongs to the male line of descent from the person to whom it was granted. If you are not directly descended you cannot use the arms. The term 'Armiger' refers to someone who is entitled to use a coat of arms.

Heraldry is a complex and fascinating subject with each element and its position carrying a significant meaning. The College of Arms in London (college-of-arms.gov.uk) and the Heraldry Society in Surrey (theheraldrysociety.com) would both be able to offer advice on investigating and identifying your family's coat of arms.

Chapter 13

TO THE GRAVE

There is a genealogical saying that 'you must always remember to kill off your ancestors'. Quite harsh you may think, but what this actually means is that you cannot fully prove a direct line of descent until you have checked that each individual has led their lives and not died in infancy, making it impossible for them to have children of their own later on. It may be a little clichéd but you must complete the 'circle of life' and follow each ancestor's story through to the end.

AN UNTIMELY END?

During the eighteenth and nineteenth centuries, the possibility of an early death hovered over people from all walks of life, with diseases like tuberculosis, typhoid or cholera being a constant threat. High infant mortality, poor sanitary conditions and overcrowded housing increased the exposure to these chronic illnesses, making people aware that life expectancy was short and death never very far away.

The prospect of an undignified pauper's funeral, in which a coffin made from rough pine with little or no adornment was carried on the shoulders of local men with little thought given to respect and decency, was a deeply troubling one. As a result, in order to pay for the burial of a loved one – and to avoid borrowing from friends and family – those closest to the deceased would take their few remaining valuables to the pawn shop or even resort to the use of moneylenders. Others on lower incomes were prompted to join burial clubs or 'friendly societies', where a weekly amount was paid to ensure that members' funeral costs were covered.

There are a number of funeral customs – some still performed today – which have their roots set firmly in the past. These 'rites of passage' were carried out in the hope of pleasing the spirit of the deceased. Holding a wake was an attempt to keep watch over the body in full view of all those gathered and was intended to be a celebration of life as well as a time to bring comfort to the deceased's family.

Other funereal rituals, imbued with superstition, included sprinkling holy water on the deceased in the belief that it would protect them from evil demons. For those that warranted it, a volley of rifle fire would mark their passing, a procedure mirroring early tribal communities who threw spears in the air to scare away any unwanted spirits which hovered over the body.

Some Victorians still believed in the pagan tradition of lighting fires to protect the living which, in turn, brought about the custom of lighting candles during prayer. The wearing of special mourning clothes meant that any spirits returning to take their next 'victim' back with them would fail to recognise the person in their new attire and overlook them.

What were the Victorian 'rules' of mourning?

In the later part of the nineteenth century, Queen Victoria set the standards for mourning following the death of her husband Prince Albert of Saxe-Coburg Gotha in December 1861. From that day forward she went into mourning for the rest of her life, staying out of the public eye for a number of years before resuming her official duties, but continuing to wear black until her own death in 1901.

Not everyone had this option to 'retreat' from life but the rules for mourning were stricter for Victorian women than they were for men. To provide a curtain of respectability, widows were expected to wear deep mourning for a year and a day which included a dress of the coarse, depressing fabric known as crape with a bonnet and heavy veil. Black fur and seal skin were traditionally used to trim wraps and capes. After eighteen months, the crape could be removed and after two years purple could be added to their wardrobe with other items and fabrics gradually incorporated to show that their period of mourning was coming to an end. At this point, the middle and upper classes were permitted to send out small cards announcing that they were re-entering society and were happy to receive callers and invitations. Fortunately, these harsh stipulations ceased with Victoria's death.

By comparison, the men got off lightly and were allowed to remarry as soon as they liked, abandoning their widower's mourning outfits at the altar in exchange for a new life with their next wife.

What was 'mourning jewellery'?

Its colour and elegant appearance made black Whitby Jet the perfect gemstone to use as part of the fashionable range of mourning jewellery worn by the Victorians. These highly polished decorative pieces could be intricately carved, surrounded by diamonds or mounted on gold settings to provide a lasting memory of the deceased. The ultimate dedication was to have a lock of the relative's hair encased inside a clear panel or receptacle within a locket, brooch or even inside a mourning ring. Today, these items of jewellery are highly collectable and provide a glimpse into a time when some aspects of death were actually made fashionable. Look closely at the jewellery pieces handed down within your family. Could any of them have been created to mourn the death of a loved one?

What were mourning cards and why were they sent?

Mourning or funeral cards were reminders to pray for the soul of the deceased and were sent out after the funeral had taken place. They could be elaborate printed affairs, the paper pierced and cut depicting designs of willow trees, urns and caskets, with a space on the front for details of the departed (although designs became much simpler in later years). This was undoubtedly an added expense for the family but these cards provided a lasting keepsake, helping ensure that the deceased was not forgotten. You may have inherited a mourning card relating to a member of your family, in effect confirming that the deceased has definitely not been forgotten and is still thought about generations later.

I have discovered a number of funeral cards and documentation relating to an ancestor, what information is this likely to tell me?

The documentation has the potential to explain the cost of the funeral and how they were buried, whilst the quality of the cards may show whether they were upstanding within the community. Condolence cards could also shed light on other members of the family and their feelings towards the deceased.

Why was the plot or location of burial so significant to our ancestors?

The burial location held status and importance. Burial in a mausoleum, tomb or vault was normally only an option for those with position or rank. These chambers could be situated in a churchyard, cemetery or on private land depending on the individual's wealth. For others, the preferred situation was within the church or, if you were influential enough, inside a dedicated chapel.

Those less fortunate could end up in an area at the far side of the churchyard which was set aside in unconsecrated ground. Sometimes a communal grave for those at the lower end of society was used to hold up to twenty bodies, covered with a scattering of soil and, incredibly, left uncovered until it was full. This health hazard brought about the call for non–church–related burial sites in the form of cemeteries.

What can I read into the elaborate carvings on my ancestor's gravestone?

Headstones with lasting memorials and symbolism were used to provide a permanent marker for the deceased and a focus for mourning and remembrance for the living. Stonemasons were engaged to create precise carvings of family inscriptions and symbolic images which carried hidden meanings or loving dedications about those departed. Some of the most common depictions include:

A bird	Peace, a messenger of God
A boat	A voyage or journey to the next world
A book or Bible	A Bible usually depicted a clergyman or religious person, whilst an open book may be used to convey the good deeds carried out by the deceased
A broken or severed flower	A premature or sudden death. A bud denotes a child
A calla lily	Represents beauty
A palm	Life after death through resurrection
A square and compasses	Usually found on the grave of a Freemason
A tied knot	Marriage or unity
A tree	Life and regeneration
A willow	Grief and mourning
An anchor	The hope of salvation (or the deceased was a sailor)
A broken chain	A loss within the family
Clasped hands	The hope of reunification in the next life, a symbol of farewell
A crown	To triumph over death
An hourglass	The passage of time
Ivy	Immortality and friendship
A laurel wreath	Symbolising life's achievements
A lily	Purity
A lion	Strength
An olive branch	Peace and harmony
A Star of David	Divine protection

Why is it important to visit a family grave in person?

Where possible, always try to visit a known family grave in person – this is all part of the family history trail. As well as this connection you can expect to uncover more facts just by reading the headstone. There may be information on family members who have been buried in the plot together, extra dates and even details or images which represent their previous occupation. The inscription may give clues as to how they died – my own great-great-grandaunt's inscription has the words 'died in an accident in Cholmondley', which enabled me to further research her death. The headstone carving could hint at the life of your ancestor, i.e. an anchor could suggest a nautical past whilst a young angel could be used to portray the death of a child. Even the epitaph could explain how they were perceived by their family.

DON'T FORGET

All is not lost if you are unable to travel to your ancestor's place of burial. Try contacting the Federation of Family History Societies who may have already collected and transcribed the memorial inscriptions in the parish you are researching. Visit ffhs. org.uk and follow the website's sidebar links to their 'project' section for details of their monumental inscriptions undertaking which is now in its thirtieth year.

What is the National Burial Index and where would I find it?

The NBI was conceived by family historians in the 1990s that used the International Genealogical Index (IGI) to search for baptisms and marriages but were hindered in their quest by the lack of available burial records. Compiled by the Federation of Family History Societies, this resulting collaboration gives you access to over 18 million burial records in England and Wales taken from Anglican registers and bishops' transcripts, as well as Nonconformist, Roman Catholic, Quaker and cemetery records. The CD version is simple to install and easy to navigate via an index which consists of a county-by-county breakdown of the parishes included and the years covered.

Search online at findmypast.com or invest approximately £30 for your own copy on CD – which is well worth the initial outlay if your ancestors are scattered throughout England and Wales. Those wishing to compile a one-name study will also find it an extremely useful resource to have at their fingertips.

What am I likely to find by looking at original burial registers?

Usually the registers record basic details such as the name of the deceased, place of abode and date of burial; you might discover that extra notes have been added in the margins by the truthful incumbents, which can highlight individual entries and explain that there may well have been more about the dear departed's character than first thought. 'Womaniser', 'binge drinker' or 'of fragile state of mind' are just some of the descriptions to be found, and if your ancestor met a less-than-ordinary death such as by drowning, peculiar accident, epidemic, poisoning or even murder, the opportunity to add a comment to the pages of the registers was just too much for some incumbents to pass up. Rather than being looked upon as gossip these notes provide essential clues, especially when the registers date back before civil registration. From 1837 onwards we rely on the death certificates to give us the cause of death, but for earlier dates, the burial register can provide an indispensable source of information.

Original registers can be viewed at the local archives but, in some cases, remain at the church to which they relate. Most churches are extremely helpful in allowing access and only ask for a donation to be offered towards the upkeep of the building – a small price to pay for the possible leads you may uncover.

Have you tried?

The website deceasedonline.com is an ever-growing database of burial and cremation records, digital scans of books of remembrance, photographs of gravestones, memorials and even cemetery maps – ideal for helping to pinpoint the final resting place of your ancestors. Search registers by country, region, county, burial authority or crematorium free of charge, then buy credits to access further information.

What is a coroner's inquest?

Since the twelfth century, it has been the duty of coroners to hold inquests on the bodies of any person who has died in sudden, accidental or suspicious circumstances to try to establish a reason for their deaths. Although these records are usually closed for 75 years, the success rate of finding existing documents varies from location to location.

A county record office should be able to direct you to the repository where the records are likely to be held, but if you come across a surviving document this could uncover the final piece of the puzzle in your ancestor's life. The reports often have details about the deceased and the day they died. Statements and witness accounts can help to build a bigger picture of the victim's final hours and even the signatures and verdict of the jurors can be included. Depending on the individual case, inquest papers may feature maps to demonstrate where the event occurred, photographs (depending upon the period) and drawings of machinery if the death was the result of an industrial accident.

A clue as to whether an inquest has been held into the death of your ancestor can often be found on the death certificate where – in England and Wales – the name of the coroner may be sited as the informant, with details of the date of the inquest and the cause of death. Follow this up with a search through the local newspapers of the time where the original incident, circumstances surrounding the death and later inquest may well have been reported.

The conclusion of an inquest not only determines the cause of death, which may have been accidental or suicide, but can also result in the seizure of property or the conviction of a murderer. Verdicts may find other members of the deceased's family guilty of their murder or manslaughter, leaving the possibility of imprisonment, transportation or hanging as the fate of another of your ancestors. Be prepared for every eventuality and record all aspects of your family history honestly.

What is an obituary?

An obituary is a biography of the deceased's life which has been placed in the newspaper by family, friends or other interested parties. It can include details such as the place and date of birth, names of siblings, parents, and other surviving relatives, occupations, military

BARROW.

FUNERAL OF MR. SHALLCROSS.—One of the oldest inhabitants has passed away in the person of Mr. Joseph Shallcross, of Little Barrow, whose death occurred at the ripe old age or 82 years. Deceased was one of the oldest members of the Little Barrow branch of the United Methodist Free Church, and was really the originator of the new chapel which was built in 1865. The interment took place at Barrow Church on Friday, a short memorial service having previously been held in the chapel at Little Barrow, conducted by Mr. George Parker, Kingsley. The chief mourners were Mr. Charles Shallcross, Didsbury, and Mr. Henry Shallcross, Ashton (brothers), Messrs. W. Shallcross, Liverpool, T. Shallcross, C. Shallcross and H. Shallcross, Little Barrow (sons), Mrs. Bate, Winsford, and Miss Shallcross, Little Barrow, daughters, Mr. Bate, Winsford, and Mr. George Moss, Helsby (sons-in-law). The following also attended:—Mr. and Mrs. Challinor (Long Green), Mr. and Mrs. Newport (Park Hall), Mr. and Mrs. G. Owen and Mr. and Mrs. S. Newport (Broomhill), Mr. Brandreth (Helsby), and Mr. Noden (Frodsham). The burial service was read by the Rev. H. A. Arnold, who was a regular visitor to Mr. Shallcross during his illness, and of whose kindness in this respect the bereaved family wish to record their high appreciation.

Obituary. This is a newspaper cutting of the obituary of my great-great-grandfather. Obituaries are fabulous for gleaning those extra details about your forebears. Other family members are also often mentioned.

PCC Will. Prerogative Court of Canterbury (PCC) wills were made between 1384 and 12 January 1858. Canterbury was one of the most important courts dealing with relatively wealthy individuals living mainly in the south of England and most of Wales. The wills are copies of original probates written by clerks of the church courts with some of the earlier examples written in Latin. This example shows the will of Samuel Pepys proved on 25 June 1703. Courtesy of thegenealogist.co.uk. PROB11/470 The National Archives UK.

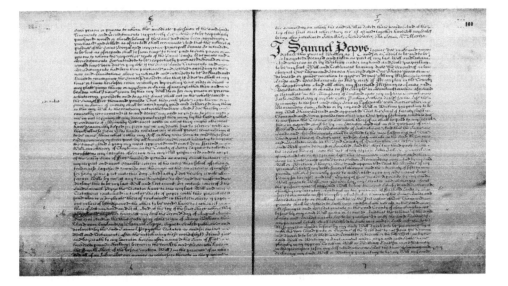

service and even the church where the funeral was held. Not everyone had an obituary but if you know when the individual died, study the newspapers to see if you can find an entry. Bear in mind that these notices can appear several weeks *after* the actual date of death.

What is the relevance of a will?

A will is a written statement detailing how a person wishes to dispose of his or her property and rights after death. It can reveal family links and details of personal possessions, and expose who was in or out of favour at a particular time by the kind of 'goods and chattels' which were bequeathed. By using the knowledge you have already gathered, you can even work out other family specifics such as who was married to whom, whether spouses, siblings or children had already died and even if new grandchildren had been added to the family.

Before the Second World War about 10 per cent of the population left a will. If you do find one relating to your family members then you may be able to uncover some unique data which is not recorded anywhere else. Bear in mind that very few women before the late nineteenth century left a will as their property and possessions would automatically pass to their husband. The discovery of such a will may indicate that they were well-off, widowed, childless, or that their offspring had predeceased them.

What is the procedure for searching for wills and probate?

From the fourteenth century up until 10 January 1858 the proving of wills came under the jurisdiction of the church so can be found deposited in a number of locations. Your first port of call should be the county record office closest to where your ancestor lived and died, but also try The National Archives when searching a wider area. Similarly, the national archives of Ireland and Scotland should be able to help you, whilst scotlandspeople.gov.uk holds many Scottish wills from 1513–1901.

From 11 January 1858 onwards, the Probate Act made the proving of wills a civil matter and across the country a probate court and registries were established. These probates can be obtained from the Principle Probate Registry in London or one of its subsidiaries. Go to willsprobate.co.uk.

DON'T FORGET!

On the internet, thegenealogist.co.uk enables you to search wills proved at the Prerogative Court of Canterbury and allows you to view the original will online. The current coverage goes back to 1600 but will eventually cover 1384–1858.

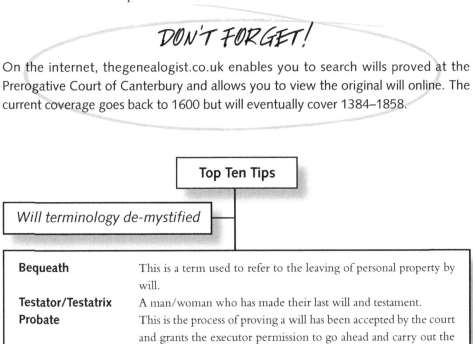

Top Ten Tips

Will terminology de-mystified

Bequeath	This is a term used to refer to the leaving of personal property by will.
Testator/Testatrix	A man/woman who has made their last will and testament.
Probate	This is the process of proving a will has been accepted by the court and grants the executor permission to go ahead and carry out the terms of the will.

Intestate	This describes a person who has died without leaving a will or a valid will cannot be found.
Administration	Refers to a grant allowing the right to administer the estate of a person who has died without leaving a will.
Executor/Executrix	A man/woman who has been appointed by the testator/testatrix to dispose of their estate following the terms of the will.
Estate	This is the term used to describe the assets and liabilities of the deceased.
Inventory	This is a list of the household goods and possessions of the deceased often with details of their value.
Holograph Will	This is a will that has been written out entirely in the deceased's own handwriting.
Codicil	Describes any addition made to a will by the testator/testatrix after it has been drawn up and signed. Any number of codicils can be made as long as each one is witnessed and signed.

INVENTORY.

The State of Nebraska, Saline County, ss.
In the Matter of the Estate of Benjamin Thompson, Deceased.

The following is a full and perfect inventory of the Real and Personal Estate of the said Estate so far as the same has come to the possession or knowledge of the undersigned Special Administrator of said Estate:

REAL ESTATE.

Part of Section or Name of Town	Lot	Bl'k	Sec.	T.	R.	Acre
S 1/2, SE 1/4-32-6-3			32	6	3	80
N 1/2, S 1/2,NE 1/4 & N 1/2,SE 1/4,			4	5	3	160
N 1/2,NW 1/4,			5	5	3	80
S 1/2,NE 1/4 & NW 1/4,NE 1/4 & E 1/2, NW 1/4,			8	5	3	200
Pt of S 1/2, SW 1/4,			22	5	3	7
NW 1/4 & Pt. of NW 1/4, SW 1/4			23	5	3	200
SE 1/4			34	5	3	160
Lot 1 Block 6 Swanton	1	6				
Section of Kansas			35	9	35	640

Chattel Property

Articles	Value
8 tons of hay	$120.00
Mare & Colt	100.00
Manure Spreader	25.00
Hay stacker	10.00
" Loader	25.00
Side Rake	15.00
Binder	50.00
1 load wood	4.00
Wagon	50.00
Buggy	5.00
Single Harness	1.00
Stock Bank	5.00
Corn 200 bu.	150.00
Oats 700 bu.	350.00
Feed Oats 200 bu.	50.00
P. Hay 8 ton	80.00
2 hole sheller	25.00
Spring Wagon	10.00
Sled	1.00
Overland Car	100.00
Gasoline Tank	5.00
Coal Oil "	5.00
Crude " V "	2.00
Cobs 4 load	5.00
Wash house goods	15.00
Household goods	
2 stoves, piano, side board, china closet,	
ward robe, book case, center table, 5 beds	
and bedding, 3 dressers, 2 rugs, some carpet and	
other goods,	252.00
20 bu. potatoes	10.00

Inventory. This 1917 inventory accompanied the will of one of my ancestors and shows the land he owned at the time of his death along with a partial list of some of his possessions and their value.

KNOW all Men by these Presents, that we *William Newport of Barrow in the County of Chester Farmer Thomas Hayes of the City of Chester Gent and William Davenport of the same City Gentleman*

are holden and firmly bound unto the Right Reverend Father in God *George Harry* by divine Permission, Lord Bishop of CHESTER, in the sum of *One hundred* Pounds, of good and lawful money of the United Kingdom of Great Britain, and Ireland, current of that part of the said Kingdom called England, to be paid unto the said Right Reverend Father, his lawful attorney, executors, and administrators, or assigns : To which payment well and truly to be made, we bind ourselves, and every of us, severally, for and in the whole, our heirs, executors, and administrators, and the heirs, executors, and administrators of every of us, firmly by these Presents. SEALED with our Seals, and dated the *Twentieth* day of *January* in the *fifty ninth* year of the Reign of our sovereign Lord GEORGE the Third, by the grace of God, of the United Kingdom of Great Britain, and Ireland, King, defender of the faith, and in the year of our Lord God, one thousand eight hundred and *Nineteen.*

THE Condition of this Obligation is such, that if *the above bounden William Newport the natural and lawful Nephew one of the next of kin and* ADMINISTRAT *of* of all and singular the goods, chattels, and credits of *Matthew Newport late of Barrow in the County and Diocese of Chester a Bachelor deceased without parent Brother or Sister* do make or cause to be made, a true and perfect inventory of all and singular the goods, chattels, and credits of the said deceased, which have or shall come to the hands, possession, or knowledge of *him* the said *William Newport.* or into the hands and possession of any other person or persons for *his use* and the same, so made, do exhibit or cause to be exhibited into the Registry of *the Consistory Court of Chester* at or before the *20th* day of *July* next ensuing; And the same goods, chattels, and credits, and all other the goods, chattels and credits of the said deceased, at the time of *his* death, which at any time after shall come to the hands or possession of the said *William Newport* or into the hands and possession of any other person or persons for *him* do well and truly administer according to law; and further do make, or cause to be made, a true and just account of *his* said administration, at or before the *Twenty first* day of *January* which shall be in the year of our Lord, one thousand eight hundred and *twenty* and all the rest and residue of the said goods, chattels, and credits, which shall be found remaining upon the said administrat *ors* account, the same being first examined and allowed of by the judge or judges for the time being of the said court, shall deliver and pay unto such person or persons respectively, as the said judge or judges, by his or their decree, or sentence, pursuant to the true intent and meaning of an act of parliament, made in the two-and-twentieth and three-and-twentieth years of the reign of his late majesty King CHARLES the second, entitled, *An act for the better settling Intestates estates,* shall limit and appoint. And if it shall hereafter appear that any last will and testament was made by the said deceased, and the executor or executors therein named do exhibit the same into the said court, making request to have it allowed and approved accordingly, if the said *William Newport* above bounden, being thereunto required, do render and deliver the said letter of administration, (approbation of such testament being first had and made in the said court) then his obligation to be void and of none effect, or else to remain in full force and virtue

Sealed and Delivered
in the Presence of }

Sam Baker

William Newport
Tho Hayes

Will. This example is a copy of the 1819 will left by my ancestor detailing their bequests and beneficiaries.

PCC Will. This is the will of authoress Jane Austen proved on 10 September 1817. Each will usually starts with the name of the testator / testatrix and the parish in which they lived. It then lists the names of beneficiaries, details of the executor who would be responsible for carrying out the wishes of the deceased, the testator's signature and witnesses, as well as the probate date when the will was proved. Finding the wills of your ancestors enables you to find out more about the deceased, their property and possessions and their closeness to family and friends. Courtesy of thegenealogist.co.uk. PROB11/1596 The National Archives UK.

Chapter 14

PRESERVE AND PROTECT

Du.uring the early stages of research we are always encouraged to track down any personal belongings and memorabilia which may have belonged to our ancestors. These items – which have not seen the light of day for many years and yet have stood the test of time – can take the form of paper ephemera such as letters, cards, documents and even diaries.

Receipts can help us to understand the cost of items during a particular period.

Even the smallest items of ephemera can build a bigger picture of your ancestor's life.

Once unearthed, you can give these riches a new lease of life. They provide a snapshot of a particular period and, although they are of obvious importance to your family, it is worth remembering that they do not necessarily have to belong to a member of your own family for you to be able to glean a captivating insight into the era in which your ancestors lived.

Why are diaries important?

Offering us invaluable personal details, diary keeping became increasingly popular from the seventeenth century onwards, with many factors contributing to an interest in this pastime of recording daily activities and memories. Advances in the education system saw a growth in literacy, whilst religious beliefs resulted in people noting down and perhaps questioning their faith or chronicling the births, marriages and deaths of family members, describing these events in detail for future generations. This was also an era when paper production became cheaper and more affordable for personal use, allowing the journal to become a sanctuary for the author's feelings and observations. Depending on the period, diaries can showcase these thoughts in immaculate copperplate writing, describing a 'lost' world which is difficult for most of us to comprehend.

How can a letter, diary or document which does not belong to my ancestor help me with my family story?

Is there a specific occupation that you would like to find out more about? Unusual trades with illustrated letterheads can shed light on business dealings and prices charged for services offered. From the simple transactions of a rural grocer to the commerce of traders in exotic locations, documents still exist with vivid explanations of everyday life in a different century.

If you are inspired by military memorabilia, look out for war diaries, regimental diaries, letters from remote outposts or heartfelt love notes written from the trenches. Perhaps you are drawn towards social history with a fascination for Edwardian life, the clothes worn and daily routines carried out?

There are literally thousands of manuscripts, letters and documents up for sale on websites such as ebay.com – it is just a matter of hunting for items and subjects that interest you. Whittling down your search with phrases such as 'travel', 'military', 'WW2' or 'naval' can help you pinpoint the gems that are out there. Book fairs, attic sales and antique fairs are great places to track items down. Do not forget to rummage through

Period birthday and Valentine's Day cards can help give clues to relationships.

Inherited postcards and memorabilia provide clues about family life and travels.

boxes of junk at car boot sales for those long-forgotten treasures and search the sites of specialist ephemera dealers to see what kind of documents they have on offer. Remember that each example is unique so consider that factor when setting yourself a budget.

How should I approach the study of an old document?

Always read the document through once to get a general idea of what it contains and then, with a 'critical eye', take a closer look at what you've got. Note down all the facts, dates and addresses along with any assumptions that you may have made. Consider the type of writing instrument used – quill, metal-tipped ink pen, pencil. Ask yourself – is the paper handmade or mass produced, is there a watermark of the maker? If the item is a letter – has the envelope survived and is the stamp and postal mark intact giving you an obvious indication to the date? Can you follow up on the address of the recipient or sender; does the place still exist?

Become an investigator and look beyond the written words for clues. Trade and commercial correspondence can be explored from the headed notepaper, travel schedules shed light on the transport arrangements of the era and gentle terms of endearment can chart the love affairs of days gone by. Where diaries are composed in a plain notebook and only the day and month dates are recorded, use an online calendar calculator, such as calwiz.com, to try and pinpoint the year in which it was written. The same technique can be used on other letters and documents where the year has not been noted. Occasions recorded within the manuscript may also help to provide a time frame; and where specific events are mentioned, try to track down these details in local newspapers – you may discover even more if the incident was interesting enough to be reported.

I find some of the words difficult to read in early documents, have you any tips on how to make this easier?

Where possible, take a few photocopies of the same document so that you can work on it at your leisure. This enables you to make notes on the copy and even use a highlighter to emphasise the problem areas without damaging the original.

Try breaking the word down into individual letters and creating your own reference guide to how the majority of letters are written in each piece of text. Find a word that you can read and compare each letter against those in ones that you cannot.

If your troubles persist, read the document aloud – this will help you to understand the flow of the wording and the message it is trying to convey. Remember that spelling could be a little hit and miss before the nineteenth century – and similar to the spelling of surnames (*see* Chapter 9), many words were spelt phonetically. If the document was created in an area with a strong regional accent or dialect, take into consideration that a phonetically spelt word in Cornwall may sound different to the same word in Newcastle.

I own a travel diary made in the early 1900s. Are there any online resources where I could find out more about this trip?

The site ancestorsonboard.com is perfect for the era your diary covers. It holds information on passenger lists and vessels sailing from the UK between 1890 and 1960, leaving for destinations including Australia, Canada, India, New Zealand, South Africa and the USA.

I have inherited an old map detailing the area where my ancestor once lived, but it is slightly discoloured in places. What could this mean?

First check for any age toning which refers to the darkening of the paper over time. This could indicate that the map was originally created on poorer quality material or has possibly been badly stored. 'Foxing' is a term for brown spots caused by damp or impurities within the paper, whilst tiny holes may be caused by 'worming' when the larvae of insects have eaten through the paper in storage. Follow the procedures below for preservation techniques that will prolong the life of your item.

I have been given a number of original family documents. How can I best preserve them?

Keep items in as near perfect condition as possible by storing them in a cool, dry place out of direct sunlight. Wrap in archival paper which is acid- and lignum-free to help with long-term preservation. Do not be tempted to use cheap plastic folders in which to store your items – over time the acids in the plastic can react with the old documents and cause irreparable damage. It is worth paying that little bit extra for specialist protectors.

Paper ephemera can rip easily and, after years of being folded in a certain way, can become very fragile along fold lines. If the item is extremely delicate consider wearing cotton gloves whilst handling. Do not overfill storage boxes and check on a regular basis to ensure that mould or pests have not contaminated the documents inside. Avoid using paperclips and staples, which can leave rusty stains, or sticky adhesive tape which over time will leave a brown residue on the document or photograph.

Contemplate transcribing entries which are difficult to read onto your computer helping to make future reference easier, but never write notes – even in pencil – on your original copy. Do not cut or remove any loose pieces; always store everything together and, where possible, make a copy of the document – this will help save on wear and tear during your research. Use a photocopier with an adjustable panel which will allow the copying of larger items like books and diaries and ensure that the spine is not bent, broken or creased. Remember to store copies away from the originals so that if one becomes lost or damaged you will always have the other.

If you're contemplating framing certain items, limit their time on display – perhaps rotate them with other pieces of interest – and do not hang them above radiators, where they may dry out and become brittle. Use low lighting to showcase them to prevent deterioration.

Consider using products from a specialist company such as Conservation by Design via their website timecare.co.uk. Their extensive range – used by organisations such as the National Trust, National Archives and British Museum – covers the preservation of everything from photos and certificates to clothing, medals and maps.

If you're looking for large or important items to be preserved, repaired or conserved for the future, take a look at the Institute of Conservation's website at icon.org.uk. There are tips on mounting and framing documents, explanations on how to avoid deterioration, and how to safeguard and store items such as fashion accessories, paintings, silver, clocks and books – all items you could potentially inherit from your family's past. Their guidelines to choosing and working with a conservator and finding an expert in both your region and specific area of interest is invaluable to anyone worried about letting a 'stranger' loose on their precious heirlooms.

FOLLOWING THE PHOTO TRAIL

Photographs are a hugely important resource when used in conjunction with our family history research. Not only do they enable us to put a face to the names of our ancestors, but they also have the potential to help us place a location, home or business which may have long since disappeared. By capturing a moment in time they allow us to visually witness what clothing, housing, transport and everyday life was like from the Victorian era onwards.

There are a number of different types of photograph in my family collection. Can you account for the differences?

Although photography began in 1839, it was initially just a pastime for wealthy individuals and not yet accessible to the masses. The first types of images appeared on polished silver plate – a process invented in France and known as daguerreotype after creator Louis Daguerre.

Ambrotypes were introduced in the 1850s and consisted of a negative image on glass which could be seen as a positive image when backed with dark material or paint, whilst tintypes enabled the cheap process of producing an image on a thin metal plate to be created. The majority of photographs from these early days were one-offs, but by the late 1850s the world of photography changed forever when the processes involved became available to all.

The *carte de visite* – a small portrait photograph backed with a piece of card – became popular, and when larger versions, known as cabinet cards, were made from 1866, families saw the potential for capturing each individual's image for posterity and displaying the results in decorative albums.

As well as being extremely useful, photographs can prove to be tantalisingly frustrating if they have not been labelled, leaving you unable to positively identify the subject. The

Old photographs/ snapshots can show outfits of the day, methods of transport and even gadgets and equipment used – in this case, an old box camera.

following tips should help you to date the image to a particular period, and by combining your findings with a little sleuthing through the branches of your tree, you may be able to get one step closer to solving the puzzle. Study the image and ask yourself:

– Are you able to tell what type of photographic process was used?

– Is the image mounted as a *carte de visite* or on a cabinet card?

– Is there a photographer's name and address on the back or front of the photograph? Could you locate this photographer and details of his career in a trade directory?

– What are the sitter's clothes, accessories and hairstyle like? In what era would they have been fashionable? Do you recognise any of the jewellery being worn and could it have been handed down to other members of your family?

– Are there any props or paraphernalia in the background that could help you with identification and dating such as hats, guns, walking sticks or even medals?

Cartes de visite and photographs capture our ancestor's image. Small yet useful inscriptions may have been added by other family members.

Advertising on the back of *cartes de visite* can help us track down who the photographer was and match family groups if unidentified photos were taken by the same photographer.

Before the advent of the flashbulb, photographs were often taken outside to make use of the natural light. Look beyond the subjects of the picture and into the background – are there any clues in the buildings, street names or general scenery that could help you with identification?

DON'T FORGET!

Always aid future generations by adding a small description on the back of each image with a special photo marker.

How can I find out more about the photographers operating in Britain during the late 1800s?

Trade directories (*see* Chapter 7) are worth investigating if you know the area in which the photographer you are looking for worked. These details can then be cross-referenced with the census allowing you to follow the individual's career over the decades.

Photographic directories were produced which listed every studio but can be difficult to find. A fabulous site created by Robert Pols can be found at early-photographers.org. uk which enables researchers to look at transcriptions of his original directories from Norfolk, Suffolk and Cambridge, listing each photographer and his address alphabetically. You will also find indispensable links to websites where directories relating to other parts of the country have been added.

Similar is cartedevisite.co.uk, a website about photographers in Britain and Ireland from 1840–1940 with details of their studios and even some of their customers. There are plenty of links to various resources as well as teaching aids and images to help you understand the photography world during this period.

DON'T FORGET!

Photographs do not have to have belonged to or be taken of your ancestors to be of use in your research. Perhaps you're looking to flesh out your ancestor's world by adding images of where they once lived; francisfrith.com is a compilation of 120,000 photographs taken by Francis Frith during the Victorian era. His business was based in Reigate, Surrey, but his photographs were taken all over the British Isles and in locations as far afield as Egypt. The archive he left upon his death in 1898 is indispensable for today's family and local historians, so why not search the site, order your copies online and discover how your village has changed in the last 150 years?

What advice would you give regarding the storage of old photographs?

Again, invest in acid-free photo albums which will help preserve them for future generations. Question older relatives to discover the identities of those in the images and take time to attach a label to the backs detailing their names and – where possible – a date to help with later research.

Some of my ancestors immigrated to America and I've inherited a scrapbook filled with what I believe are 'Trade Cards'. Can you explain exactly what these were used for?

Throughout the 1800s, most merchants and shopkeepers had decorative cards produced which would be given away to promote either their business or products sold. The idea is thought to have originated from similar cards used by craftsmen in the 1700s to publicise their particular line of work. This became extremely fashionable in America and, whilst many European countries had their own decorative versions, it was not quite so popular in Britain until a smaller type of card was later issued with cigarettes and brands of tea that became collectable in its own right.

The Victorian cards varied in size from tiny 3cm x 7cm versions to large 14cm x 21cm creations, often given out at Christmas or other significant times of the year. Victorians were hoarders – their houses were crammed with ornaments and trinkets ensuring that a cluttered room adorned with ornate accessories met the strict fashion guidelines of the day. At the time, the pretty designs featured on the trade cards made the perfect collectable for the modern Victorian, who would paste examples into scrapbooks and arrange them in subjects that were appealing ensuring that products were not forgotten as their collections grew. The craze for collecting increased as people sought out the more complex designs when colour lithography of the 1870s became more accessible.

New inventions played a huge part in the subjects chosen for illustration. At the time, the introduction of a lawnmower which could be pushed by a man (rather than pulled by an animal) was a commercial success. The creation of a side-wheel machine (developed in England), which was lightweight and inexpensive, caught on all over the world and gradually found its way onto trade cards that showed the ease of operation to its customers. Even Kodak chose to use this method of advertising to showcase its latest camera equipment. Victorian trade cards can give a fascinating glimpse into life during this era.

The use of trade cards reached its peak in the 1890s. Advertising policies began to change as magazines and newspapers began offering more and more advertising space within their pages. This wider readership outshone the amount of coverage a business could receive by handing out trade cards to each customer; it was also more cost effective.

This period marked the beginning of the postcard age. Those who had previously collected trade cards now switched allegiance and sought out the latest themed postcards of locations they had visited.

In a box of family heirlooms I came across two First World War medals. How can I best preserve them, and what extra information could they help me discover?

Campaign medals are usually inscribed with the recipient's name, regiment and number; these are extremely useful in helping you to track down their service record. By discovering the regiment they belonged to you can try to establish if a dedicated

Trade Cards help to explain the types of products available to the general public during the Victorian era.

regimental museum exists that could help you fill in a little background as to where the recipient was stationed and the campaigns in which he was involved. Many regiments have war diaries and your ancestor could well have been mentioned.

Consider mounting the war medals and any badges, insignia and photos in a shadow box – a deep-set frame that will not only protect the medals but showcase them for family and friends to see. This can be done professionally using dust-sealed units, whilst any metalwork damage can be easily restored and any frayed ribbons replaced. War medals are not just valuable but hard-earned and well-deserved – so why not display them with pride?

Family heirlooms exist in a number of guises: from patchwork quilts and tapestries, that may have been sewn by your ancestor's hand, to decorative buckles and combs which may have adorned their clothing or hair. From the smallest item to a real gem of a find, such as an old cine-film recording, once you start looking you could be surprised by what has survived the passage of time.

Chapter 15

COLLATE AND COLLABORATE

T he purpose of genealogy is to chart your ancestors' lives. To understand how they were affected by the world around them and write up their story for future generations, you will need to take a closer look at each individual to see if your investigations are nearing completion and whether you're finally ready to sum up your case.

If you have trouble finding information in one area, try varying your sources. For example, if a death date is proving difficult to locate on the BMD index, check out cemetery records, monumental inscriptions or even family bibles. If you still cannot find specific details after completing a thorough search, move on to another family member – some ancestors do not want to be found whilst others will surprise you, their particulars cropping up in a resource where you least expect to find them.

The checklist below will help guide you through the main records and make writing up your findings in a chronological order much easier.

Birth	Parish registers for those born before 1837
	Birth certificates for those born after 1837
Baptism	Parish registers and church records for all religious denominations
Schooling	Log books, attendance registers, public school and university records
Apprenticeships	Apprenticeship indentures and Poor Law records for parish apprentices
Work/Occupation	Censuses, trade and historical directories. Company records and memberships
Military Career	Army, Royal Air Force, Royal and Merchant Navy service records, pensions, enlistment papers, medal index cards
Home/Family	Census returns, electoral registers, poll and rate books, directories, deeds, mortgage indentures
Marriage	Marriage certificate for unions after 1837
	Anglican marriage church records between 1753–1837
Children	Parish registers if born before 1837
	Birth certificates if born after 1837
	Bastardy/Poor Law records for illegitimate children

Emigration	Passenger lists and manifests, passport applications, government schemes encouraging migration
Transportation	Criminal records, court proceedings, newspaper reports, transportation records and ships' lists
Health	Hospital, asylum and workhouse records
Death	Death certificate if died after 1837. Burial registers if died before 1837. Obituaries and newspaper notices
Inquest	Coroner's reports and inquest records. Newspaper reports
Burial	Burial Registers
Will/Probate	Probate registers

What should I take into account when trying to write up my family story?

Firstly, consider how you want to display your results – in electronic format as a blog or website which can be accessed online, or in a paper format, which can be read and digested at leisure by your relatives? Don't be put off by thinking that the mammoth task of writing a book is the only way to tell your story – why not consider creating a newsletter, scrapbook or artistically drawn family tree, making use of copies of the photos, certificates and ephemera that you have collected along the way?

Don't try to include every single date and detail; concentrate initially on one branch, surname or the descendants of one couple. If you've found an interesting ancestor start by focusing on them, or, if your forebears specialised in a specific trade, weave the story around that occupation to create an historical archive for future generations.

However you decide to present your finding, you do not want a boring list of facts and figures but instead want to bring the story of your ancestors to life. You have spent so long compiling all this information that it is important to ensure your final tribute is not just given a cursory glance and shelved forever.

My ancestors weren't famous and led ordinary lives. How can I capture the reader's attention?

The majority of us will be in this situation, but the world has changed so much over the centuries that even the most ordinary of lives are of interest. Start by taking a look at the section of this book entitled 'Anchoring your Ancestors' and work out what was going on in Britain and beyond during the period in which your ancestor lived. Set the scene for your readers and then begin to interweave your facts and findings. Research the areas in which they lived and describe the streets as they once were, perhaps illustrating them with old family photographs. Do not be disheartened if you lack photographs; topographical postcards are often available which instantly take you back to a town or village from the Victorian and Edwardian eras. Keep your eyes peeled for examples related to your areas of interest at antique, book or ephemera fairs, with specialist dealers or on auction sites such as eBay.

Local history publications will help you depict what life was like in a specific village or, alternatively, study historical directories in greater detail to add extra depth about the types of shops and facilities which would have been open for business at that time.

In genealogy, the importance of confirming correct dates and locations cannot be denied, but it is often the combination of personal family history facts and local history colour which truly brings our ancestry to life, and if we really want to pass on our fascination with the subject then we need to hold the reader's attention and awaken their curiosity.

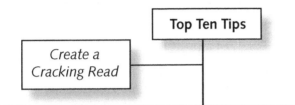

Top Ten Tips

Create a Cracking Read

Decide who your prospective reader will be. Do you want this to be a 'for your eyes only' compilation for your family or close friends, or would you like your finished work to have a broader appeal? Consider how you could do this – would students benefit from your knowledge of a certain occupation or could you gear it towards tourists to the area who would love to find out more about life in the region?

Create a theme. You owe it to yourself to pass your enthusiasm for your subject on to others, so don't become bogged down with endless lists. Try to make it more than a chronological timeline about 'family X'. Centre it on a location, incident or event and build your information around this.

Identify the conflict. You may think that your family story does not feature conflict – but you would probably be wrong. Did your ancestor flee Ireland after the Potato Famine to make a new life for himself in England or even America? Or struggle to get his invention noticed, or desperately fight to survive and return to his loved ones after battling on the front line in France? You have to create drama to hold your reader's interest. The conflict will help give your story a beginning where your story is explained, a middle where the struggle or problem is faced and an end where the conflict is overcome. Remember – the simplest problem can create conflict.

Creating your characters. You may think that because you didn't know your ancestors personally that you cannot characterise them – again this is not true. A photograph allows you to describe their appearance, clothing, style and accessories, but what you have learnt about their lives also helps you to determine whether they were happy, strong-minded, resilient or stubborn, weak, troubled or even cowardly. Try compiling a mini biography for each person who you wish to involve in your story and you will soon find that these people were more than just a name.

Dialogue. There is nothing more tedious than pages and pages of unbroken narrative. Break it up with dialogue in the form of snippets of conversation or anecdotes that you remember hearing. Recall their memories or recount their letters as though they were reading them aloud. Alternatively, break up text with 'Box Outs' – these are separate boxes of information which relate to the story but don't fit directly into the narrative. For example, a section on your ancestor's work as an apprentice shopkeeper could be broken up with a small box out on the currency of the period or the types of food and their cost at that time.

Crafty construction. Structure your narrative into sections or manageable chapters. Don't try to include every last piece of information you've found out – limit yourself to the interesting facts and anecdotes which provide pace and help move the story along.

Keep it simple. Don't waffle or feel the need to spin your story out. Don't say it in five pages if you can make it more punchy and dynamic without losing anything of importance in two. Give your chapters catchy headings which relate to the content and try to keep them all a similar size to make it a consistent read.

Tantalising titles. As informative as 'The Brown Family Story' is, you should avoid it like the plague. Really give your title some thought, make it intriguing and encourage the reader to want to find out more. If you can't live without it, use it as the subtitle in smaller text below your main heading.

FROM RUSSIA WITH LOVE

The Brown Family Story

Designer style. It's now time to have some fun. The simplest 'publisher' program on your computer or even contained on your family history software can produce fantastic results. Enjoy playing around with the layout, inserting photographs, scans of certificates and letters, as well as changing the font to a readable size and colour, and generally making your creation pleasing to the eye.

Check, check and check again. Your work is complete and all that is left is to print it out; but before you do, check back through your text for spelling mistakes, bad grammar or inconsistencies – there is nothing more annoying than printing out the results of your research on that expensive paper you bought especially for the job, only to find that you've spelt 'Aunt Matilda' three different ways and have her living at the wrong address.

What is print on demand?

Print on Demand (POD) (sometimes *publish* on demand) is a service where copies of a new book or document are not printed until an order is received. Previously, the printing of single copies of a publication was not commercially viable, but the introduction of digital printing has now made this possible. This technology is a bonus for family and local historians who may only require a small print run of their own book, minimising their costs and overheads and making their publishing dream a reality.

From a research point of view, POD has also opened up access to old resources, where some previously out of print titles can be brought back to life via this service and read once again. The bookseller and publishers Phillimore and Co. are just one of the companies that offer this service for some of their historical titles. Go to phillimore.co.uk for more information.

I'm not great with words. Is there any other way that I could present my family story?

The world of papercrafting is now nearly as big a pastime as that of genealogical research. Many historians are using this medium as a way of displaying their findings in a fun and attractive way which is visually appealing to the reader and extremely pleasurable to create.

Scrapbooking allows you to present your family history by displaying your photos, journals and ephemera on beautiful pages with decorative embellishments and, in effect, to produce your own 'coffee table' book. The information is imparted in snippets and illustrated with images which can include anything from personal photos and newspaper clippings to theatre programmes and old birthday cards – in fact, any mementoes from your family's past. Each page is constructed independently and then slotted into a protective plastic sleeve within the album. Scrapbooking is a huge industry with many towns now having their own craft shop which will be able to supply you with an endless range of decorative elements to enhance your work. This is an artistic way to add your own touch to your research. If you would like to find out more, or for ideas on how to go about assembling your pages, pick up a copy of *Scrapbook Magazine*.

Perhaps you like the idea of producing an eye-catching piece of artwork that can be enjoyed by all the family but are not that enthusiastic about the 'cutting and sticking' part of the task. There are many others who feel the same and instead are able to come up with similar results by becoming digital scrapbookers. The techniques of generating your own family history page with embellishments are applied but instead carried out on screen, allowing you to manipulate your photographs, add complementary backgrounds or scan in your prized pieces of ephemera. You can then either print out your results or email them to members of your family. Type 'digital scrapbooking' into any search engine and you'll be surprised at just how many online tutorials there are and like-minded scrapbookers who are only too willing to help.

Ancestry.com have seen the potential for this kind of presentation facility and added a publishing feature to their ever-expanding site. They offer the chance for you to relive

My Gran - Mary Ann Donald
born in Troon, Scotland on
the 6th November 1919.
This glamorous photo was
taken in her late teens.

Some people,
no matter how old they get,
never lose their beauty –
they merely move it from
their faces into their hearts.

Martin Buxbaum

Scrapbook pages.
Just one of the ways
to capture your
family memories.

your memories by building a family history book, family tree poster, photo book or calendar using the research and information you have discovered. Creating these keepsakes is made surprisingly easy thanks to their online demos and tutorials with plenty of ideas and samples that show you what can be achieved. Once you have uploaded your information, the step-by-step process guides you through each stage allowing you to arrange, alter and customise it on screen. When you are happy, you can simply have your finished piece bound, published and delivered, or print individual pages at home for free. This is a fantastic facility, allowing the creation of heirloom-quality keepsakes which make ideal presents for anyone within your family. Do not just think of this as a way of capturing the lives of your ancestors – this service can also be used to record the lives of your children and grandchildren for future generations. Go to ancestry.co.uk and follow the links via the 'publish' button on the top toolbar.

My children have shown an interest in my research. How can I get them involved?

Bringing other family members in on your family history project is always a good idea. Not only will you be able to share the thrill of your findings but they may even see things from a different perspective from you, suggesting areas of research that you may not have considered before. Now that you have amassed a wide selection of data to work with, consider how you can expand upon this with the addition of a twenty-first-century twist. Get the children or grandchildren involved at home. If you're feeling adventurous, contact the local school with the idea of creating a 'time capsule' as a lasting legacy.

Would you recommend sharing the information I have found with others outside my immediate family?

Definitely – share your information and you are guaranteed to reap the rewards. There is the possibility that you could tap into an undiscovered source or new ground will be opened up to further your research. Be selective with the details you give out, but you may find that by swapping data you can solve a problem in your tree that has been troubling you or even give you access to family photos from a distant relative that you previously never knew existed.

Consider social networking. Genes Reunited (genesreunited.co.uk) has over 9 million members around the world – all of whom are eager to share their findings using the search and messaging facility. This site also has the added benefit of access to basic records such as the England and Wales censuses and the General Record Office BMD indexes, as well as First and Second World War death records.

Ancestry trees at ancestry.co.uk provide another fabulous way of adding new connections to your tree. This easily navigable yet comprehensive facility allows you to move around the various branches of your chosen tree, zoom in on individuals and their information and print areas specific to you. Contact with the 'owner' of each online tree is via Ancestry's connected emailing service where you can make enquiries or ask for access to certain trees which require permission. As with Genes Reunited, uploading your own tree is easily done using a Gedcom file from your family history software.

Do not dismiss facebook.com as just a place where young subscribers meet for an online chat. It also has a dedicated genealogy applet that already has in excess of 50 million users. Initially, you create a 'profile' page, sharing as much or as little as you want your online 'friends' to know. You are then provided with space known as a 'wall' where you can post comments, thoughts and photos to share with your friends and an area where you can send or receive private messages. The genealogy application 'We're Related' works in the same way and once loaded allows you to manually build a tree (as yet there is no Gedcom facility to import your existing tree), add details of your family through information shared by other Facebook users and create a basic pedigree chart.

It must be noted that this is not a serious contender for the other genealogical packages out there, but nor does it pretend to be. If you use it as a fun way of keeping in touch with living relatives and swapping photos and family information then there are benefits to using it alongside your existing software.

Once you start searching there is a variety of websites onto which you can upload your family tree but, before you do, consider the subscriber base and how relevant it is to your own research. An American site may attract limited numbers of UK users and result in very few contacts, so be aware of the potential before you part with money.

However you decide to share your data online, always remember:

- Set privacy levels when sharing family details with your Facebook friends and other networkers.
- Out of consideration and to avoid the possibility of identity theft, do not upload the detailed information of living relatives – there are usually options to replace their names with the word 'living'.
- Don't use your mother's maiden name as a password.
- Use each site's internal messaging service to contact others rather than your own email address to avoid unsolicited mail and attachments until you become familiar with the other networker.
- Read each site's terms and conditions about their sharing of your content before you upload any of your family information which you later wish you had kept private – once it is in the public domain there is no going back.
- Give credit to anyone who has given you data and always ask first before you reproduce any of their information.

Another option is to advertise in local newspapers to see if anyone out there has the information you need. Similarly, you could place an advert on one of the specific boards which are usually set aside for such requests at family history centres and archives – you may find that you are sharing your research facility with a distant relative. Even a chat to other genealogists at your archives can give results. People travel far and wide to view original records – I got chatting to a lady who now lives in the area where my ancestors once lived. She kindly agreed to go around and take photographs of the addresses and properties which still existed and were connected to my family. This was such a kind gesture and her knowledge of the area meant she could locate these addresses much quicker than I would have been able to. As a result, she has brought this part of my research to life and we continue to keep in touch, every Christmas describing all our latest finds and the genealogical brick walls which we have overcome.

Although you may not be related, other people's knowledge of an area, time period or occupation can be indispensable in adding to your story.

I seem to have hit a brick wall with my research. How can I overcome this?

At some point this happens to us all; the information we have gathered swirls about our heads to the extent that we cannot see the wood for the trees. Take time to sit down and re-read your findings. Sift through your old notes and you will be surprised that one little snippet of information will usually start to recharge your batteries and give you a new avenue of research to pursue. Carry out the same procedure on your genealogy software package – look for gaps and work out how you are going to fill them.

Another tip is to take time away from your own notes and familiarise yourself with the resources that are available to you. There are new databases being added online all the time and there may well be a fresh set of records that hold the key to your problem. Consider joining a specialised tutorial online to hone or expand your skills in the area which is proving to be a struggle.

Family and local history go hand in hand so perhaps this is the time to do some in-depth research on the areas where your ancestors lived. Seek out local history publications and acquaint yourself with the workings and day-to-day life of a particular town or village; read local newspapers from the time and get a feel for the period. This sideways shift in your investigations may throw up new questions and get your ancestral mission on the move again.

Would you recommend I join a family history society?

Definitely. Join a local group or become a member of a number of societies in locations where your ancestors once lived. The benefits include access to indexes of monumental inscriptions from local churches and burial grounds, parish register indexes and the advice of enthusiasts who are usually very happy to help with any queries and may even already be researching the same surnames as you. If you can attend their meetings, expect to find a calendar of guest speakers on varying subjects enabling you to pick up a few tips along the way. If you live too far away to visit, most societies publish a quarterly journal or magazine which is posted to you as part of your membership fee, detailing member interests and the latest news. The Federation of Family History Societies, online at ffhs. org.uk, will help you to find the group that will be of most benefit to you.

DON'T FORGET

There are family history societies that specialise in railway ancestors, Romany and traveller forebears, Anglo-Italians who have settled in Britain, and more – try googling your area of interest and see what other enthusiasts are out there.

What can I expect to find if I visit a family history fair?

I can guarantee that if you have become hooked on family history then a visit to a fair will not disappoint. From genealogy software to document storage, stallholders offer a huge range of products to aid and inspire your research. You may find companies offering to print out your family tree for display, or to show the dispersal of your surname across the country. Second-hand book dealers may have the out-of-print local history guide you were looking for or a family history society may have transcribed the memorial inscriptions in the churchyard where you believe your ancestors are buried. And, of course, there's always the opportunity to chat to other family historians and perhaps arrange to attend other genealogical social events. Every fair will have something new to offer, but try to attend those held in regions connected to the lives of your ancestors where you are likely to find a greater percentage of local history publications and experts on the area.

Of course, if you need a family history 'fix' then you can visit the annual Who Do You Think You Are? event in London, linked to the BBC TV series of the same name. Representatives from the majority of genealogical companies and organisations are on hand to answer your questions, date your photographs, offer advice and educate you on some of the most fascinating areas of British and world history. Celebrities from the TV series explain their experiences in the theatre, workshops are held by experts in their genealogical field and there are plenty of opportunities to shop for much-needed supplies and publications, and perhaps even pick up a few freebies along the way. Their website at whodoyouthinkyouarelive.co.uk will explain more about the next show or visit the site of the magazine at bbcwhodoyouthinkyouaremagazine.com to keep you updated with genealogical news if you cannot wait for this yearly event to come around.

What is the Society of Genealogists and what are the benefits of becoming a member?

The Society of Genealogists (SoG) is the national library and education centre for family history, online at sog.org.uk. Now that you have caught the 'family history bug' it is likely that you still have numerous unanswered questions and want to find out more. Membership allows you access to many unique collections as well as parish registers, marriage licences, poll books, directories, wills and apprenticeship records – the list is endless, and ensures that you can take your research to the next level. Based in London, the society holds regular talks on all aspects of genealogy but if you are unable to visit in person they offer online courses, information leaflets and a Family History Advice Line to answer any queries you may have.

What is DNA testing and how can it help?

DNA testing is used to determine if two people share a common ancestor and is therefore a useful tool to help validate the paper research you have already carried out. But it also has the means to go far beyond this paper trail by helping to show if there is a connection between two people with the same surname – a theory difficult to prove by any other means if you have no documentary links.

There are two main tests available for family historians. The Y-DNA examines the markers on the Y chromosome, passed down through the generations via the direct paternal line. The more matching markers that two people share, the more likely they are to be related.

Women do not inherit the Y chromosome so they must rely on the males within their family to take this particular test in their place. Instead, mt-DNA looks at specific markers in mitochondrial DNA which follows the direct maternal line. The test can be taken by both men and women because, although only women can pass it on to the next generation, men receive the X chromosome of their XY from their mothers. This procedure is not as useful to anyone researching a specific surname match, as the female surname tends to change with every generation, so a Y-DNA test would be better for this purpose where the male surname is inherited. Each test is carried out in the form of a simple cheek swab which is then analysed and compared against other genetic information within each company's database.

When deciding which company to choose to complete your DNA tests you must consider that a genetic genealogical database is only as valuable as its size – the larger the database, the greater the likelihood of a positive comparison of results with its other members around the world.

By evaluating genetic material, it is possible to determinine if two people share a common ancestor, to prove or disprove a research theory, trace family lineages and others to whom you could be related, as well as obtaining clues about your ethnic origins. Tests usually cost in the region of £100; do your research into what each company offers and decide whether this route is for you. Oxford Ancestors (oxfordancestors.com) offers a free information pack and a detailed website which may be able to answer some of your questions, whilst DNA Worldwide (dna-worldwide.com) also offers a comprehensive online description of what is involved and what you can hope to discover.

I keep in touch with some of my 'new' relatives via email but would really like to meet them face to face. What advice would you give about organising a family reunion?

For a really successful event allow plenty of time for planning and tracking down as many people as possible to attend. Remember that everybody has busy lives these days so organise the date a good few months in advance and send out invitations to spread the word. Always include an RSVP so that you can begin to calculate numbers as the invites are accepted.

Do not underestimate how much the reunion will cost. You'll need a venue and will probably have to lay on food. Consider meeting in a restaurant, café or pub – that way you can keep food costs to a minimum as everyone pays for themselves. Remember to make group bookings in advance and you may even receive a discount.

A chat and a catch-up is all very well but you want to make the reunion relevant – after all, you are all meeting because of your family history – so why not plan an itinerary, with a tour of the village where your ancestors lived or a visit to the church where many of them were baptised, married or buried? Compile a selection of photocopied maps, photographs and relevant documents to add interest and maybe even a basic family history chart featuring all the names of those who are attending – you can create this on your genealogy software and print out copies.

If your reunion is to be a large gathering, consider getting the local newspaper involved who may send out a photographer and record the event for posterity. The publicity may even uncover some new facts about the people in your tree if you request readers to write in with their memories or related information.

Enjoy the whole process and don't get too ambitious. If you would like to share the work involved then get the like-minded enthusiasts within your family to help out. You really could have a fantastic day.

Can you ever say that your family history research is complete?

This can depend upon what your initial goals were. You may only have wished to find all the descendants of your great-great-grandparents, or you could have embarked on a one-name study of your surname. Along the way, your priorities could have changed so that now you feel so intrigued by a branch of your tree that you want to find out more. Don't worry – this is completely natural and an affliction suffered by many family historians who do not feel able to stop searching. Genealogy can be a pleasant pastime that can be dipped in and out of when time allows or an all-encompassing body of work; it is entirely up to you.

Subscriptions to any of the dedicated magazines are a worthy investment, so pop into your local newsagent and see which publication best suits your needs. Each month you will be kept informed of the latest databases that become available for public viewing which could help you to unlock the previously unopened areas of your tree. Magazines on offer include *Family History Monthly*, *Family Tree Magazine*, *Your Family Tree* and *Your Family History*.

But wherever you decide to draw the boundaries, the most important thing is that you enjoy what you're doing, which in itself broaches the question – if you enjoy it, why stop?

The benefits of becoming a 'family history detective' far outweigh those frustrating times when you think you will never rise above the brick wall which has presented itself, but if you keep in mind a very apt quote by one of the most famous detectives of all time, then you can't go far wrong.

> *'Eliminate the impossible and whatever remains,*
> *however improbable, must be the truth.'*
> **Sherlock Holmes**
> *The Sign of the Four* **by Arthur Conan Doyle**

Chapter 16

ANCHORING YOUR ANCESTORS: HISTORICAL TIMELINES

I n order to 'place' a particular ancestor in history, it is important to understand the period in which they lived, perhaps who was on the throne at that time and what significant events were going on in the world that they may have experienced first hand. The following timelines are a general guide from the sixteenth to the end of the twentieth century and can help to build the backdrop to your forebear's life or raise even more questions which you would eventually like to answer.

MONARCHS

The Tudors

1485–1509   HENRY VII
1509–47   HENRY VIII
1547–53   EDWARD VI
1553   LADY JANE GREY
1553–58   MARY I
1558–1603   ELIZABETH I

The Stuarts

1603–25   JAMES I
1625–49   CHARLES I

The Commonwealth

Declared 19 May 1649
1653–58	OLIVER CROMWELL
1658–59	RICHARD CROMWELL

The Stuart Restoration

1660–85	CHARLES II
1685–88	JAMES II and VII of Scotland
1689–94	MARY II (with WILLIAM III of Orange)
1702–14	ANNE

The Hanoverians

1714–27	GEORGE I
1727–60	GEORGE II
1760–1820	GEORGE III
1820–30	GEORGE IV
1830–37	WILLIAM IV
1837–1901	VICTORIA
1901–10	EDWARD VII

House of Windsor

Known as the House of Saxe-Coburg and Gotha until 1917
1910–36	GEORGE V
1936	EDWARD VIII
1936–52	GEORGE VI
1952–present	ELIZABETH II

BRITISH PRIME MINISTERS

Who was Prime Minister of the country during your ancestor's lifetime?

Eighteenth Century

1721–42	Sir Robert Walpole
1742–43	Spencer Compton, Earl of Wilmington
1743–54	Henry Pelham
1754–56/57–62	Thomas Pelham-Holles, Duke of Newcastle
1756–57	William Cavendish, Duke of Devonshire

1762–63	John Stuart, Earl of Bute
1763–65	George Grenville
1765–66	Charles Wentworth, Marquess of Rockingham
1766–68	Earl of Chatham, William Pitt 'The Elder'
1768–70	Augustus Henry Fitzroy, Duke of Grafton
1770–82	Lord North
1782–83	William Petty, Earl of Shelburne
1783/1807–09	William Bentinck, Duke of Portland

Nineteenth Century

1783–1801/04–06	William Pitt 'The Younger'
1801–04	Henry Addington
1806–07	William Wyndam Grenville, Lord Grenville
1809–12	Spencer Perceval
1812–27	Robert Banks Jenkinson, Earl of Liverpool
1827	George Canning
1827–28	Frederick Robinson, Viscount Goderich
1828–30	Arthur Wellesley, Duke of Wellington
1830–34	Earl Grey
1834/35–41	William Lamb, Viscount Melbourne
1834–35/35–41	Sir Robert Peel
1865–66	Earl Russell
1852/58–59/66–68	The Earl of Derby
1852–55	Earl of Aberdeen
1855–58/59–65	Viscount Palmerston
1868/74–80	Benjamin Disraeli
1868–74/80–85/86/92–94	William Ewart Gladstone
1885–86/86–92/95–1902	Robert Gascoyne-Cecil, Marquess of Salisbury
1894–95	Earl of Rosebery

Twentieth Century

1902–05	Arthur James Balfour
1905–08	Henry Campbell-Bannerman
1908–16	Herbert Henry Asquith
1916–22	David Lloyd George
1922–23	Andrew Bonar Law
1923/24–29/35–37	Stanley Baldwin
1924/29–35	James Ramsay MacDonald
1937–40	Arthur Neville Chamberlain
1940–45/51–55	Sir Winston Leonard Spencer Churchill
1945–51	Clement Richard Attlee

1955–57	Anthony Eden
1957–63	Harold Macmillan
1963–64	Sir Alec Douglas-Home
1964–70/74–76	Harold Wilson
1970–74	Edward Heath
1976–79	James Callaghan
1979–1990	Margaret Thatcher
1990–1997	John Major
1997–2007	Tony Blair

FURNITURE, STYLE AND ARCHITECTURE

Tudor	1485–1588
Early English	1558–1625
Puritan	1649–60
Baroque	1620–1725
Rococo	1720–70
Neo-classical	1775–1810
Regency	1812–30
Eclectic	1830–80
Arts and Crafts	1880–1900
Art Nouveau	1895–1920
Art Deco	1910–25

EVENTS

1536	The Dissolution of the Monasteries begins.
1588	Defeat of the Spanish Armada.
1599	Opening of the Globe Theatre by William Shakespeare's playing company.
1605	Foiling of the Gunpowder Plot to blow up Parliament.
1620	The Pilgrim Fathers set sail for America on board the *Mayflower*.
1642	Outbreak of the English Civil War.
1665	The Great Plague strikes Britain.
1666	The Great Fire of London destroys many of the capital's buildings.
1677	The first stone of St Paul's Cathedral is laid.
1715	The first Jacobite Rebellion breaks out, followed by a second in 1745.
1768	James Cook leads his first expedition to the Pacific.
1771	Britain's first cotton mill opens.
1775	The American War of Independence begins.
1776	The American Colonies proclaim their independence.
1787	The first convict fleet sails for Australia.

1788	The first edition of *The Times* is published.
1789	The French Revolution begins with the storming of the Bastille.
1805	Admiral Nelson leads his fleet to victory in the Battle of Trafalgar.
1807	Britain abolishes the Slave Trade.
1811	Jane Austen's first novel, *Sense and Sensibility*, is published.
1815	The Battle of Waterloo is fought.
1825	The world's first steam locomotive passenger service begins between Stockton and Darlington.
1829	Robert Peel establishes the Metropolitan Police.
1833	The Factory Bill is enacted to restrict the hours worked by women and children.
1834	A new Poor Law is introduced to give relief outside the workhouse.
1836	Charles Dickens' first novel *The Pickwick Papers* is serialised.
1838	The first public record office is established.
1839	Slavery is finally abolished in the colonies.
1842	The Mines Act is introduced to prevent females and boys under the age of 10 working down the mines.
1843	William Wordsworth becomes Poet Laureate until his death in 1850.
1848	The Public Health Act introduces health boards and inspectors to oversee improvements in Britain's water supplies, drainage and sanitation.
1851	The Great Exhibition opens at London's Crystal Palace.
1882	Suicide victims are allowed to be buried in consecrated ground for the first time.
1914	Outbreak of the First World War.
1918	Women over the age of 30 are given the right to vote.
1936	King Edward VIII abdicates to marry Wallis Simpson.
1939	Outbreak of the Second World War.
1948	The National Health Service is established.
1948	An influx of West Indian immigrants arrive in Britain onboard the SS *Empire Windrush*
1951	The Festival of Britain takes place, 100 years after the Great Exhibition.

INVENTIONS

Could your ancestor have witnessed the invention of any of these new products below? Perhaps they read about them in the newspaper, operated these devices or bought the items when they first appeared in the shops.

Clock:	1656, The Netherlands – Christian Huygens (pendulum model).
Spinning:	1764, England – James Hargreaves (spinning jenny).
Steam engine:	1769, England – James Watt.
Hot air balloon:	1783, France – Joseph and Jacques Montgolfier.
Loom:	1785, England – Edmund Cartwright (power-driven loom).
Electric lamp:	1801, England – Sir Humphrey Davy (arc lamp).

Locomotive:	1804, England – Richard Trevithick (steam powered).
Electric motor:	1822, England – Michael Faraday.
Matches:	1826, England – John Walker.
Typewriter:	1829, USA – W.A. Burt.
Lawn mower:	1830/31, England – Edwin Budding, John Ferrabee.
Postage stamp:	1837, England – Rowland Hill.
Telegraph:	1837, USA – Samuel F.B. Morse.
Rubber:	1839, USA – Charles Goodyear (vulcanisation process).
Photography:	1841, England – William Fox Talbot (first paper negative from which prints could be made).
Sewing machine:	1851, USA – Isaac Singer (continuous stitching).
Antiseptic:	1867, England – Joseph Lister (for use in surgery).
Telephone:	1876, USA – Alexander Graham Bell.
Lightbulb:	1878, England – Joseph Swann (longer-lasting electric lightbulb).
Bicycle:	1884, England – James Starley (first modern model).
Fountain pen:	1884, USA – Lewis E. Waterman.
Motorcycle:	1884, England – Edward Butler (motor tricycle).
Motor car:	1886, Germany – Gottlieb Daimler (first four-wheeled motor vehicle).
Hand-held camera:	1888, USA – George Eastman.
Zipper:	1891, USA – W. L. Judson.
Motion pictures:	1893, USA – Thomas A. Edison.
Radio:	1895, Italy – Guglielmo Marconi (wireless telegraphy).
Vacuum cleaner:	1901, England – Hubert C. Booth.
Frozen food:	1924, USA – Clarence Birdseye.
Television:	1926, England – John Logie Baird.

Intrigued to find out more? Why not visit the British Library's decade-to-decade timeline which covers major events from 1200 to date. This is a fabulous resource with images and audio clips that help to bring each period to life. Just choose your century of interest and enjoy the animated adventure as you learn about everything from the first Bible that was printed in English instead of Latin, to the invention of photography and beyond. The addition of newspaper cuttings, illuminated manuscripts and interactive pages makes this a massive resource for anyone wishing to write up their family history findings and include details of world events in their narrative. Visit bl.uk/timeline.

Similarly, the website of the Institute of Historical Research at british-history.ac.uk could be of help. Its digital library of primary and secondary sources boasts in excess of 1,000 volumes and data sets covering medieval to modern history in the British Isles. The ingenious features of this site allow you to track down information by century, ruling monarch, religious, scientific or local history, by region or a simple text search. Ideal for discovering what was happening during a certain period as well as learning about the important figures and innovations that would have influenced your ancestor's lives.

Appendix 1

USEFUL WEBSITES

There is a vast array of websites available to help you with everything genealogy-related from naval battles at sea to a million and one causes of death. It would be impossible to list them all, but here are just some of my favourites.

www.thegenealogist.co.uk — Essential reading with a varied and ever-growing range of data sets which can help you to expand your research possibilities. Simple to use with the benefit of an experienced team who will try to resolve any subscriber questions via their email system.

www.findmypast.co.uk — A fabulous site with an impressive search engine which enables you to narrow down your investigations and isolate your information easily. Take advantage of their online Family Tree Builder and helpful video tutorials by subscribing.

www.freebmd.org.uk — Besides being free to search, this site has the added benefit of allowing you to work out the possible spouse in a marriage. New data is being added all the time so check back for updates.

freereg.rootsweb.com — A companion site to freebmd which aims to provide free access to baptism, marriage and burial records, that have been transcribed from parish and Nonconformist registers of the UK.

/genealogy.about.com — Found your ancestor on the census but can't fathom what his occupation was? Visit this site for help with old trades and even origins of occupational surnames.

cyndislist.com   Provides access to thousands of genealogy-related websites across the internet.

familysearch.org   Home to the collections compiled by the Latter-day Saints from records and resources around the world.

londonancestor.com   If you've got 'London links' then this gateway site is definitely the place to visit.

findagrave.com   A useful resource for finding the grave of an individual or famous person. Over 49 million graves have been recorded here with links to interesting monuments and epitaphs.

rootsweb.ancestry.com   Part of the Ancestry community, Rootsweb allows you to search and browse the mailing lists and message boards covering thousands of topics and surnames.

Appendix 2

USEFUL ADDRESSES

I am a huge fan of the internet but there are times when a telephone call or visit to a repository, library or museum is definitely what's needed to help advance your research, confirm your findings or simply provide a fantastic day out. Below are just some of the contact details which you'll find essential in your searches.

The National Archives
Kew, Surrey
TW9 4DU
Tel: 020 8876 3444
Email: Use contact form on website: nationalarchives.gov.uk/contact/

The National Archives of Scotland
H.M. General Register House
2 Princes Street
Edinburgh, EH1 3YY
Tel: 0131 535 1314
Email: enquiries@nas.gov.uk

The National Archives of Ireland
Bishop Street
Dublin 8
Ireland
Tel: 01 407 2300
Email: mail@nationalarchives.ie

The National Library of Wales
Aberystwyth
Ceredigion
Wales, SY23 3BU
Tel: 01970 632 800
Email: Use contact form on website: www.llgc.org.uk/

General Register Office
Certificate Services Section
PO Box 2
Southport, PR8 2JD
Tel: 0845 603 7788
Email: certificate.services@ips.gsi.gov.uk

General Register Office Scotland
New Register House
3 West Register Street
Edinburgh
Scotland, EH1 3YT
Tel: 0131 314 4411
Email: Use contact form on website www.gro-scotland.gov.uk

General Register Office Ireland
Government Offices
Convent Road
Roscommon
Tel: 090 6632900

The Society of Genealogists
14 Charterhouse Buildings
Goswell Road
London, EC1M 7BA
Tel: 020 7251 8799
Email: genealogy@sog.org.uk

British Library National Newspaper Library
Colindale Avenue
London, NW9 5HE
Tel: 020 7412 7353
Email: newspaper@bl.uk

RAF Museum
Graham Park Way
Hendon
London, NW9 5LL
Tel: 020 8205 2266
Email: london@rafmuseum.org

The National Maritime Museum
Greenwich
London, SE10 9NF
Tel: 020 8858 4422
Email: library@nmm.ac.uk

National Army Museum
Royal Hospital Road
Chelsea
London, SW3 4HT
Tel: 020 7730 0717
Email: info@national-army-museum.ac.uk

Imperial War Museum
Lambeth Road
London, SE1 6HZ
Tel: 020 7416 5320
Email: mail@iwm.org.uk

The Institute of Heraldic and Genealogical Studies
79–82 Northgate
Canterbury
Kent, CT1 1BA
Tel: 01227 768664
Website: www.ihgs.ac.uk/

The College of Arms
Queen Victoria Street
London
EC4V 4BT
Tel: 020 7248 2762
Website: www.college-of-arms.gov.uk

The Salvation Army Family Tracing Service
101 Newington Causeway
London, SE1 6BN
Tel: 0845 634 4747

BIBLIOGRAPHY

Your Family Tree Online by Graeme Davis

A practical internet guide which concentrates on how to follow your family history via the internet.

How to Books Ltd, 2009, paperback ISBN 978-18452-8344-5

Researching Scottish Family History by Chris Paton

The perfect guide for helping you to untangle your Scottish roots.

The Family History Partnership, 2010, paperback ISBN 978-19062-8022-2

Tracing Your Irish Family History by Anthony Adolph

Packed with plenty of information and illustrations to help you with your Irish ancestry, as well as useful tips on the best resources in countries with major Irish communities.

Collins, 2007, hardback ISBN 978 0007255320

Family History for Kids by Emma Jolly

If you've awakened your child's interest in their family history then this book is perfect. Easy to follow and explained in simple terms – this is a must when passing on the genealogy baton.

Pymer Quantrill Publishing, 2007, paperback ISBN 978-09557-5780-8

The Genealogist's Internet by Peter Christian

This book is essential reading for any family historian with internet access.

The National Archives, ISBN 978-19056-1539-1

Nick Barratt's Beginner's Guide to Your Ancestors' Lives by Nick Barratt

This book combines useful research information as well as giving a fascinating insight into the social history surrounding each generation.

Pen and Sword Books, 2010, hardback ISBN 978-18488-4056-0

The Victorians and Edwardians at Work by John Hannavy

Ideal for filling in the backdrop to your ancestors' working lives during this period.

Shire Publications Ltd, 2009, paperback ISBN 978-07478-0719-3

Tracing Your Railway Ancestors by Di Drummond

A comprehensive guide featuring all aspects of railway life from working for Britain's railway companies to where to locate related records.

Pen and Sword Books, ISBN 978-18441-5864-5

British Postcards of the First World War by Peter Doyle

A small yet comprehensive book which charts the history of the First World War in postcards – ideal for anyone who has inherited this type of ephemera and wishes to use the images to illustrate their family story.

Shire Publications, ISBN 978-07478-0766-7

Scrapbooking Your Family History by Laura Best

Packed with plenty of tips on how to preserve your family memories and ephemera.

Sterling, ISBN 978-14027-5182-0

INDEX

adoption 89–91

agricultural labourers 20

Air Force, Royal 161, 162

apprenticeships 65

aristocratic links 170–3

Army, British 134–57

assisted/non assisted passengers 111

asylum 72

banns 43

baptism 43–51

bishops' transcripts 43

BMD 33–9

British Library 141

burials 43, 48, 174–9

campaign medals and service records 136, 139, 140, 146–55, 158, 159, 161, 162, 164

canal workers 86–8

Catholics 50

census 52–60

certificates 33

charts 19, 20

child migrants 117, 118

Civil Registration 33

clergy 83, 84

Coats of Arms 170–3

Commonwealth War Graves 143, 144

coroners 179

crime and convicts 66–9

death 174

directories 99–102

divorce 43, 44

DNA 206, 207

document preservation and storage 185–94

education 62–5

electoral registers 60, 61

Ellis Island 114–6

emigration 105–19

equipment advice 24–9

family history societies 205

famous ancestors 170–2

findmypast 33, 44, 54, 55, 57, 113–5, 117, 146–55, 159, 178

First World War 134, 138, 139, 140–5

Freemasonry 92

genealogical software 24–8

The Genealogist 35, 39, 45, 47, 50, 51, 53, 57, 61, 64, 76, 90, 100, 101, 121, 122, 136, 137, 145, 171, 180, 184

gravestones 176, 177

handwriting 188, 189

heraldry 170–3

historical timelines 209–14

Home Front (incl. rationing) 164–6

housing (incl. house history) 102–4

Huguenots 129, 130

illegitimacy 38, 39, 41
International Genealogical Index 48
internet security 204
Irish ancestry 126, 127

Jewish ancestry 131–3

law and order 66–70, 80–3

maps 93–9
marriage 32–8, 41–51
memorabilia 185–96
memorials 176–7

names 120, 121, 123
National Service 163, 164
Navy, Royal 158–61
networking, social 203, 204
newspaper research 73, 74
Nonconformists 49, 50
nursing 156, 157, 167

obituaries 179, 180
occupations 77–91
one-name studies 121
Ordnance Survey Maps 95

parish registers 43–51
passenger lists 109–11

passports 114
paupers 70
photographs 191–4
police 80–2
Poll Books 60, 61
Poor Laws 71
postmen 88, 89
poverty maps 97
probate records 181–4

Quakers 130, 131

railway workers 86, 87
reunions 207

school log books 62, 63
schooling (private/public) 62–5
Scottish ancestry 122, 123
Second World War 133, 134, 138, 140–4,
   146–62, 163–9
strays' index 49
surname mapping 121, 122

theatre 85, 86
trade directories 99–102
transportation 66–8

Welsh ancestry 123–6
wills 180–4
workhouses 70–2

Made in the USA
Middletown, DE
17 January 2021